IMAGES
of America

THE OHIO STATE REFORMATORY

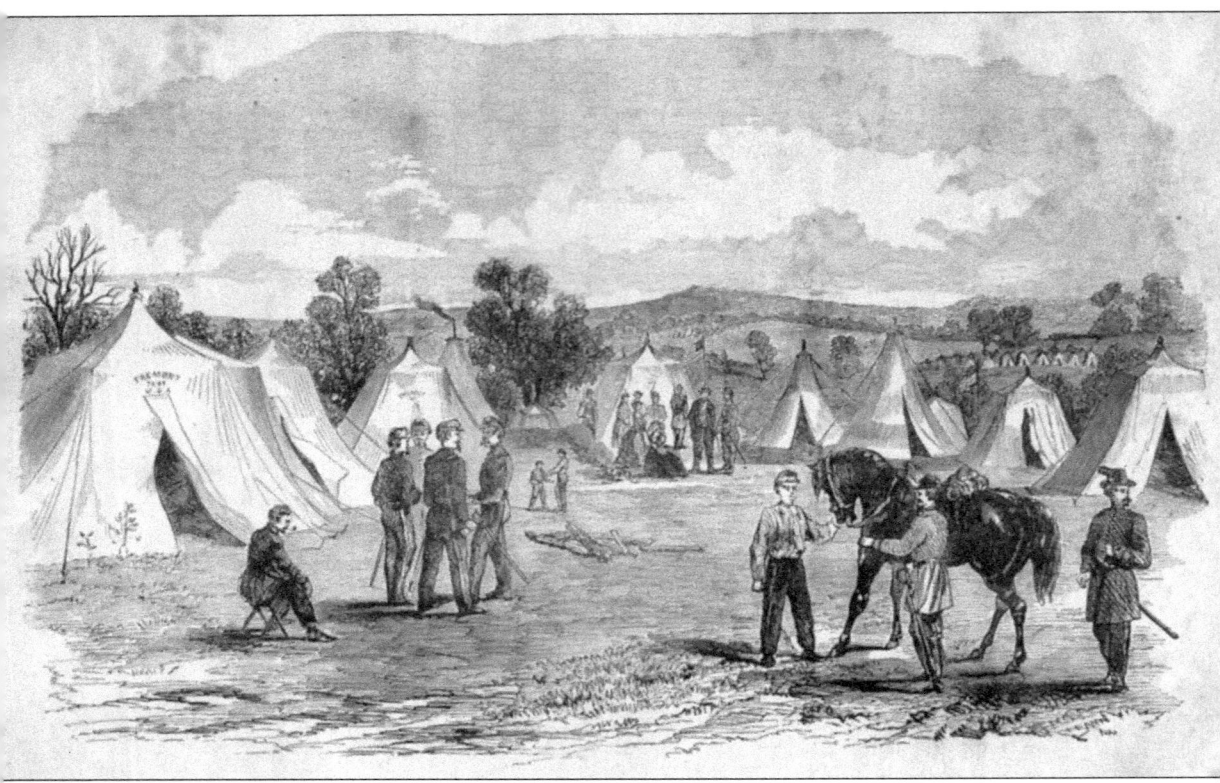

The grounds that would eventually become home to the Ohio State Reformatory was farmland belonging to the Tingley family. The Tingleys donated the land to the government when Pres. Abraham Lincoln called on the states to train recruits to fight in the Civil War. The camp, originally named after former US congressman and Ohio governor Mordecai Bartley, was home to the 15th and the 32nd Ohio Infantry. The camp was later renamed Camp Mansfield as it continued training men for service in the Union army. Volunteers from five surrounding counties continued to train at Camp Mansfield until, in October 1862, a draft was instituted in order to fulfill the quota established for this, the 10th District, of Ohio's commitment for troops. It became the 10th Ohio military headquarters. Camp Mansfield ultimately trained over 5,000 troops for the Union cause. Thomas Tingley, the owner of the property, became a sutler, a civilian merchant who traveled with the army.

ON THE COVER: While visitors could easily enter the administration wings in the front of the prison, the west gate was the only entrance into the prison proper. Security at this gate was extremely high, as it was the potential site of escapes. Absolutely every vehicle having business within the prison had to enter here. Prior to the common use of motor vehicles, horse-drawn wagons and buggies approached and waited for a guard to open the iron gate and inspect the contents. This gate was used when inmates were being transported into and out of the institution. Materials brought by truck for various workshops would come through the west gate. The gate included a watchtower that was manned by guards 24 hours a day. Other guards were positioned on the wall and could look down on the gate.

IMAGES
of America

THE OHIO STATE REFORMATORY

Nancy K. Darbey

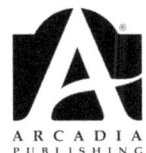

Copyright © 2016 by Nancy K. Darbey
ISBN 978-1-5316-9807-2

Published by Arcadia Publishing
Charleston, South Carolina

Library of Congress Control Number: 2015940359

For all general information, please contact Arcadia Publishing:
Telephone 843-853-2070
Fax 843-853-0044
E-mail sales@arcadiapublishing.com
For customer service and orders:
Toll-Free 1-888-313-2665

Visit us on the Internet at www.arcadiapublishing.com

This book is dedicated to the loving memory of my parents and to Gary, Judy, Dan, Stacie, Jackson, and Olivia with all my love.

Contents

Acknowledgments   6

Introduction   7

1. A Building Fit for a King: Architecture   9

2. Keepers of the Keys: Administrators   35

3. Preparing for a Better Life: Work and Training   61

4. Behind the Walls: Fun and Games   87

5. Hollywood Comes to Town: The Reformatory on Screen   119

About the Organization   126

Bibliography   127

Acknowledgments

When the Ohio State Reformatory (OSR) was envisioned, little did anyone realize that the building would become an icon of popular culture. Saved from destruction by local grassroots efforts, the building was placed in the National Register of Historic Places in 1995. Prior to the Mansfield Preservation Society taking ownership and conservatorship, much damage had been done to the building. It is a testament to the volunteers who have donated thousands of hours over the last 20 years and their tremendous commitment to the OSR, as well as members of the board of trustees and staff who have donated time and effort to restore and maintain the building and remaining grounds. Many contribute to the ongoing preservation of the Ohio State Reformatory.

I would like to thank my editor, Jesse Darland from Arcadia Publishing. His patience, encouragement, and feedback were so appreciated as I worked my way through the process.

This book would not have been possible without the generosity of so many individuals, including the following: OSR curator Becky McKinnell, for her support and knowledge; Mark and Cheryl Kneram, for their vast collection of documents; OSR staff members Paul Smith and Mary Kennard, for their technical assistance; Dan Seckel, for help with architectural background; and Scott Sukel, for his incredible talent, photograph collection, and wealth of information. Michelle Conine, Jill Keppler, Michael Humphrey, Don Zin, Becky McKinnell, Cheryl Kneram, and Mark Kneram have been invaluable in their help with checking the facts used throughout the text.

Unless otherwise noted, all images appear courtesy of the Mansfield Reformatory Preservation Society.

INTRODUCTION

Prisons, as with innumerable other social institutions, are subject to change and transition. So it was and is with prison reform. In the mid-19th century, "reform" was viewed as a new form of corrections. Rather than incarcerate all prisoners in institutions intended to isolate and punish, the "reformatory movement" promoted education, training, and variable sentencing to prepare prisoners for eventual release. Designed to house offenders between the ages of 16 and 30, reformatories would give prisoners training that would allow them to leave prison with a trade, thus reducing the chance that they would commit further offenses. Among the first and most notable of these institutions was Elmira Reformatory in Elmira, New York, which opened in 1876.

The "reformatory movement" became a focus for the Ohio State Legislature in the 1880s. In the March 1884 Ohio legislative session, "Mr. White introduced a bill providing for the erection of a State intermediate penitentiary or reformatory, to which prisoners sentenced for the first time offense are to be sent." Maintenance for the building would be provided by using one-tenth of the proceeds from the Scott Law. Unfortunately, the Scott Law, a tax on saloon owners, was declared unconstitutional by the Ohio Supreme Court in October 1884. That would leave the state to find other ways to provide funds for construction.

Influential businessmen, representing the board of trade, began petitioning the state to locate the new institution in Mansfield. They received help from two important and influential citizens. US senator John Sherman, brother of Civil War general William T. Sherman, and Roeliff Brinkerhoff, a Civil War veteran, owner/editor of a local newspaper, banker, and reformer, were early supporters of the effort. Unbeknownst to them, these men championed a unique institution that would serve the community even when the original intent was changed by social demands.

In 1885, Mansfield was selected as the site for the new facility. It was seen as a boon to the local economy, providing employment opportunities for citizens. The population of Mansfield grew from 9,800 in 1880 to 13,000 in 1890, just prior to the opening of the penitentiary. Mansfield was accessed by four railroads, which allowed for an economy that moved from agriculture to business.

Once the city had been selected, it fell upon the community to find a site that would accommodate the building and its future construction. The city began with the purchase of 30 acres north of town that had been the site of a Civil War training camp, Camp Mordecai Bartley. Soon after, the state purchased 150 additional acres of adjacent land.

Cleveland architect Levi Scofield was hired to design the building. As an architect trained in Europe, Scofield was known for his massive structures that rivaled European castles. His work, intended to create a sense of inspiration and spirituality, used a combination of three architectural styles: Victorian Gothic, Richardsonian Romanesque, and Queen Anne. Ultimately, the main building itself would encompass over 250,000 square feet. Thus began a decade-long effort to complete the Ohio State Reformatory. Over those 10 years, the project would be plagued by lack of funding and by second-guessing by the legislature. By 1891, rumblings in the legislature began due to rising costs. At one point, rumors began circulating that a better use for the building would be as an "inebriate asylum" or "drunkards refuge." An editorial in the *Mansfield Evening News* in 1884 considered this a "silly scheme" and "too silly for a second thought." It further stated, "Any twaddle about making anything else than a prison out of the intermediate penitentiary has passed."

Another possibility posed a more serious threat to the prison. On January 21, 1890, a resolution was offered to change the penitentiary to an insane asylum according to the *Delphos Weekly Herald* of January 30, 1890. To counter this proposal, a contingent of supporters appeared before the house finance committee to plead their case. They were given little reassurance by the committee. By February 6, 1890, a trip had been planned for the finance committee and members of the penitentiary board of managers to visit the reformatory in Elmira, New York. Upon their return, the legislators were fully convinced that the Intermediate Penitentiary was, indeed, an important part of Ohio's prison system. They determined that the necessary funding should be secured. The first estimate of $1 million eventually became $1.5 million; in 2015 dollars, that is the equivalent of almost $40 million.

By 1896, the Ohio State Reformatory, as it was now known, was completed enough for the first prisoners to arrive. September 17 was heralded as a day of celebration in the city. Mansfield's *Shield and Banner* proclaimed it "Mansfield's Greatest Day." On that day, the first 150 youthful offenders were transferred to the facility. These young men would be put to work immediately. Their first project was the construction of the wall that would surround the prison.

However, the completion of the building proper was not finished for another three years. On September 24, 1900, the *Mansfield News* wrote, "The last stone was set in place in the east cell wing ventilating tower at 10:30 o'clock Saturday."

The ensuing decades brought many changes to the reformatory as it continued to expand and evolve. The east cell block, completed using inmate labor in 1910, was six tiers high, with 100 cells per tier. The original west cell block had five tiers with 350 cells.

By the 1980s, the reformatory had fallen into disrepair due to insufficient funding and neglect. In 1978, the Counsel for Human Dignity, representing 2,400 inmates, sued the State of Ohio, claiming inhumane treatment of prisoners. In 1983, the US District Court ruled in the inmates' favor, ordering the building closed and the prisoners transferred to other institutions. The last inmate was moved from the reformatory to the Mansfield Correctional Institution on December 30, 1990.

While still a working prison, the reformatory was the setting of two movies. *Harry and Walter Go to New York* was filmed on the grounds in 1976. In 1989, *Tango and Cash* used not only the grounds, but also filmed within the walls. After the prison closed, Frank Darabont chose the facility for his film *The Shawshank Redemption* (1994). Much of the grounds and building were used. Since its closing, the reformatory has been used as the backdrop for a number of films, music videos, and television programs.

Little did those men who championed the Ohio State Reformatory in the 1880s realize the impact their efforts would have on the small community of Mansfield. Over its 94 years of operation, the facility transitioned from a model of the reform movement to a maximum-security prison. Today, it is a landmark of an era long forgotten.

One

A Building Fit for a King

Architecture

Architect Levi Tucker Scofield was a native Ohioan. Born in Cleveland, he was a lifelong citizen and served in the Ohio Infantry during the Civil War. Scofield returned to Cleveland after the war and began his studies. Having been trained in Europe, Scofield was influenced by the Victorian Gothic, Richardsonian Romanesque, and Queen Anne schools. He specialized in large, imposing institutions, including schools, asylums, and prisons. Scofield was commissioned to design various buildings throughout Ohio. In 1884, he was hired to design the Intermediate Penitentiary in Mansfield, Ohio, on 180 acres of land purchased by the state. His design was reminiscent of that of Chateau Chambord in France. Scofield's design of the Ohio State Reformatory was intended to create a sense of spirituality within the inmates so as to allow them to leave the institution better than when they arrived. Unfortunately, the prisoners saw the building as less spiritual, naming it "Dracula's Castle." After 10 years of stop-and-go construction, the building opened and welcomed its first 150 prisoners to great fanfare. Special touches were used to create the aesthetic tone desired by Scofield. He did not want the exterior marred by downspouts cluttering the exterior walls; instead, they were laid within the walls of the building. Later, utility trumped aesthetics. More practical innovations were used as part of the design of outbuildings and facilities. Dr. James A. Leonard, a long-serving superintendent, designed showers for the inmates that were more efficient and hygienic than prior bathing systems. Other brick-and-mortal buildings lacked the beauty and elegance of Scofield's design.

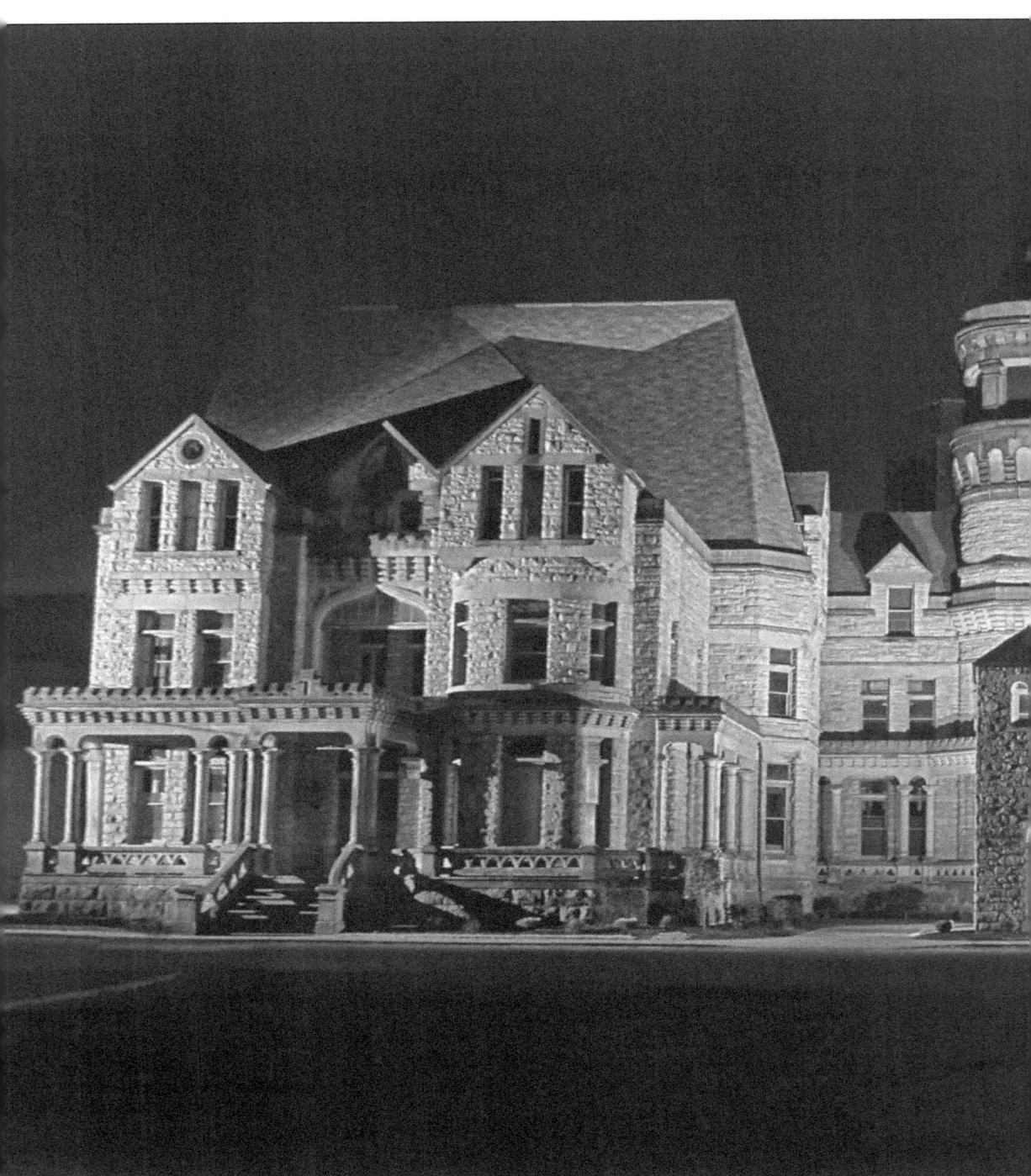

The east and west administrative wings of the reformatory are symmetrical. The two sides provided administrative offices for superintendents and their staffs, as well as residences for the warden, assistant warden, chaplain, and their families. The wardens' offices were on the first floor of the west (left) wing. A formal dining room, family living room, and personal office were on the first

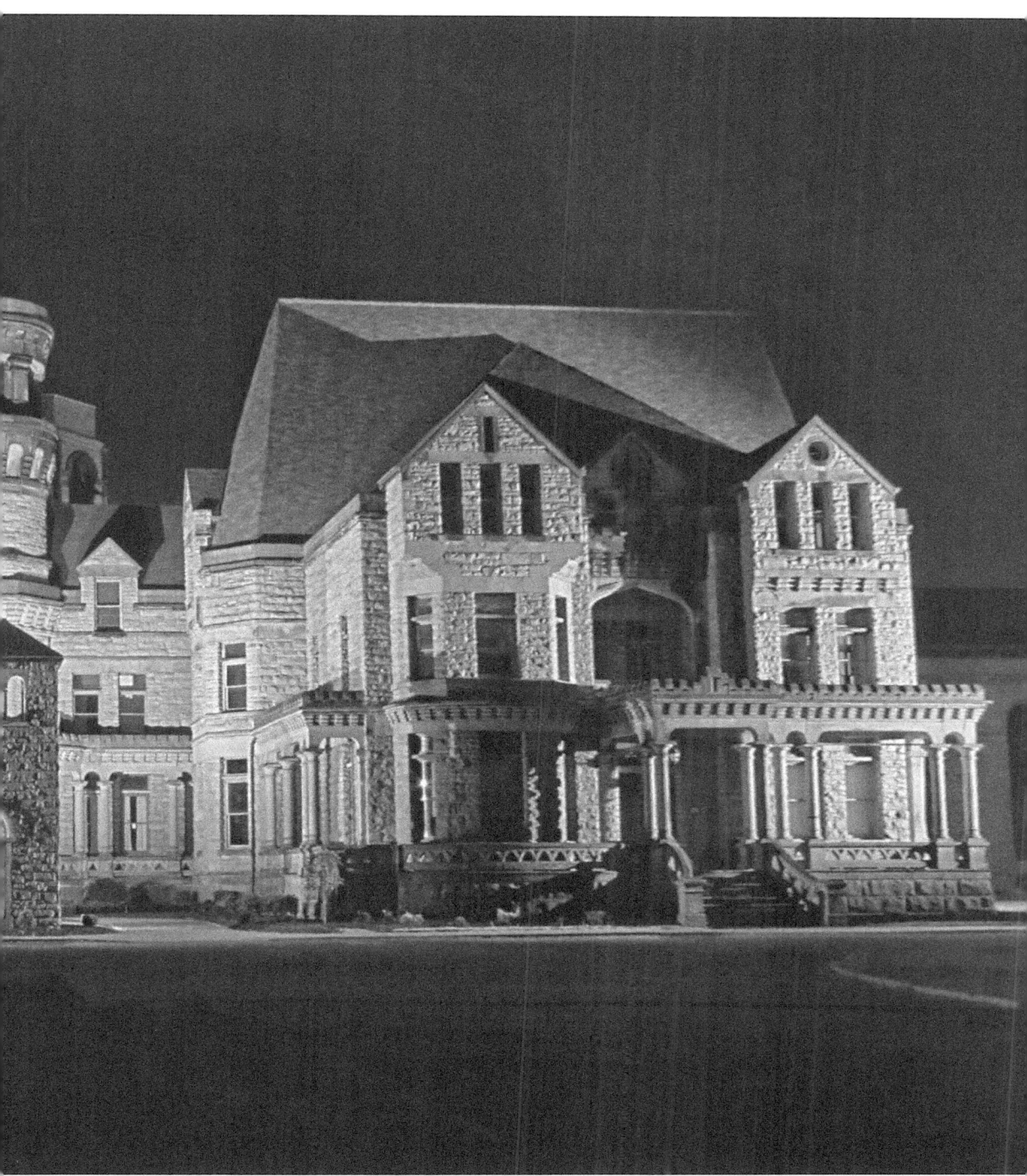

floor of the east (right) wing. Family bedrooms and sitting rooms were on the second floor, with the third floors reserved for guests and storage. The east and west administration structures, as well as the initial (west) cell block and wall, were massive. The walls alone measured between two and a half and four and a half feet wide throughout the building. (Courtesy of Scott Sukel.)

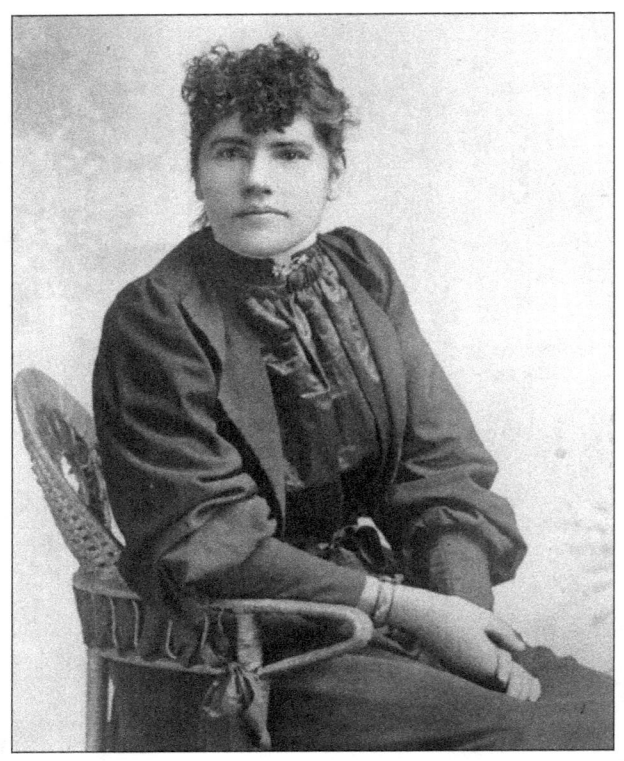

As the state was buying property to build the reformatory, the Wise family sold 34 acres of its adjoining land for construction. After her parents died and her siblings moved away, Phoebe Wise remained on a small parcel of land next to the reformatory. In December 1891, three men broke into her home, threatening her life and torturing her to get her to reveal where her rumored treasure was hidden. Later, a man labeled a lunatic stalked and harassed her. After being arrested and released, he returned to her home, attempting to gain entry. She shot and killed him. Charges were not pressed against her, and Phoebe Wise lived out the rest of her life in her small home, dying in her late 90s.

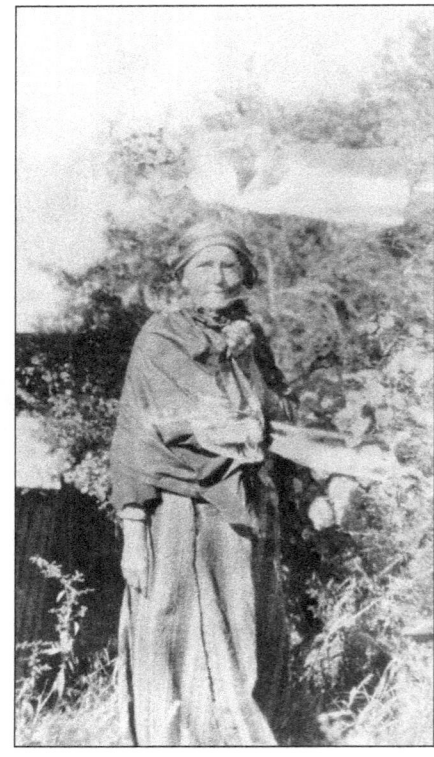

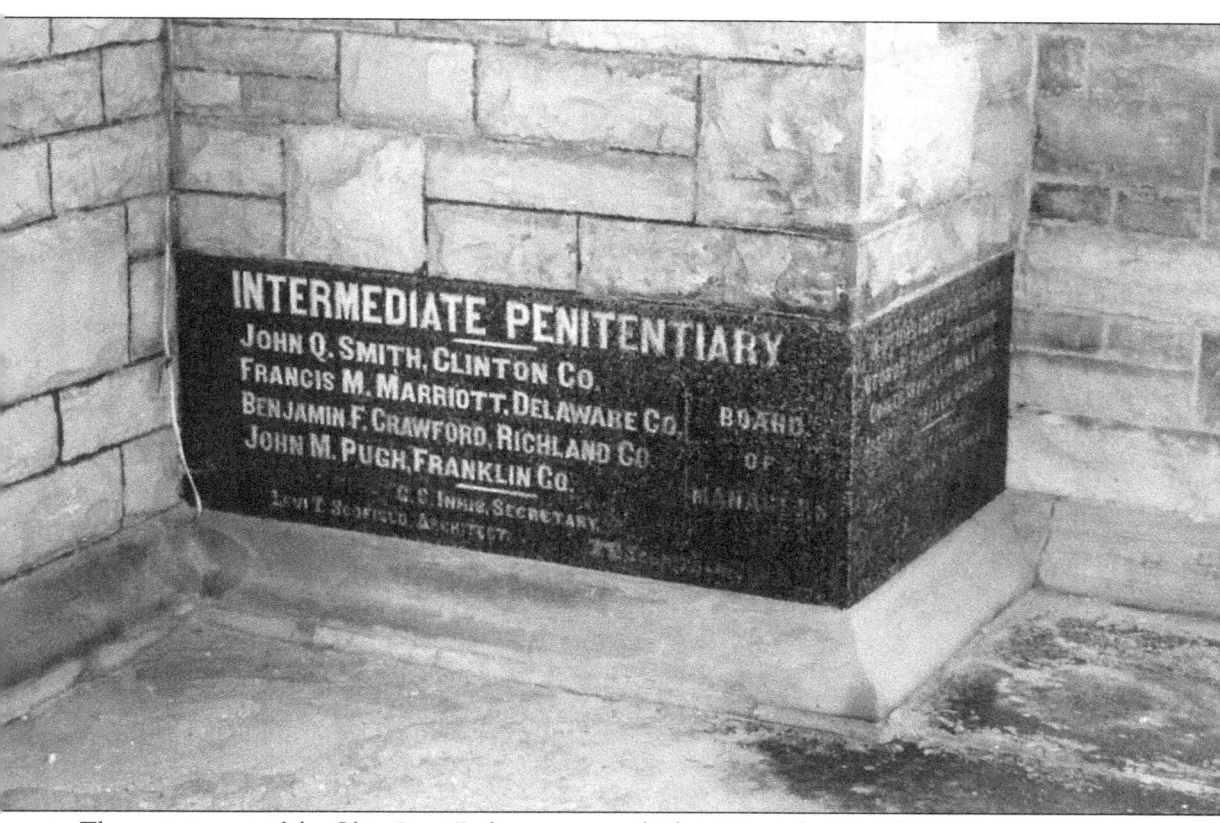

The cornerstone of the Ohio State Reformatory was laid on November 22, 1886. It was reported that 15,000 people visited Mansfield to celebrate the occasion. Within the cornerstone was a time capsule containing items representing the celebratory event and items representative of Mansfield and Ohio in 1886. Among items saved were a copy of the law creating the Intermediate Penitentiary, building specifications, lists of local and state officials, items from local businesses and fraternal organizations, a copy of the Baltimore & Ohio Railroad Red Book, proof sets of 1886 coins, copies of local and state newspapers, the names of officials and members of the Ohio State General Assembly (1884–1885 and 1886–1887), and a parchment containing the names of the board of managers and officers of the Intermediate Penitentiary.

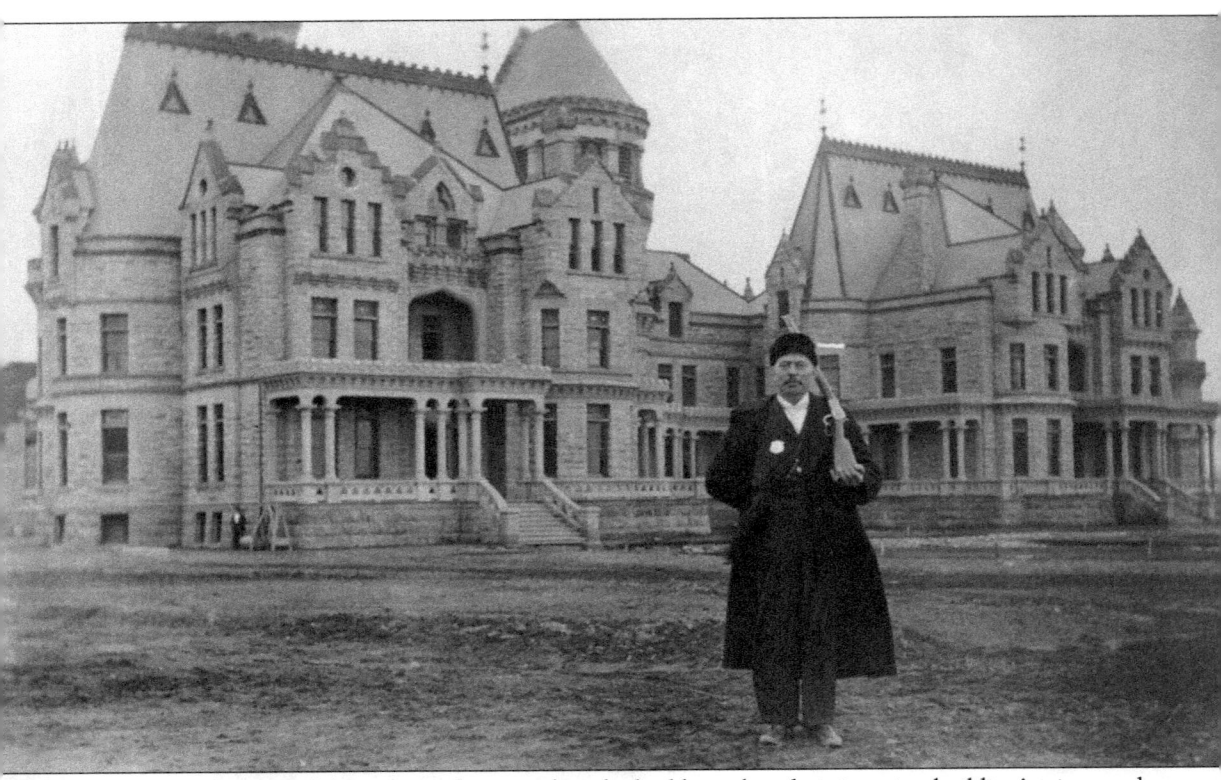

Although inmate labor was used to complete the building, the administration building's wings and west cell block were erected by local contractors and their work crews. Artisans were brought in to complete work that local craftsmen were unable to do. Some workmen continued to work after the OSR opened to inmates in 1896, with inmates as their work crews. Contractors Hancock & Dow supervised all work until the last exterior stone was set in place on September 24, 1900. As seen here, a sheriff's deputy stood guard over the outside grounds throughout the construction until the institution's guards took over. The sheriff's guard ended with the opening of the prison, but the sheriff's office remained available to provide help when needed throughout the existence of the facility. Along with the Ohio Highway Patrol, the sheriff's department responded to riots and escapes that occurred sporadically.

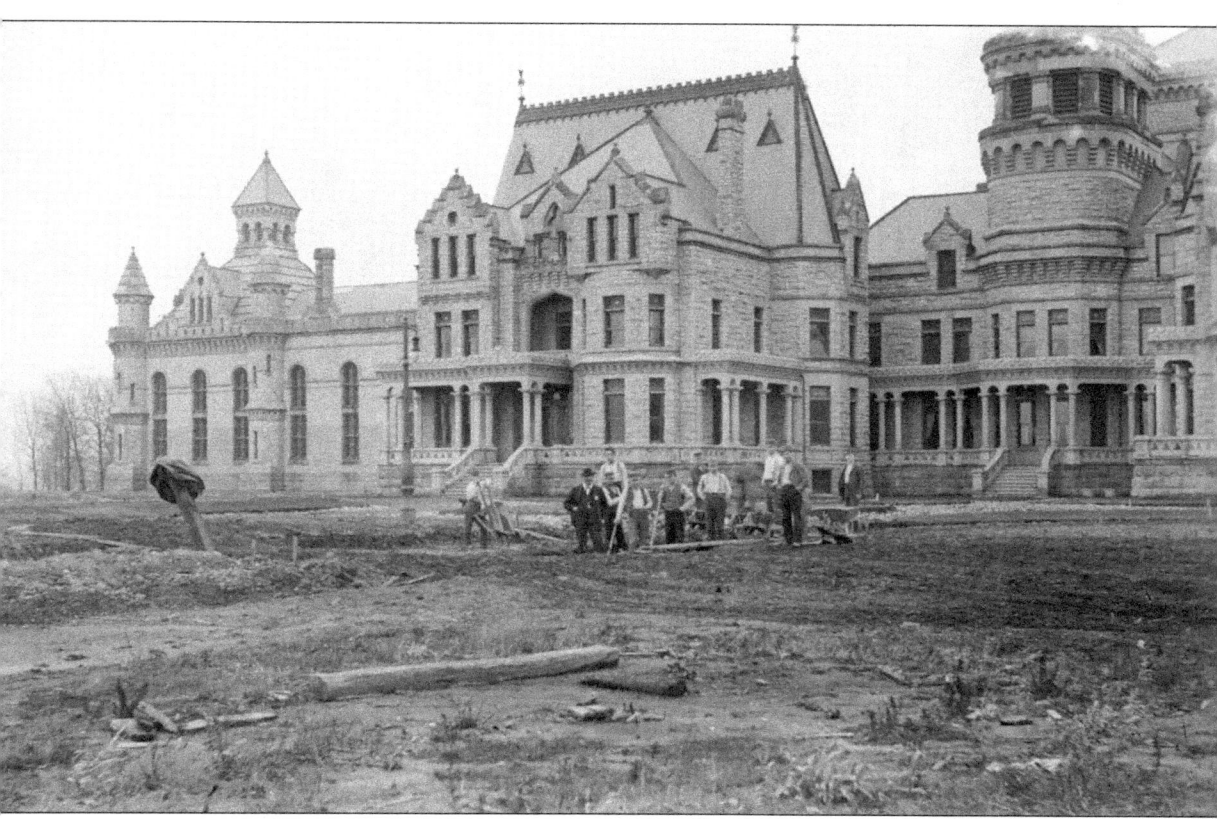

When the first inmates were moved to the Ohio State Reformatory from the Ohio Penitentiary, the first order of business was to complete the building. Inmates were put to work installing the sewer system for the administration wing and building the west cell block and roads. Another critical piece of construction was the wall surrounding the property. The stone wall surrounding the 15 acres of the prison proper was 25 feet high. Those inmates who were considered a high risk for escape were fitted with an "Oregon boot," a shackle that severely limited their mobility. Inmates were also charged with establishing and working the kitchen and beginning farm operations. In addition, seven years later, inmates were used as labor for the construction of the OSR's east six-tier cell block. By the time of the east cell block's completion, it was expected that an additional 600 inmates would be housed there.

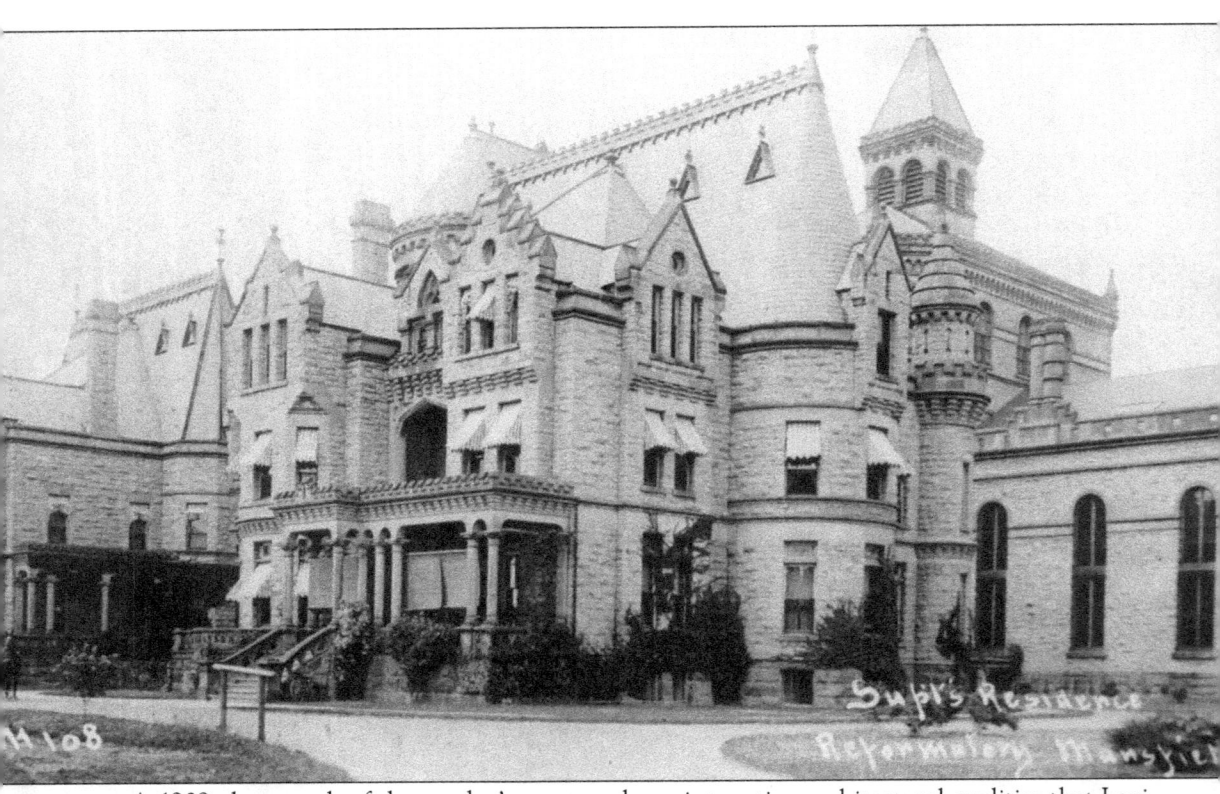

A 1909 photograph of the warden's quarters shows interesting architectural qualities that Levi Scofield used in the design. The unique building incorporates three styles. Atop the high roofline are decorative flashing ridges common in the Romanesque style. The tall tower uses tent roofing, as seen in Queen Anne architecture. The tower, used either for a bell or an additional water tower, is located over the tuberculosis ward of the hospital. Along the side is a small tower or turret with conical roof that is reminiscent of the Gothic style. Interestingly, turrets were originally developed for castle defense. Scofield, however, used turrets for exterior design. Not wanting to waste interior space, the living quarters has small, round rooms inside the turrets. These were probably used as storage by the families. Turrets were also built into the walls of the cell blocks and were initially used to store wood for heating.

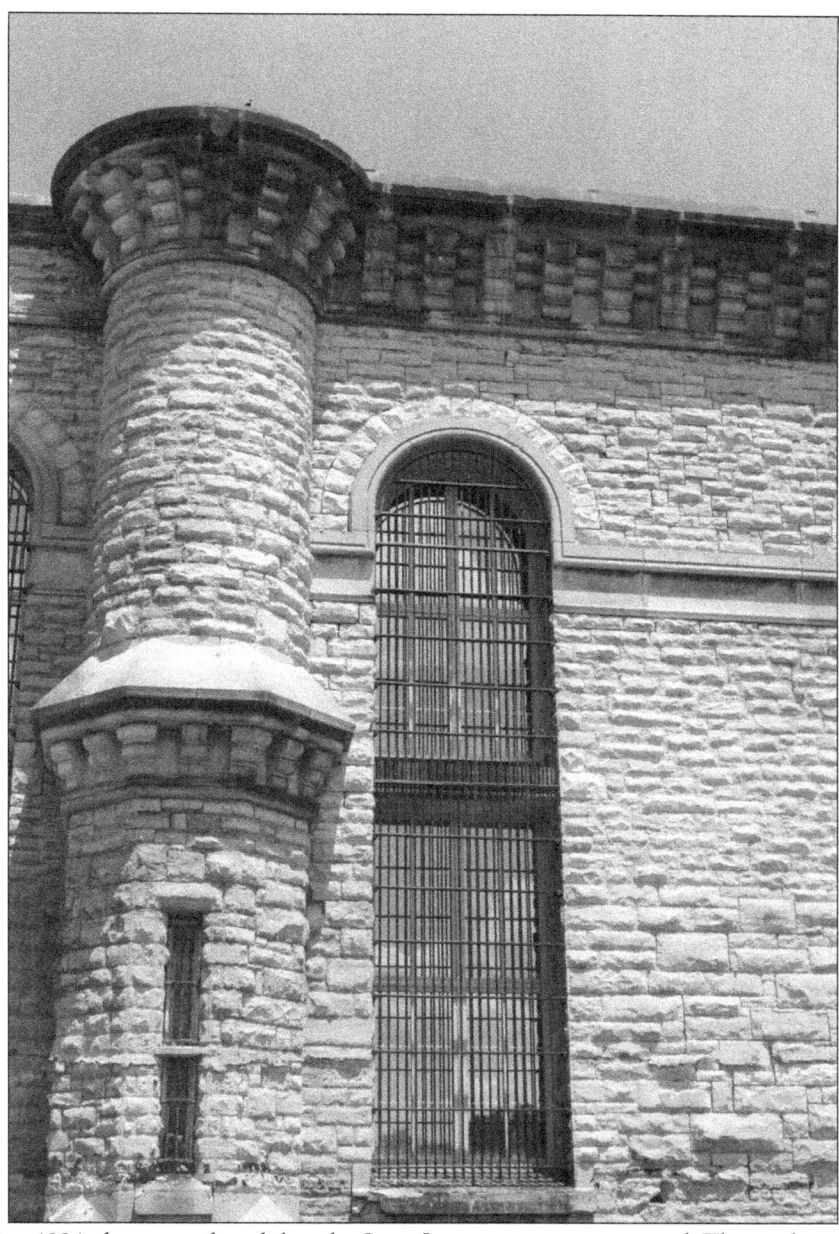

In October 1884, the courts found that the Scott Law was unconstitutional. The tax levied against saloonkeepers would have funded construction of the reformatory. As a result, the legislature would appropriate little money each year for construction. The projected cost to build the OSR was $1.5 million, and the lack of funding was frustrating to the building advocates. Finally, in the early 1890s, the legislature implemented another tax intended to complete the stop-and-go construction. A whiskey tax was imposed, not on the saloonkeepers but on those who purchased whiskey. The "whisky line" on the building marks where construction resumed after the tax was implemented. This photograph clearly shows the whisky line. Halfway up the south-facing window, the stones are dramatically smaller above the line than below. Visitors not aware of this usually do not notice the different stonework.

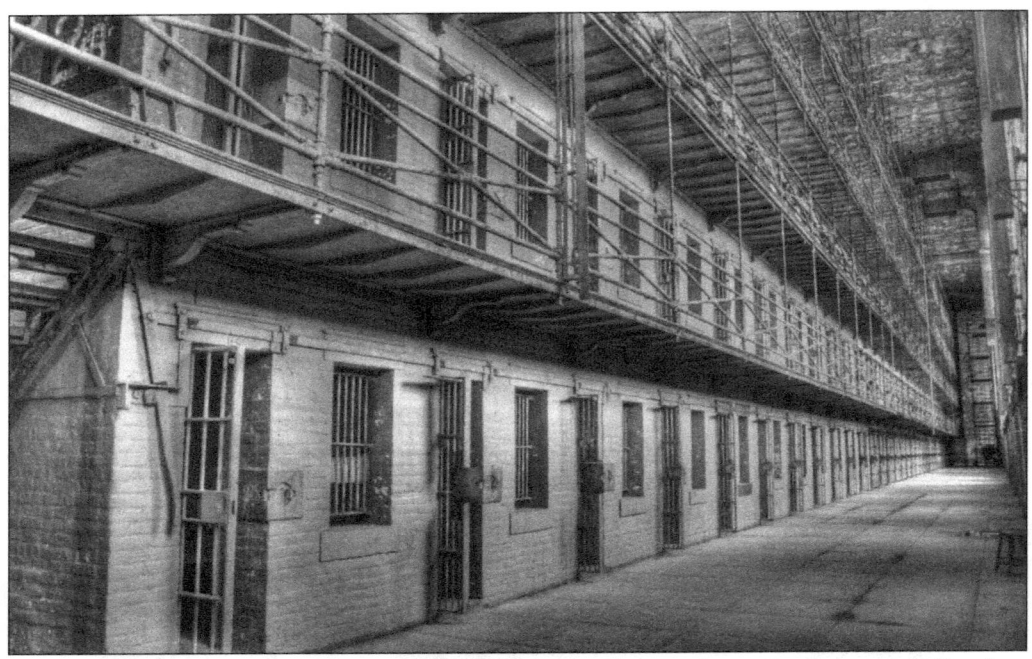

The west cell block is five tiers (or stories) high, with 70 cells on each tier. Because it is smaller than the east block, it was quieter. Inmates had to earn the right to be housed in the west cell block, and they referred to it as "the Hilton." Trustees were housed on the first tier to allow them to get to their work assignments more quickly. These positions included cafeteria workers, hospital aides, commissary workers, landscapers, and runners. Before the advent of inter-prison communications, a runner was assigned to the office of an administrator. He would sit outside the office, waiting for a message that needed to be sent to another office. He would then "run" to the other office, wait for a reply, and "run" it back to his boss. (Above, courtesy of Scott Sukel.)

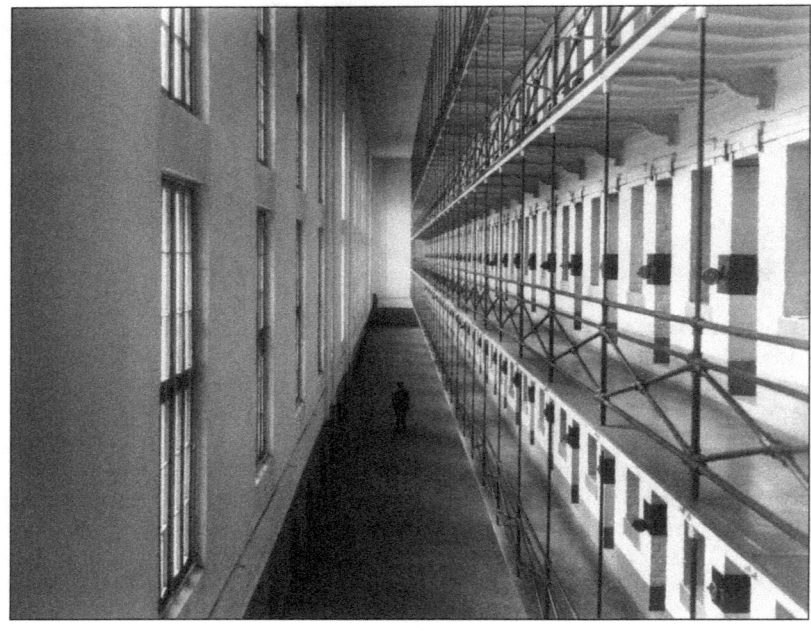

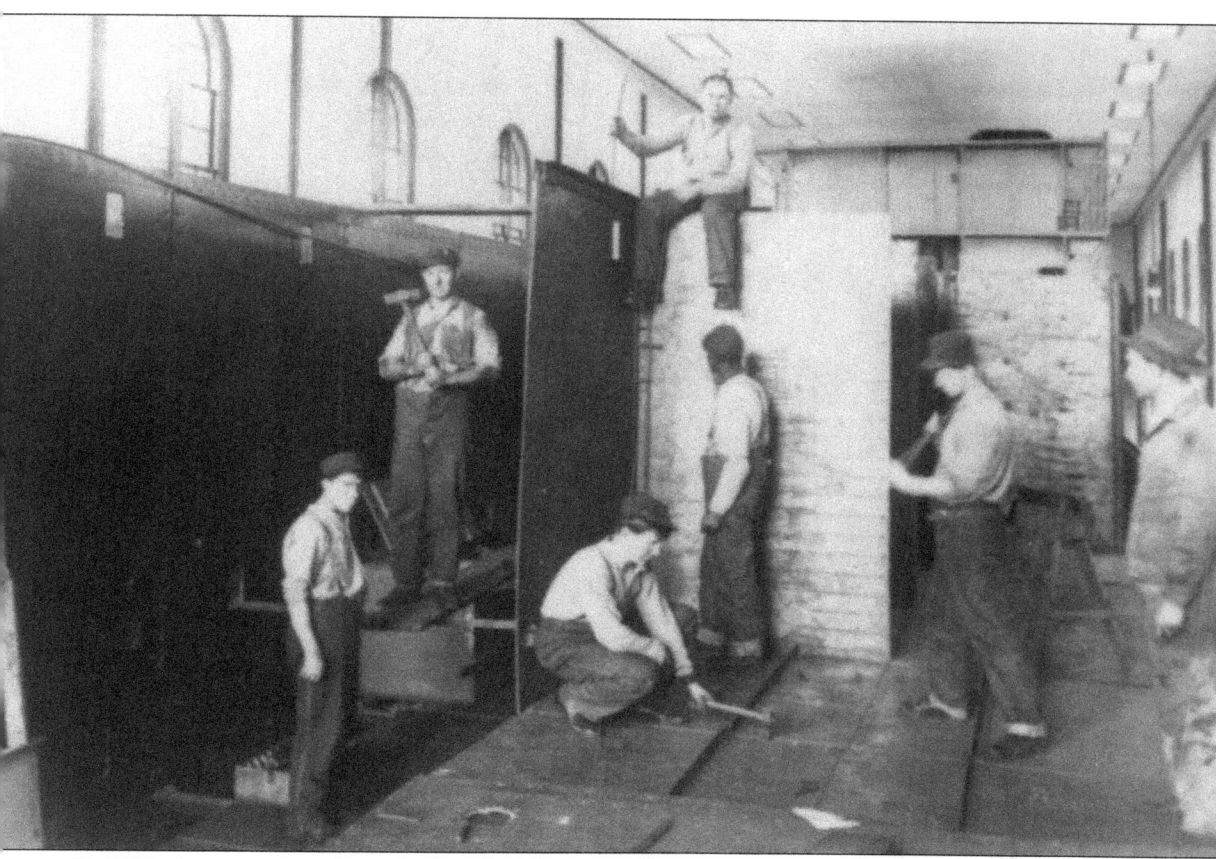

By 1908, the prison population had swelled to 988, and housing had not kept up. Anticipating this increase, work on the east cell block began in 1903. Inmates were put to work on the construction. Standing six tiers high, the structure became the largest freestanding cell block in the world. Aside from short walkways that attach it to the main building, the east block's 600 cells could, if something brought down the rest of the prison, remain standing. These 600 cells would eventually house 1,200 inmates. Supt. James Leonard included several unique touches to the extension. Innovative showers for inmates were added. In addition, six special padded cells were built, intended for malingering inmates who would feign insanity so as to get out of work details.

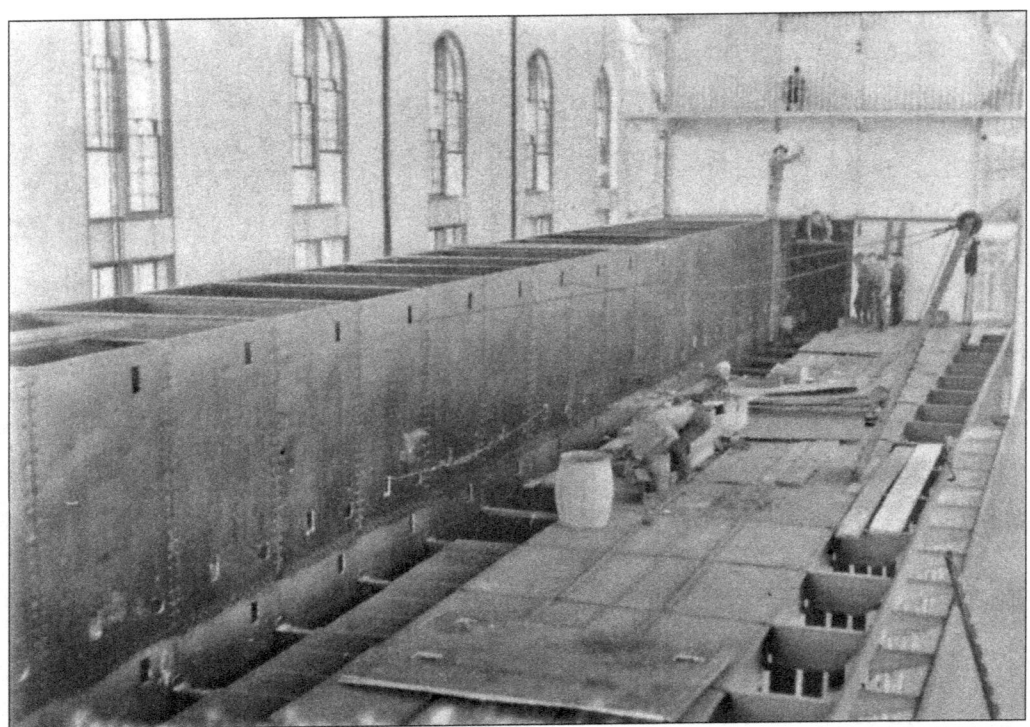

The narrow walkway behind the cells was called the catwalk. Each tier of both cell blocks contained a catwalk. Guards were required to walk the range once each shift. A ladder allowed them to climb up to the next tier without leaving its confines. The purpose of the catwalk was twofold: first, as each cell had its own electric and water supply, these could be cut off if an inmate broke a rule; second, guards could eavesdrop on inmates' conversations. (Below, courtesy of Ron and Joann Schurer.)

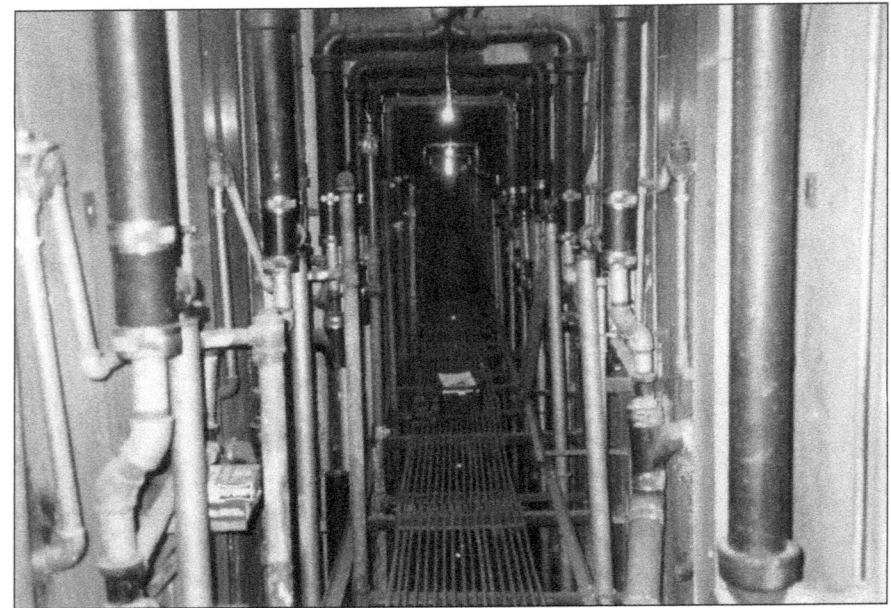

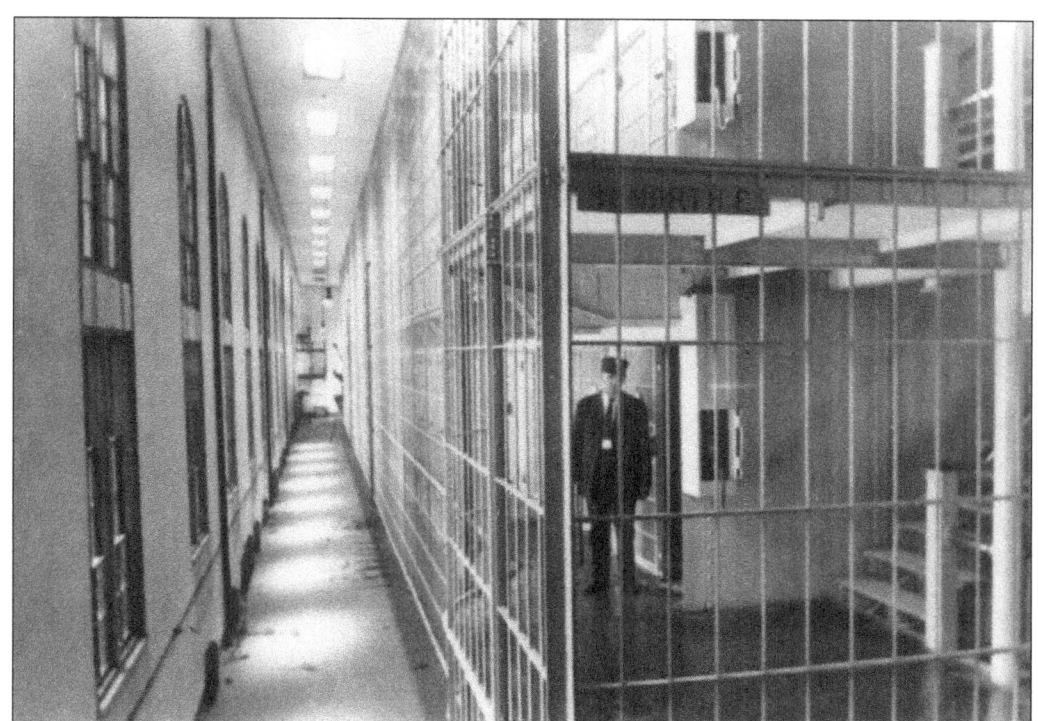

Shortly after the prison opened in 1896, plans were being made to add a cell block on the east side of the building. When completed, this block had six tiers, each with 100 cells, designated by tier and side (above). The east cell block was constructed by inmates and included premade cells. Steel mesh ran along the outside of each tier to prevent inmates from falling or being pushed over the edge to the floor of the block. The first tier was used for inmates considered too difficult to house with the general population. Rather than the typical barred doors, these cells had heavier, less-porous doors. (At right, courtesy of Scott Sukel.)

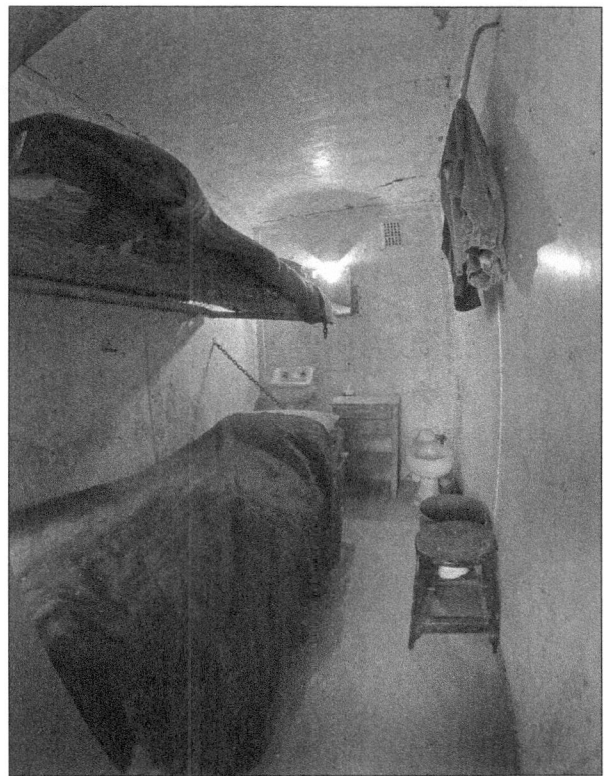

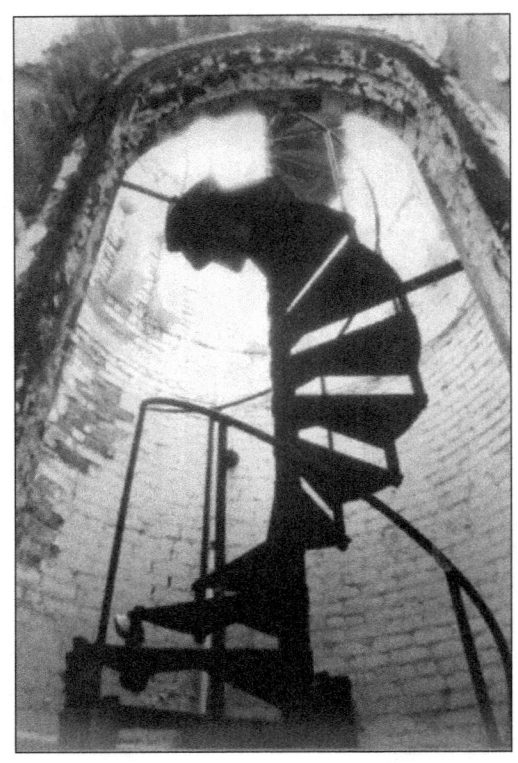

Spiral staircases are located in various places throughout the building. These narrow staircases were intended for the use of officers as they navigated the cell blocks and climbed to the wall and guard towers. For security purposes, the iron staircases are extremely narrow and steep to deter inmates from quickly making their way to the tower and overtaking guards. The photograph at left shows a staircase leading up to the wall and guard tower. Shown below is the entry to a staircase that runs from the bottom to the top tier of a cell block. (Below, courtesy of Scott Sukel.)

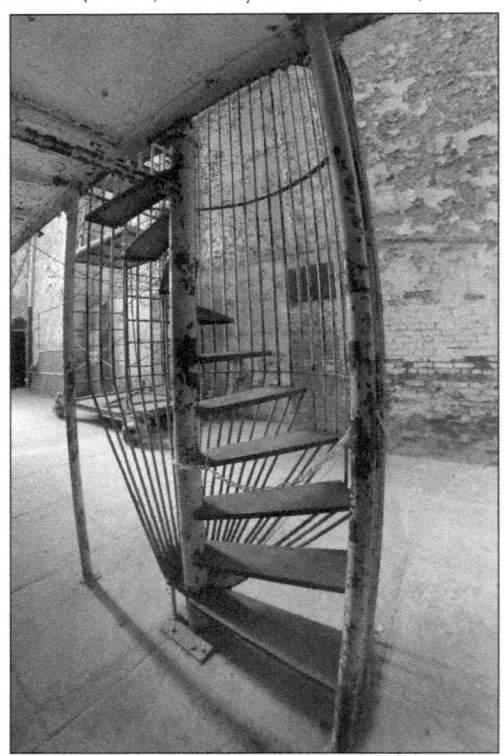

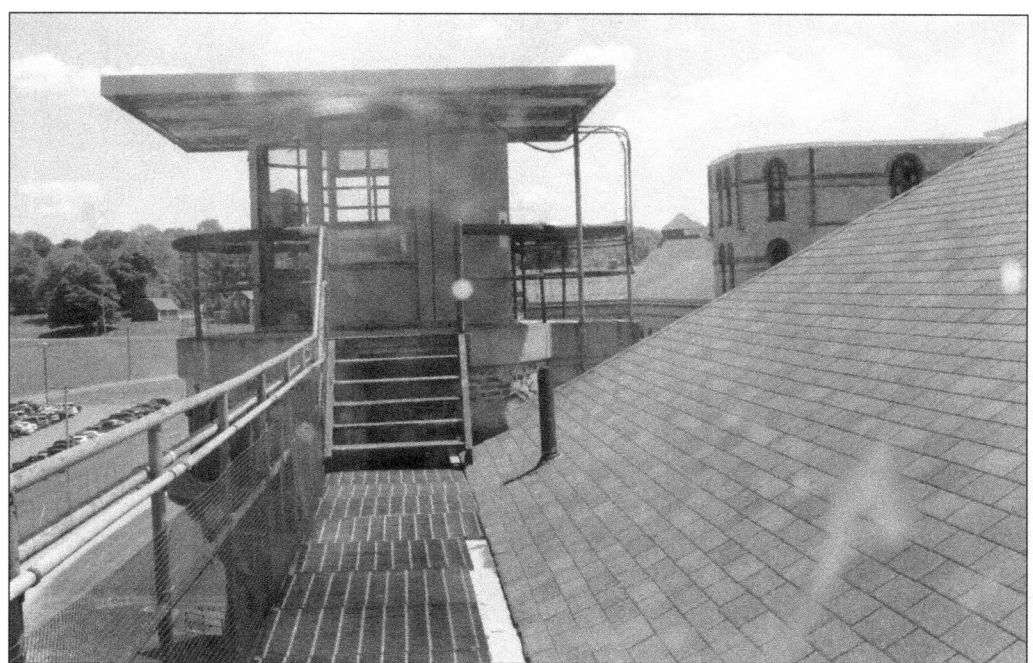

Among the guards' responsibilities was to walk the wall, which ran around three sides of the prison proper: north, east, and west. The narrow walkway along the 25-foot-high wall allowed guards to patrol and observe the inmates at all times while in the yard. Inmates crossed the yard or were there several times a day. The wall also allowed guards to have an unobstructed view of the area outside the prison to watch for activities that might cause security concerns. Towers placed along the wall were used by the guards during their eight-hour shifts. The wall and towers were built in the late 1890s by inmate labor.

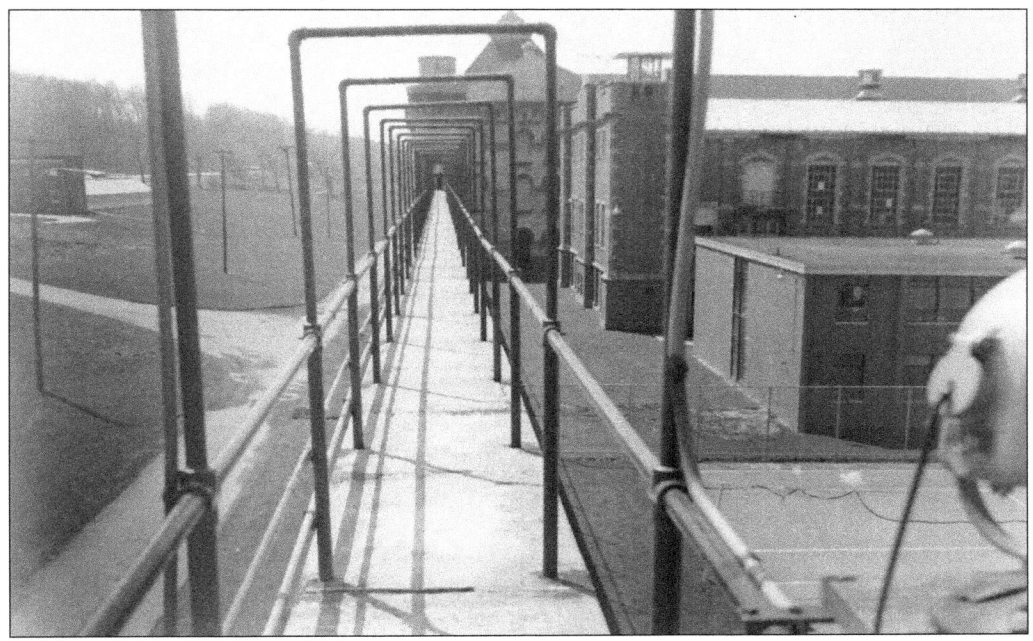

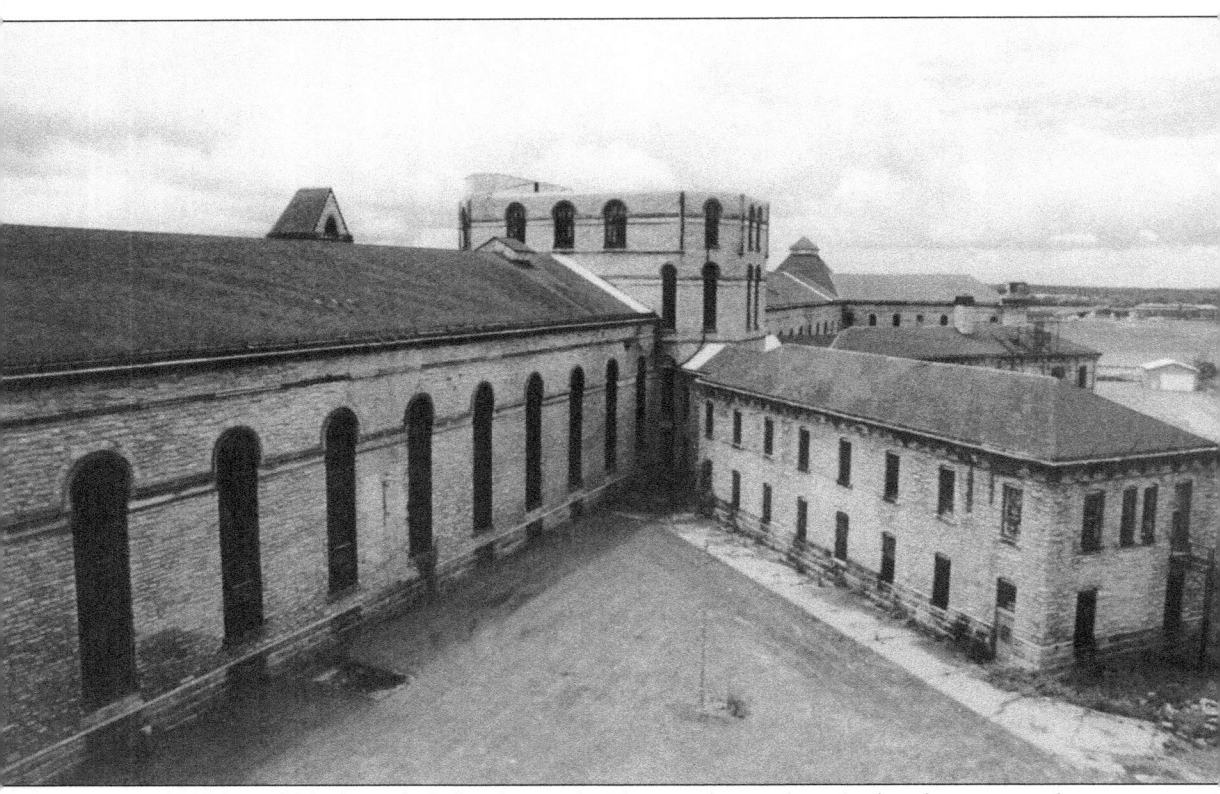

Each of the cell blocks included a "diagonal." The east diagonal was built to house an auditorium, classrooms, and special cells for difficult inmates. These cells, which included one padded cell, were primarily intended for inmates who feigned mental illness to avoid work. The light in the cells would remain on at all times, and the cells would be soundproof. It was believed at the time that the constant light and silence would be effective punishment. Later, the second floor became the training room for the barbershop. The first floor was later used for library scenes in the film *The Shawshank Redemption*. The west diagonal was intended for offices for the captain of the guard, space for inmates to meet with attorneys, and the inter-prison court for dealing with inmates who had violated rules.

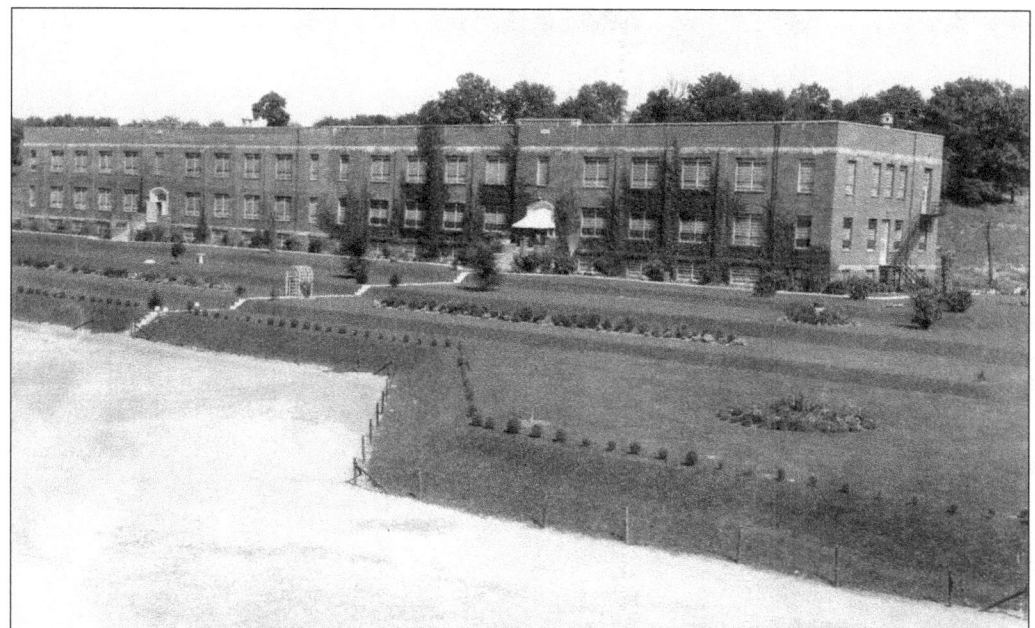

E-Dorm, built prior to 1960, was erected to house young inmates outside the prison walls when the reformatory started holding more serious offenders. Prior to this, inmates between the ages of 16 and 18 had been placed in youth correctional facilities, as they were too young to be housed in the general prison population with hardened criminals. E-Dorm, though located outside the prison walls, was still surrounded by barbed wire. The dorm had a separate school with its own teachers. The young inmates ate meals in the main dining hall but at different times than the general population, and they had a separate recreation area.

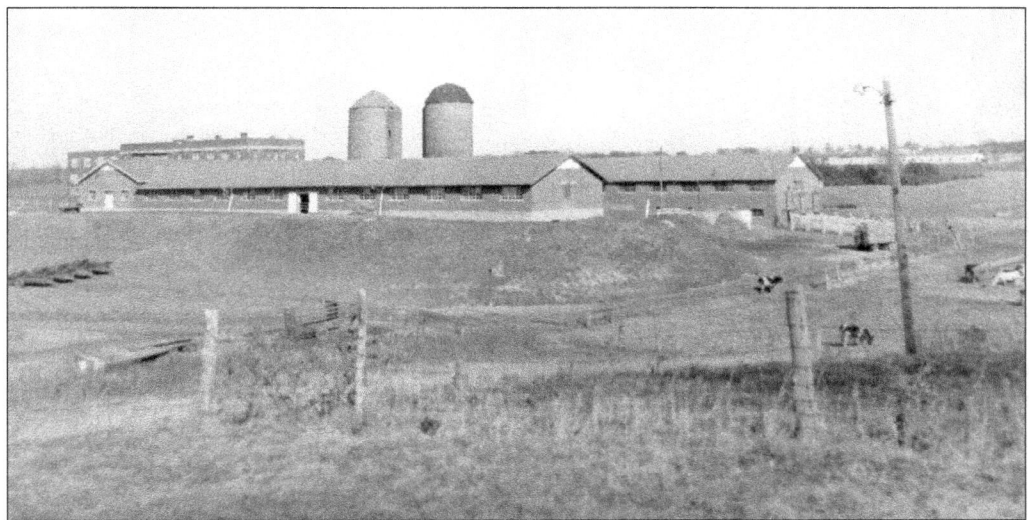

J-Dorm housed honors farm inmates. These men had proven themselves to be more trustworthy and were allowed to work the 1,600-acre farm. They worked the tillable land as well as the orchards, cattle barn, chicken and pig barns, slaughterhouse, and cannery. Near the farm was a building that stored harvested potatoes as well as coffins made in the wood shop. A portion of J-Dorm is seen here next to the silos.

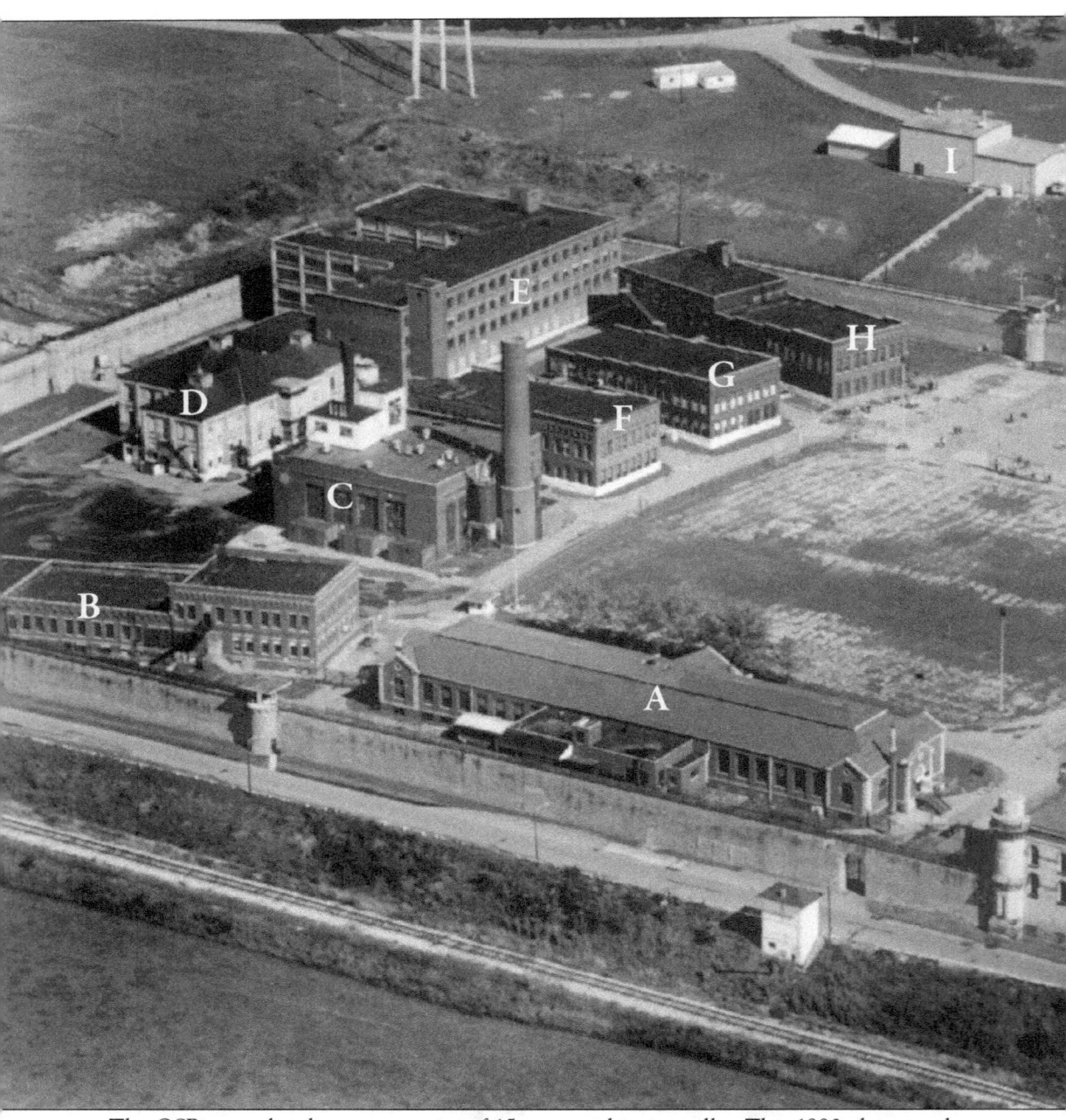

The OSR was a bustling community of 15 acres within its walls. This 1990 photograph was taken shortly before the building closed on December 31. From bottom left are (A) the mess/dining hall; (B) the maintenance and recreation building; (C) the old power plant; (D) the fire department/old furniture factory; (F) the shoe shop; (G) the tailor shop; (H) the machine shop;

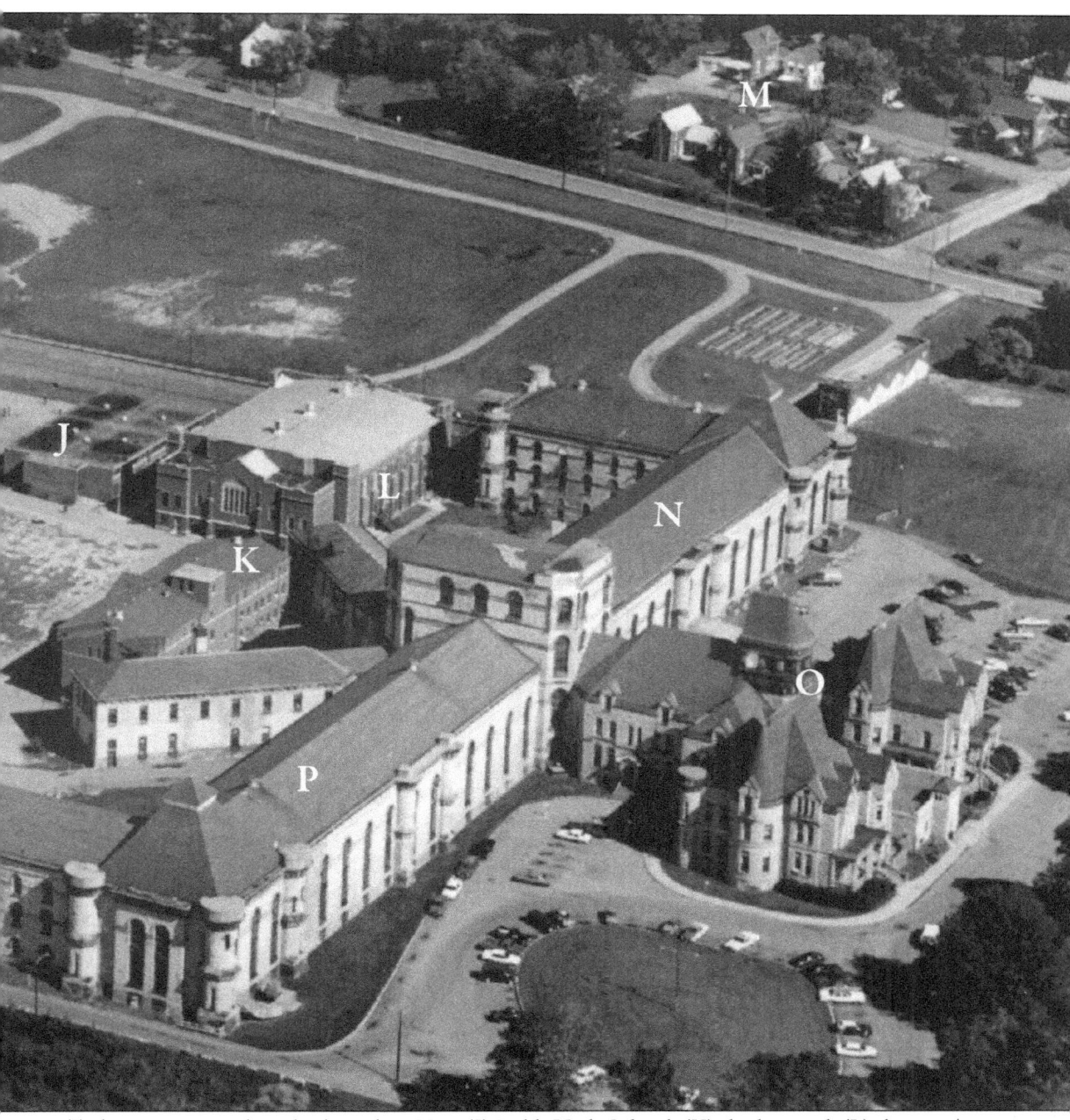

(I) the new power plant, built in the 1970s; (J) Fields High School; (K) the hospital; (L) the gym/chapel; (M) Hancock Heights; (N) the east cell block; (O) administration/living quarters; (P) the west cell block.

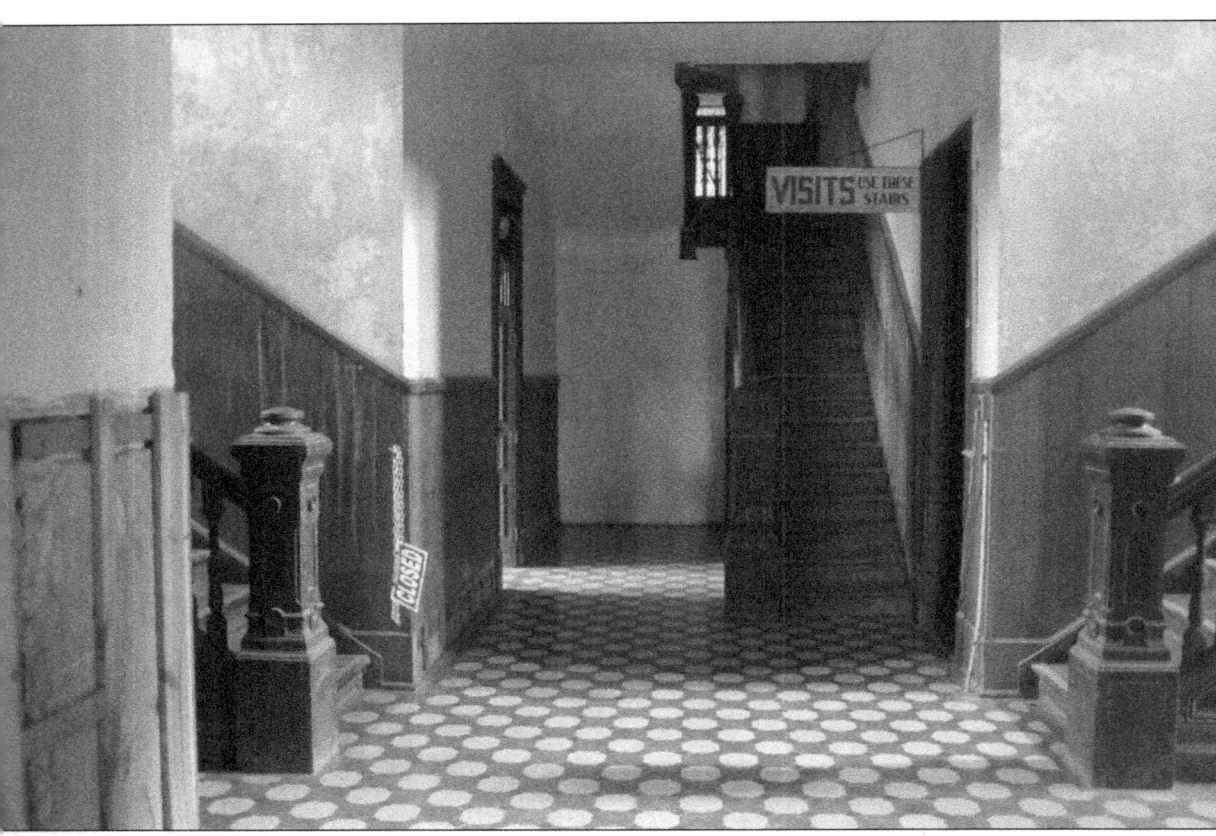

The center hall of the administrative area was integral to receiving prisoners. The stairs in the center of this photograph led to the central guard room (CGR). After being received, inmates would go to the CGR before being taken to various parts of the prison. The stairs to the left and right led to administrative offices. To the south of these stairs are doors leading from the parking areas. The west door was used to bring inmates to the facility in the early years; however, when the OSR became a maximum-security facility, cages were placed immediately inside the east door. Inmates were placed here until paperwork was signed and the reformatory took custody of them. The open doorway on the left led to the mail room. Each piece of mail to or from inmates was opened and read before delivery.

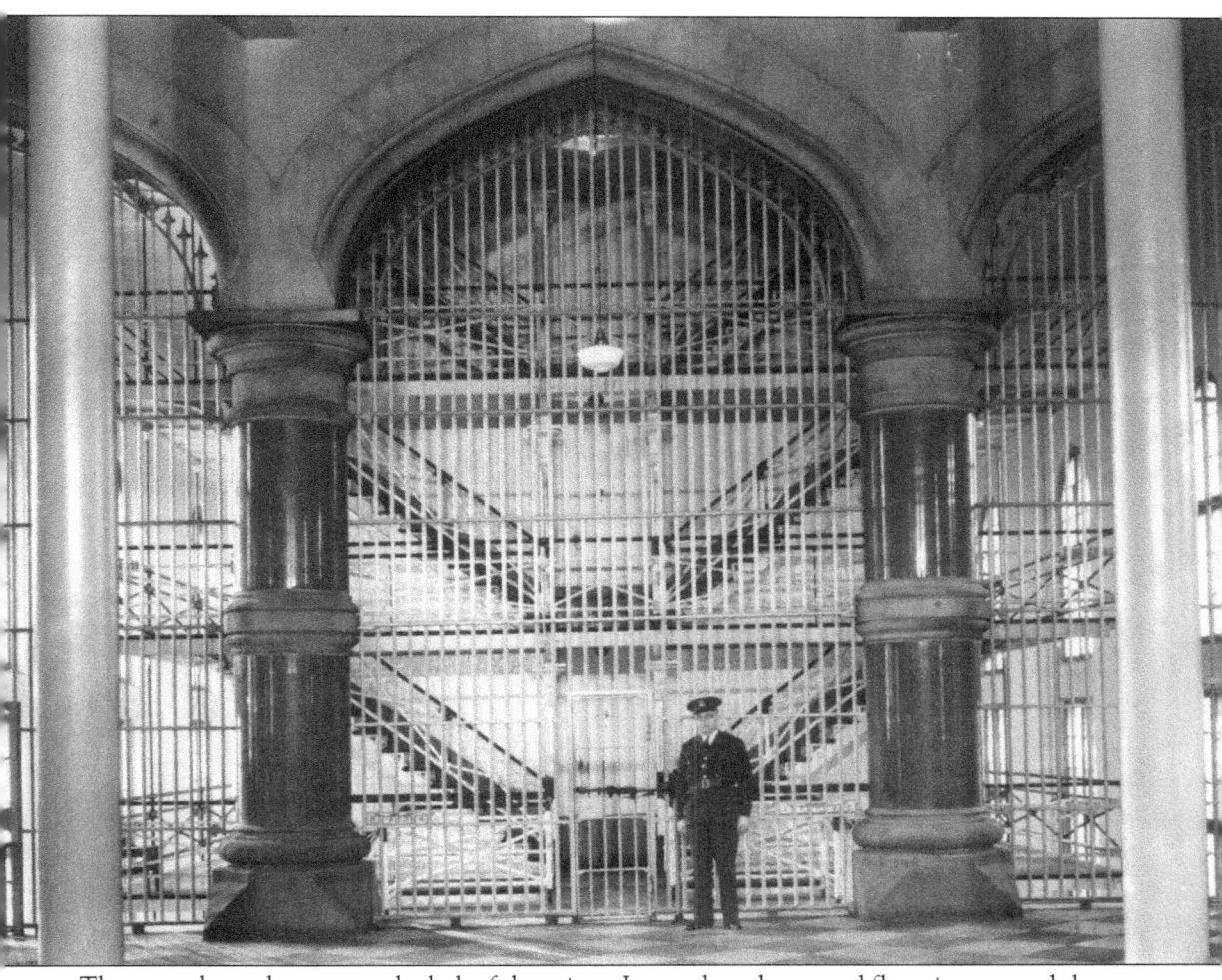

The central guard room was the hub of the prison. Located on the second floor, it separated the administration wing from the prison. Inmates entered the prison through this room to begin their sentences; likewise, they would leave the prison through the CGR upon being released or earning parole. The CGR also served as the visiting room. Inmates were allowed visits from immediate family members once a month. During visitation, curtains were pulled across the bars leading to the cell blocks to mask the sights and sounds within. Families could bring food to share, but each basket was carefully searched for contraband. Coats and handbags were also checked for items prohibited by the prison.

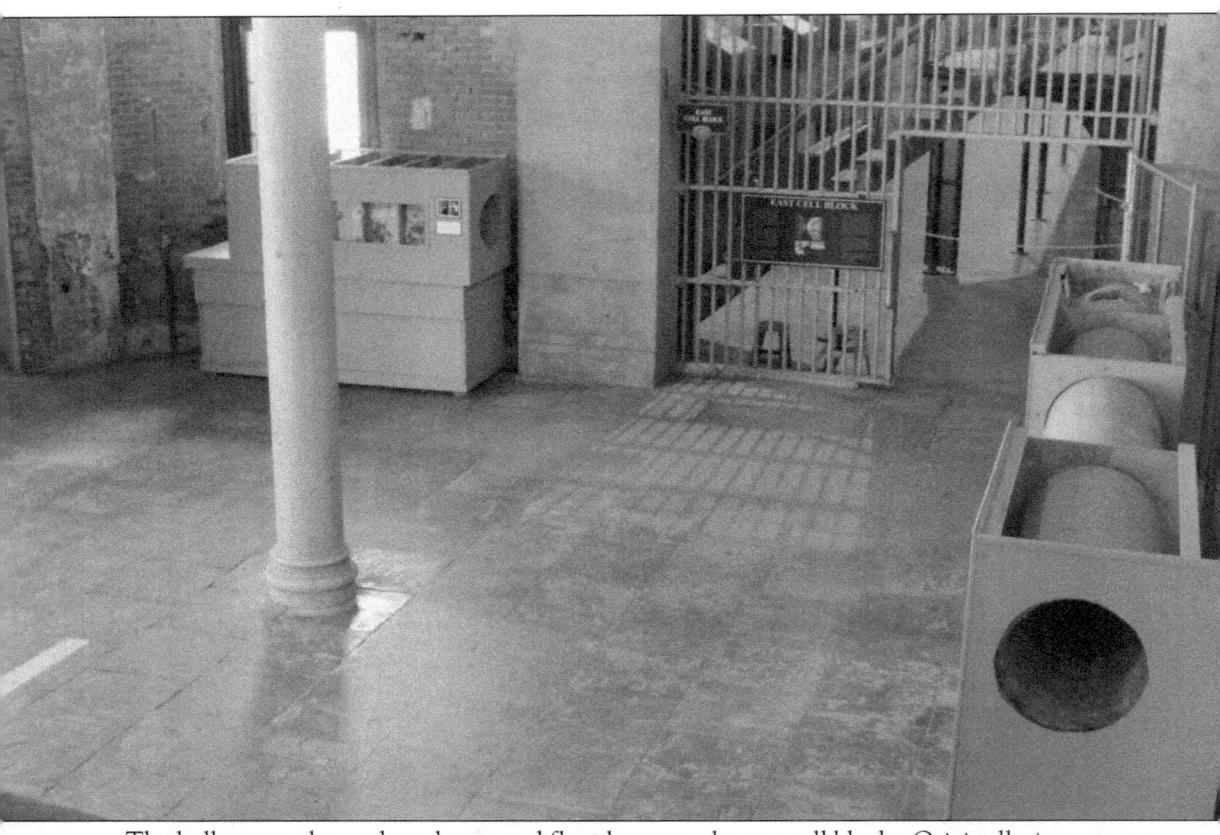

The bullpen was located on the ground floor between the two cell blocks. Originally, it was part of the cafeteria. When the new cafeteria was built, the bullpen became a pass-through to the outbuildings. Inmates were marched, by tier and block (east or west), to and from the cafeteria. They also passed through the bullpen when moving to and from any of the workshops, school, hospital, and the yard. Returning from meals, inmates were locked in their cells for the head count. In *The Shawshank Redemption*, the character Andy Dufresne and the other new inmates are marched into the prison and are lined up along a yellow line (lower left) to be addressed by Warden Norton.

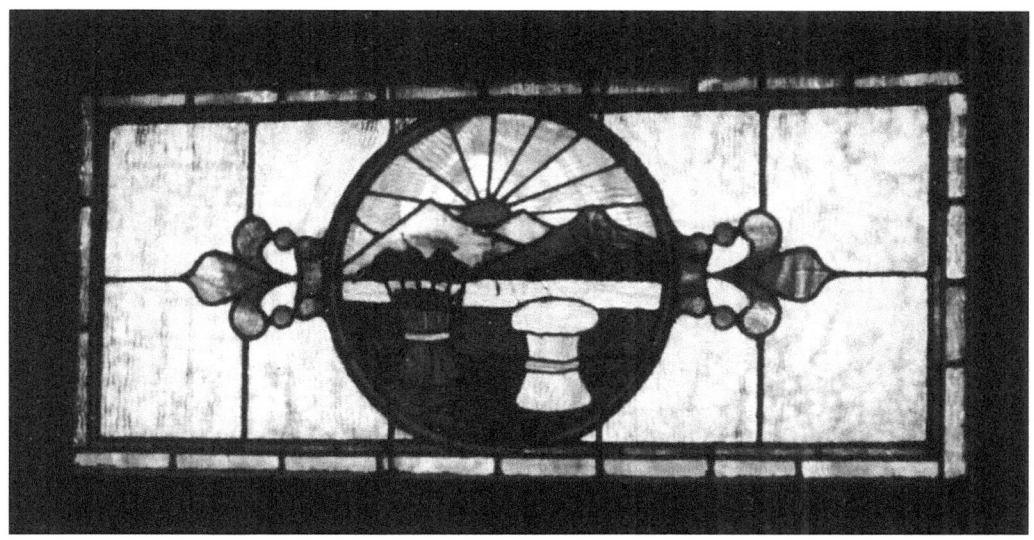

Stained-glass windows were a beautiful adornment to the administrative wings of the reformatory. Each front-facing set of windows on the first and second floors had a different set of stained-glassed windows as the upper pane. The photograph above shows a window with a representation of the seal of the State of Ohio, slightly modified to create this stained-glass representation, which hung over the center door. An oval-and-scroll design is shown below. Each set of stained glass has a separate name so as to distinguish it from the others. (Courtesy of Scott Sukel.)

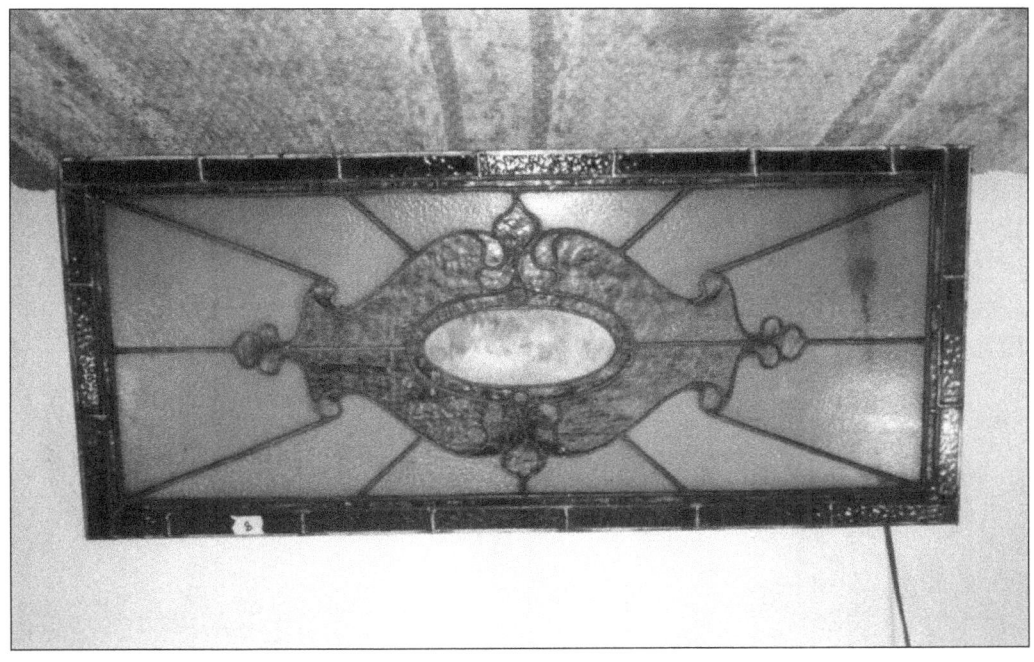

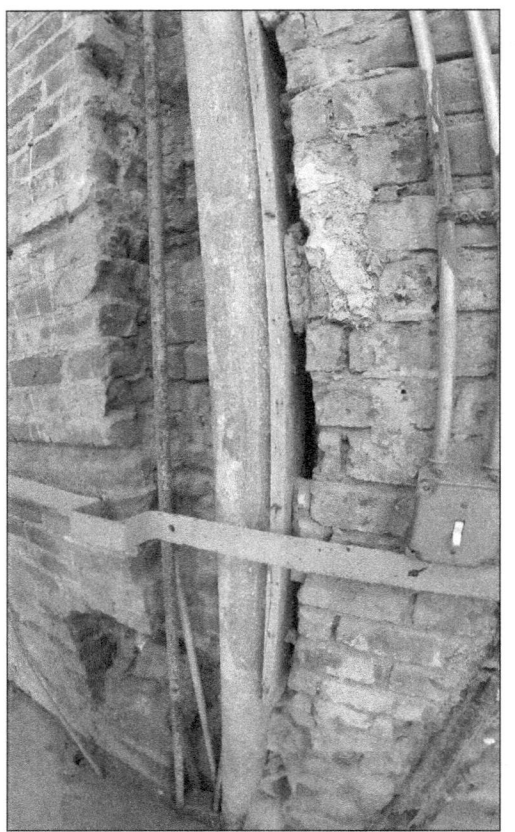

Scofield envisioned a building that would create a spiritual environment for the inmates. He wanted those incarcerated to take advantage of the time they spent at the OSR and felt that his design would give them hope and encourage them to change. Scofield's vision was manifested in the structure itself. He did not want the building to be marred by unnecessary clutter. To that end, he designed the downspouts to be built within the walls rather that outside. Understandably, these have broken over the last century and have been replaced with outdoor downspouts. (Courtesy of Scott Sukel.)

Whether intentional or accidental, the sunlight-formed "X" seen here is a curiosity. Because of the layout on the third floor between the east and west administrative wings, the feature appears on clear days. This anomaly separates two interesting areas of the building. To the left were rooms with cots that were rented to unmarried guards. To the right is where the chaplain met with inmates upon their arrival at the prison and those who were having personal problems. The stairs in the center led to the chapel. (Courtesy of Scott Sukel.)

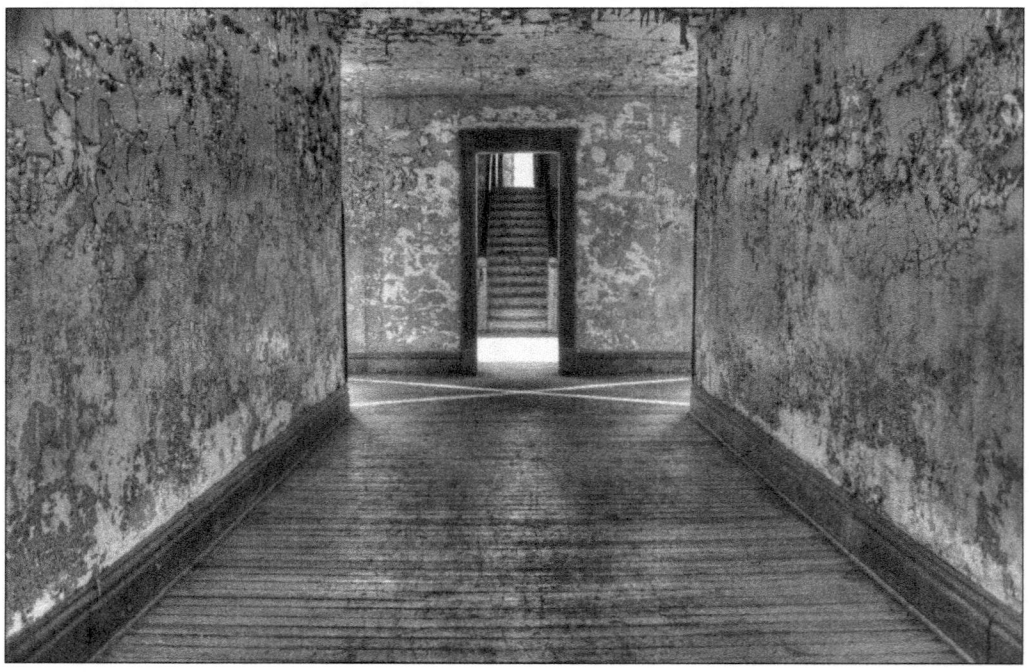

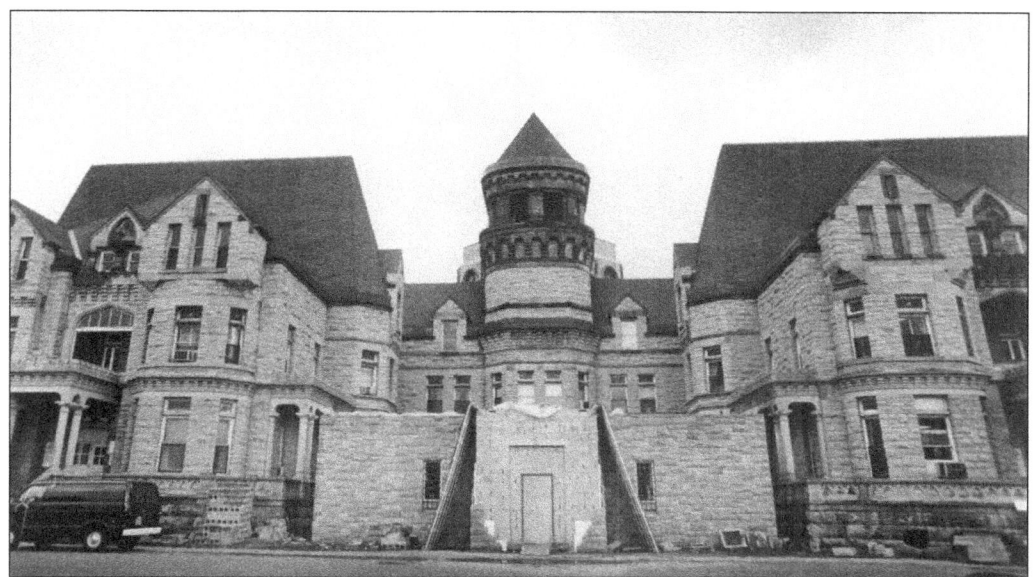

In the mid-1960s, prison security had become a higher priority. The facility was now a maximum-security prison with a death row, but no death house. The image above shows the construction of what was called the "A" building. Visitors would have their possessions searched before being admitted. Then, a staff member would be called to escort the visitor to their destination. To accommodate the new level of security, the lobby immediately inside the administrative wing was converted from the guards' dining room. To restore the building's original frontage, the "A" building was torn down in 2009, but its bell tower was retained. The view today is seen below. (Below, courtesy of Jeff Sprang/*Mansfield News Journal*.)

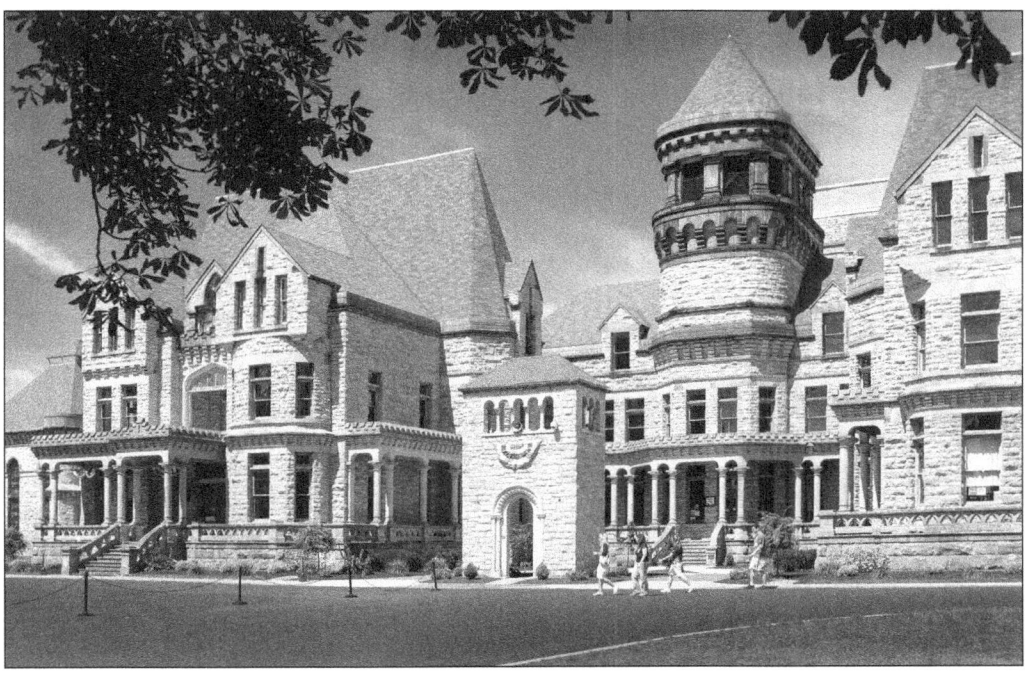

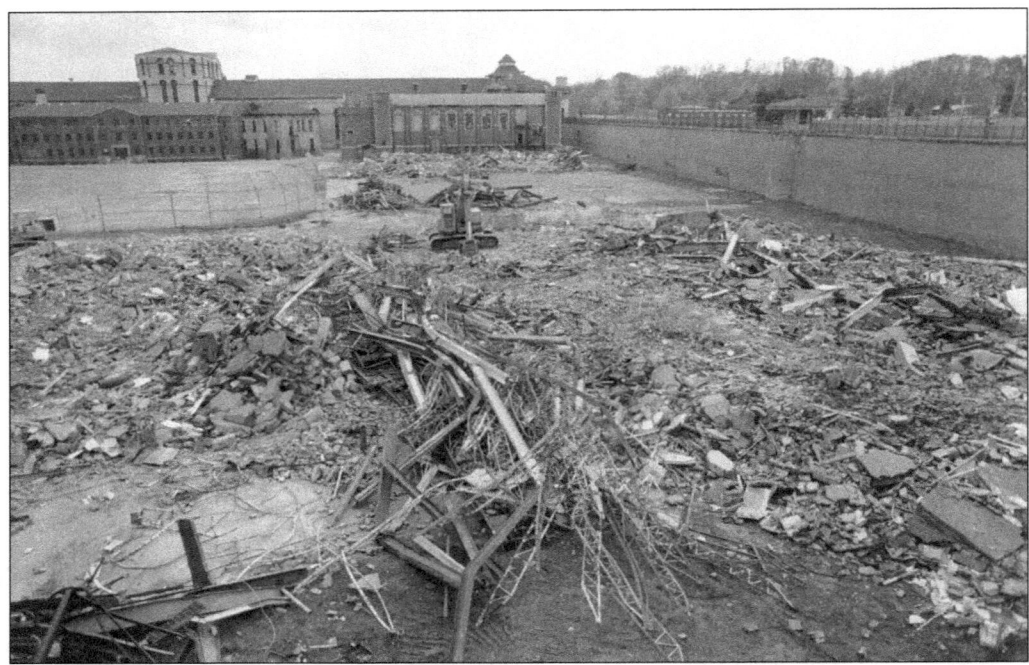

In 1983, the Ohio State Reformatory accepted the Boyd Consent Decree, the result of a lawsuit filed by the Council for Human Dignity that claimed "brutalizing and inhumane" treatment in the 90-year-old prison. The lawsuit cited the facility's ever-deteriorating conditions. The court ordered that the cell blocks be closed. On September 26, 1990, the first 31 inmates were transferred from the OSR to the new Mansfield Correctional Institute (MANCI), located next to the old prison. After the reformatory closed, discussion began on what to do with the massive building. Soon after the filming of *The Shawshank Redemption*, plans for demolition started. The photograph above shows the beginning of demolition of outbuildings in 1993. (Above, courtesy of Jeff Sprang/ *Mansfield News Journal*.)

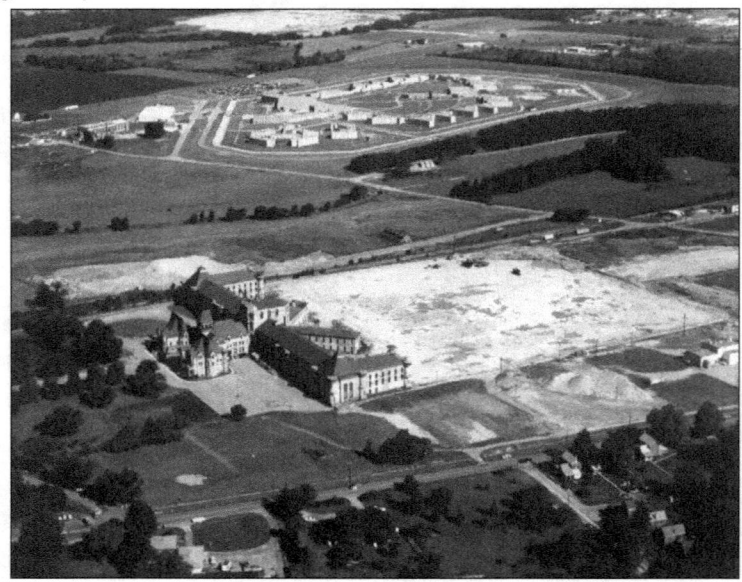

Two

KEEPERS OF THE KEYS

ADMINISTRATORS

During its 94 years, the Ohio State Reformatory had 11 wardens. Called superintendents, these men had varying degrees of influence on the reformatory's mission. Those who served the longest provided the most innovative and progressive opportunities for inmates. In the first half of the 20th century, three men, James Leonard (1904–1918), Thomas C. Jenkins (1918–1935), and Arthur Glattke (1935–1959), served a total of 55 years as wardens. The other wardens served 35 years: W.D. Patterson (1896–1897), W.E. Sutton (1897–1904), George Allarding (1959–1966), Bennett Cooper (1966–1970), Bernard Barton (1970–1972), Robert White (1972–1975), Frank Gray (1975–1983), and Eric Dahlberg (1983–1990). As the era of horse-drawn carriages gave way to the modern age, the superintendents brought the most up-to-date technology into the training and work programs available to inmates. These programs allowed inmates to gain experience in areas of interest that would allow them to work in that field after their release. The superintendents placed a high value on learning and continued to expand educational opportunities at the prison. By the time the reformatory closed, high school diplomas could be earned through the accredited high school, Fields School, and inmates could work toward a college degree by studying with visiting professors. The educational and training opportunities would not have been possible without the support of dedicated superintendents.

Guards were also part of the prison administration. They were charged with keeping order and controlling the prisoners. In a very real sense, the guards were on the front line every day. In the history of the OSR, three guards lost their lives at the hands of inmates, former inmates, or those trying to break inmates out of the facility. When inmates violated the rules of the prison, it fell to the guards to carry out punishment. When an infraction was reported, the inmates went before the prison's "Court of Appeals," headed by the assistant superintendent. If the inmate was found guilty of a rule violation, the result was loss of privileges or "lost time," which resulted in days or months being added to his minimum sentence. No matter the level of punishment, it fell to the guards for enforcement.

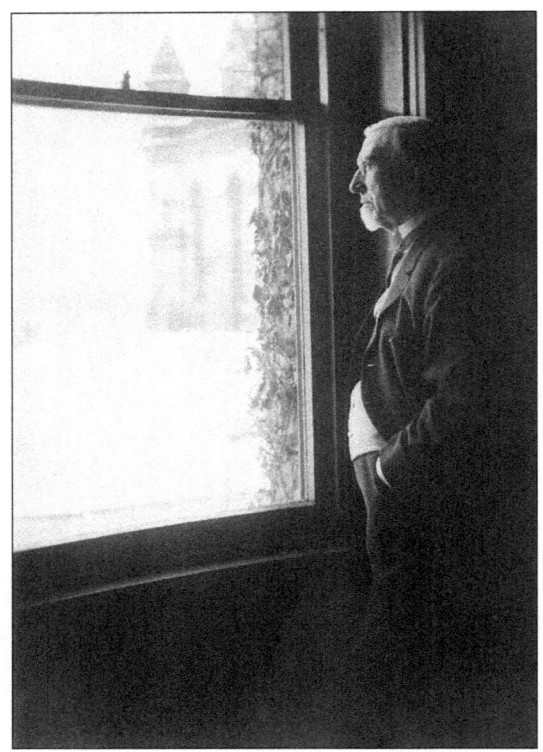

Dr. James A. Leonard (at left) was the third warden at the OSR. Serving from 1901 to 1918, he instituted some progressive ideas in penology. He believed that young men should be punished for their crimes but that they should have the opportunity to be rehabilitated. He believed that the "reformatory movement" was essential to avoiding recidivism. Leonard lived at the reformatory with his wife and four children. During his tenure, he and his wife hosted local, state, and national officials in the warden's quarters with lavish dinners and overnight accommodations. In 1918, Leonard's daughter Laura had her wedding at the residence (below). In keeping with the esteem with which the warden and his family were held in Mansfield society, the event was reported in great detail in the July 19, 1918, edition of the *Mansfield News*.

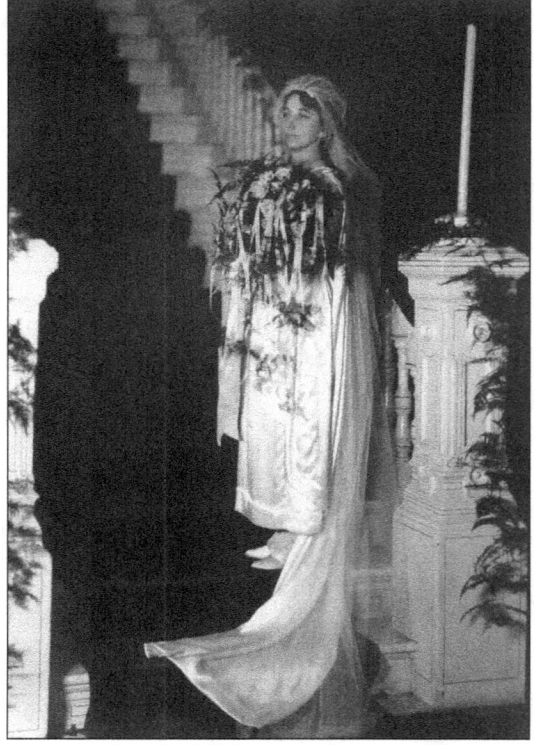

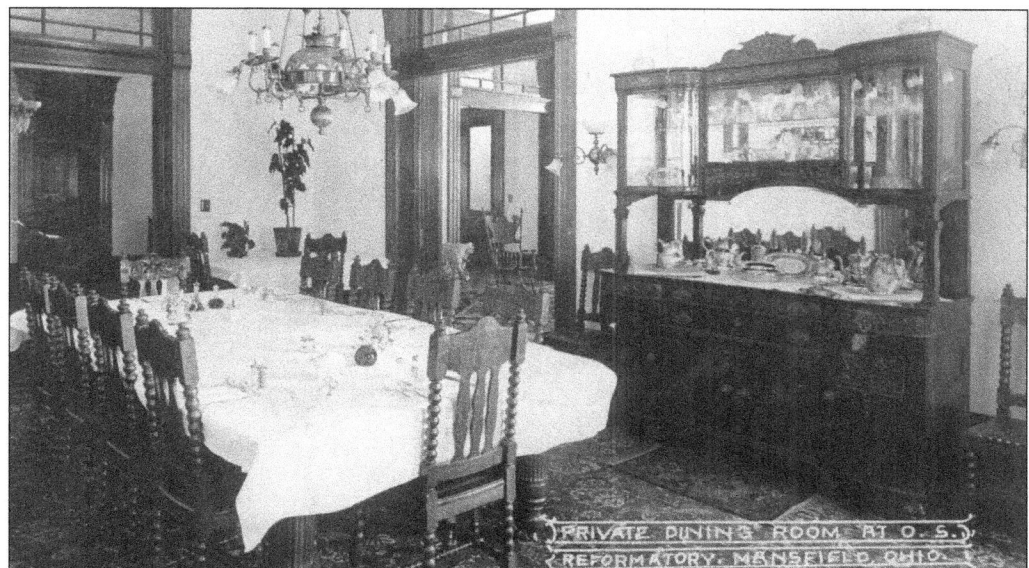

The formal dining room hosted many state dinners. Visitors to Ohio would be brought from Columbus to the reformatory for ornate dinners that showcased the building. The meals were cooked in the kitchen and delivered to the area by dumbwaiter. Servers were "trustee" inmates who made sure each guest was properly waited on. When the room was not being used for formal dinners, it was the family dining room. The image above shows the elaborate credenza and dining chairs. Those pieces, along with the carved table, were made in the furniture factory. The doors in the background led to the warden's parlor. As seen below, aside from the credenza, the newly restored dining room does not contain original furniture, as it was removed many years before. The door on the right leads to a catering kitchen, which kept food warm prior to being served.

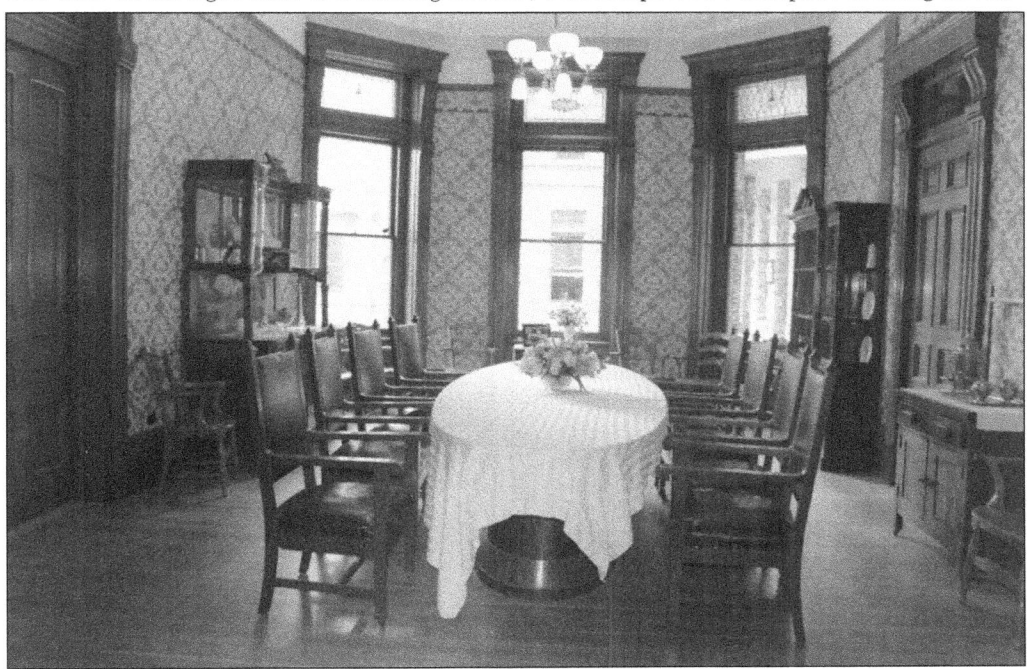

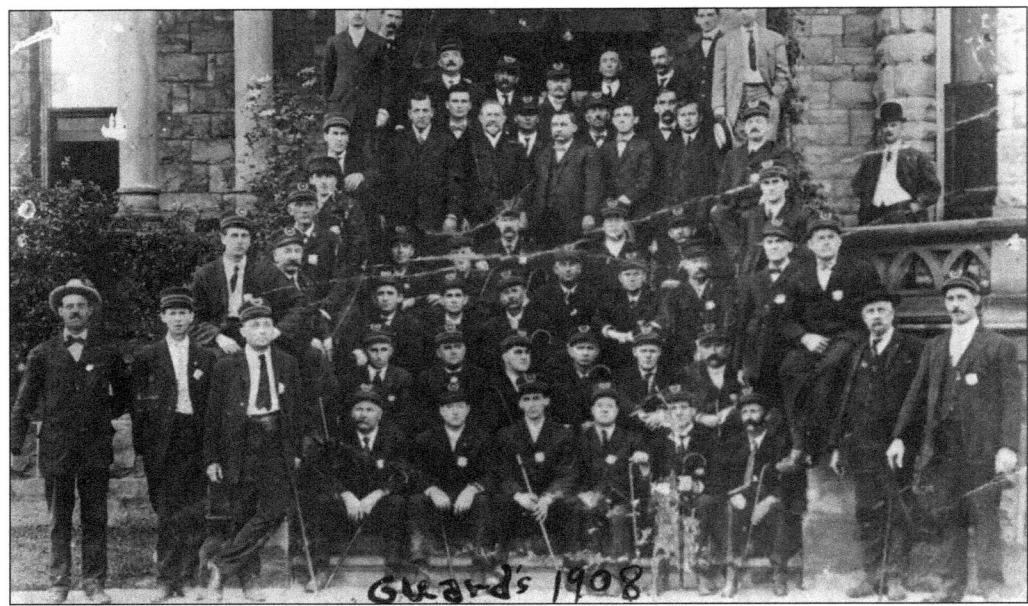

The initial guards employed by the Ohio State Reformatory began work upon the arrival of the first inmates in 1896. The guards were scheduled to work six days a week and were paid a salary of $500 a year. Their duties included walking the wall and guard tower, patrolling the grounds, walking the cell blocks, and supervising inmates. Guards locked and unlocked each cell door in the morning and after the inmates were confined at night. For many years, the inmates were only placed in their cells to sleep. Much of the guards' duties involved supervision of inmates while they were in school or workshops. Guns were never a part of a guard's equipment except while on the wall; instead, they carried billy clubs.

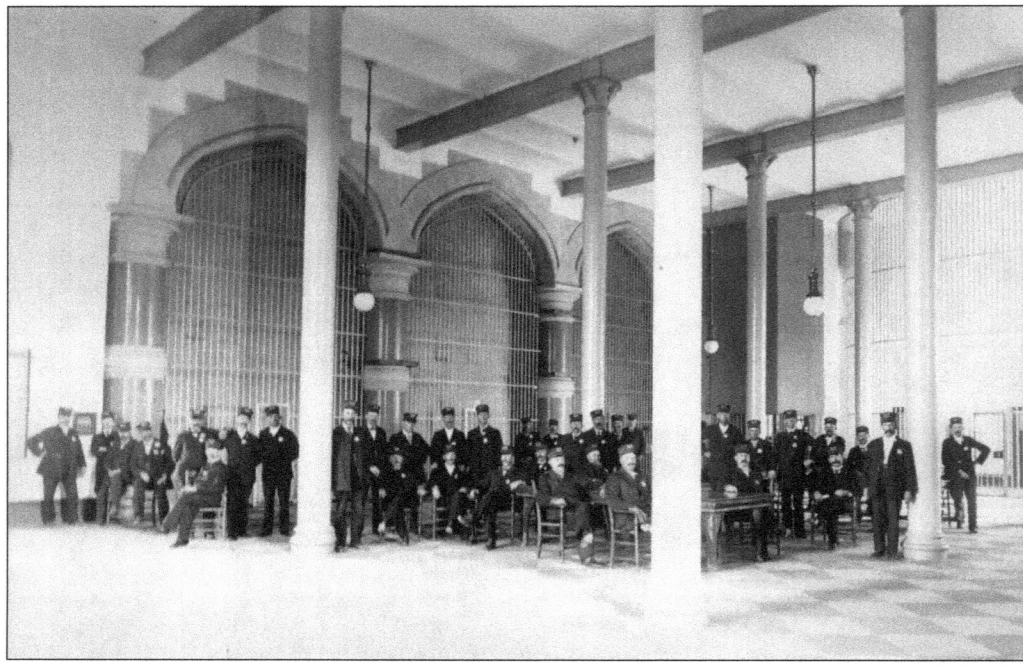

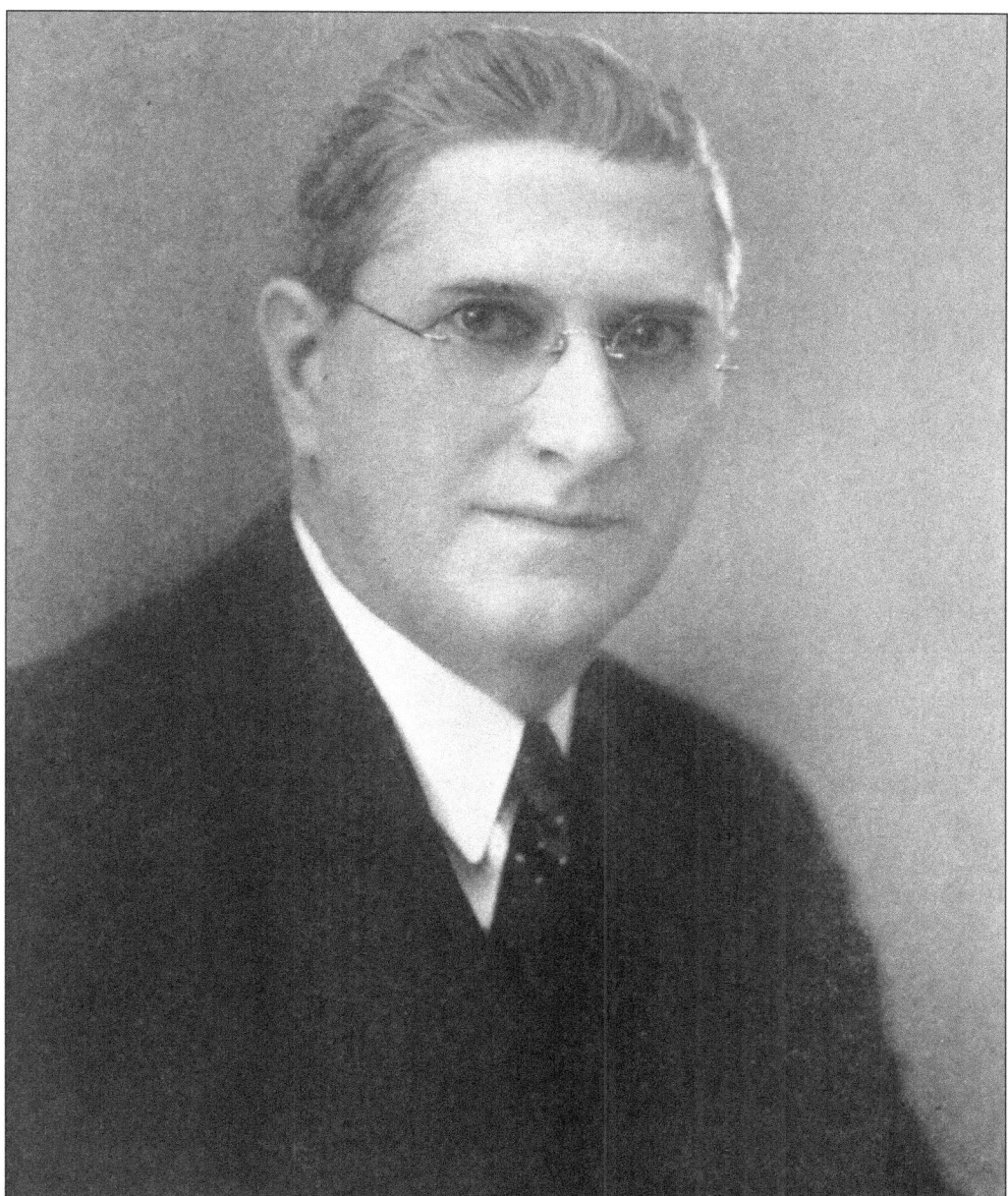

Supt. Thomas Jenkins began his work at the Ohio State Reformatory in 1905. Leaving a post as a public school teacher, Jenkins's plan was to work at the reformatory for one year before moving on to another job. Fortunately for the OSR, his plans changed as he was promoted, from guard to teacher to field officer and then to assistant superintendent. In 1918, Jenkins was appointed superintendent and served until he was transferred in 1935. During his 30-year tenure at the reformatory, Jenkins witnessed or supervised tremendous growth. The east cell block was only partially completed, with 201 cells, in 1905. A cutting room in the tailor shop was added, and the furniture factory was rebuilt and expanded following a fire. The power plant was constructed, as was a new school, dining room, and chapel. When the population expanded beyond capacity, E-Dorm and J-Dorm were built outside the prison walls.

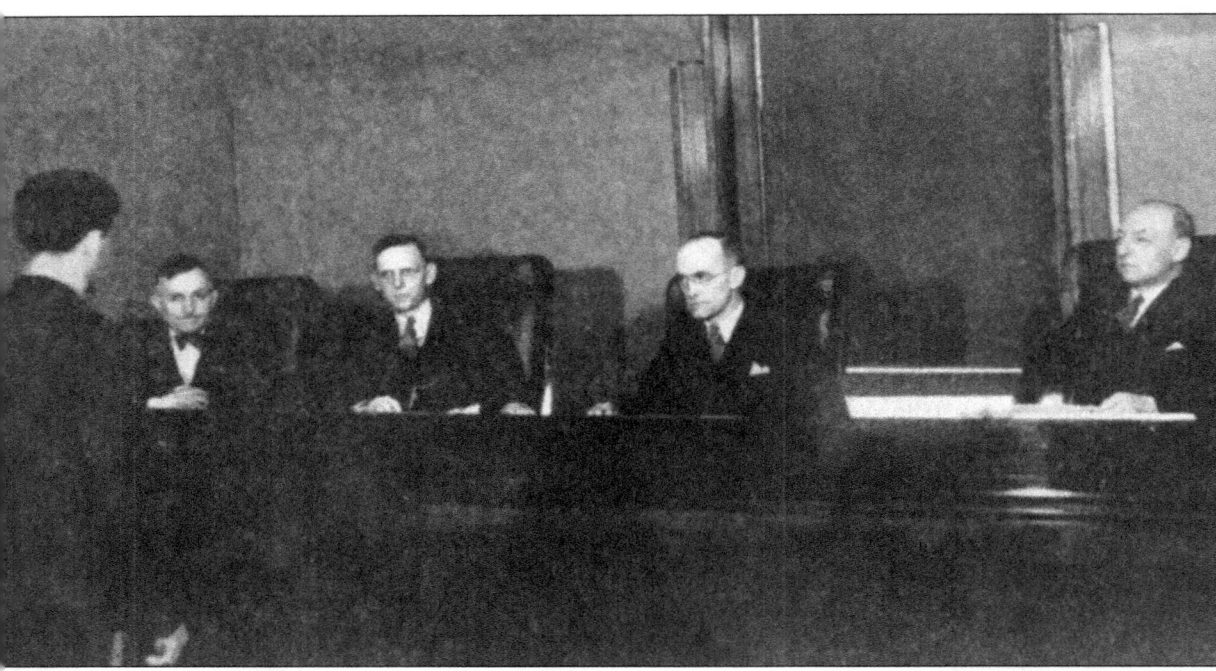

The parole board was charged not only with ensuring that the release of a prisoner posed no safety issue for the community, but also that the inmate was prepared for a successful life after prison. Comprising four men from around the state, the board met once a month at the OSR to hear cases of inmates eligible for parole. The parole board reviewed a resume of the inmate and a record of his time at the reformatory. The hearing took on the appearance of a trial. The prisoner was questioned to determine if time in the reformatory had successfully rehabilitated him. He was also asked about his crime, his attitude toward his time in prison, and his feelings about a society had that sent him to the OSR. About one third of those who came before the board were granted release.

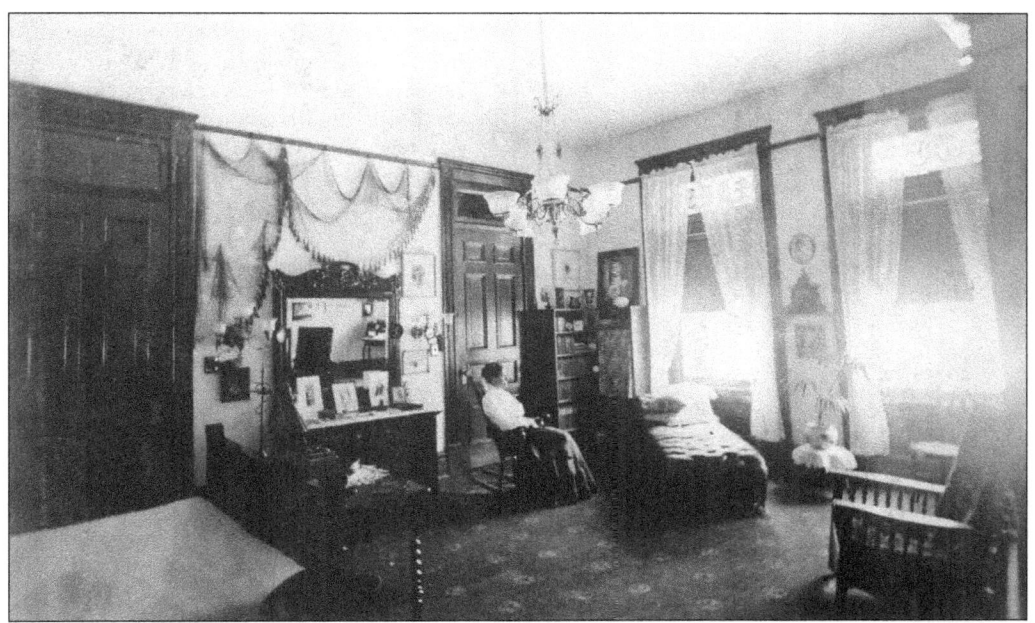

The spiritual life of the inmates was considered an important part of their rehabilitation. The first chaplain, Dr. W.H. Locke, was present with Supt. W.D. Patterson when the first 150 prisoners arrived in 1896. Locke and his family lived in ornately decorated rooms in the chaplain's quarters in the west administrative wing. From the earliest days of the OSR, the administrators' quarters were attended to by "trustees" who cleaned and served meals to the families and looked after young children, who resided in the residence until they reached an age of majority. Locke retired from his position in 1907. Mrs. Locke is in the living room (above) and bedroom (below) of the chaplain's quarters in the early 1900s.

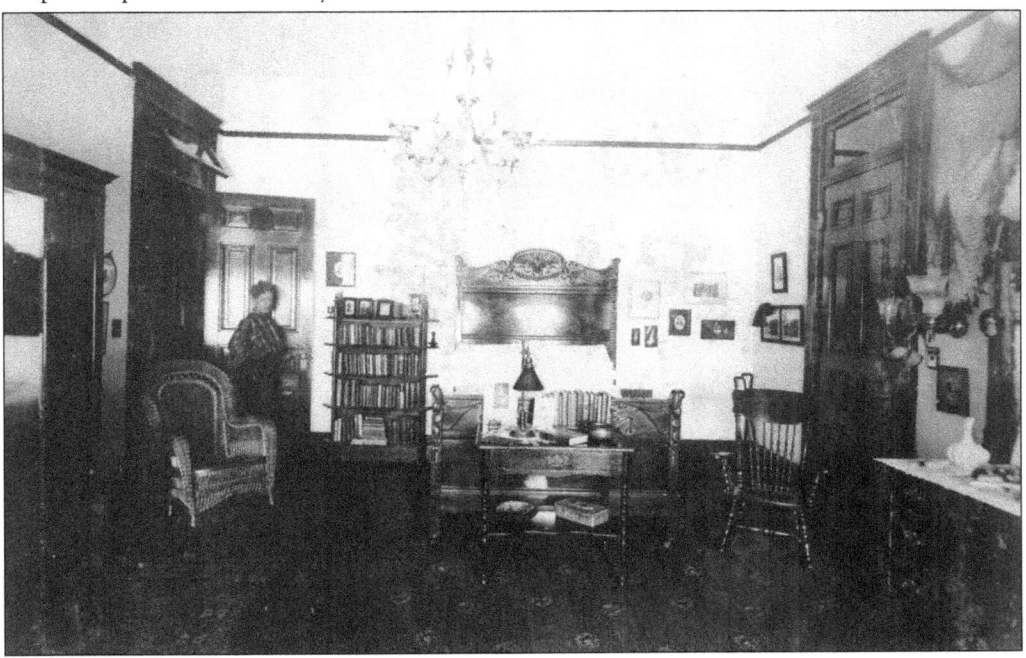

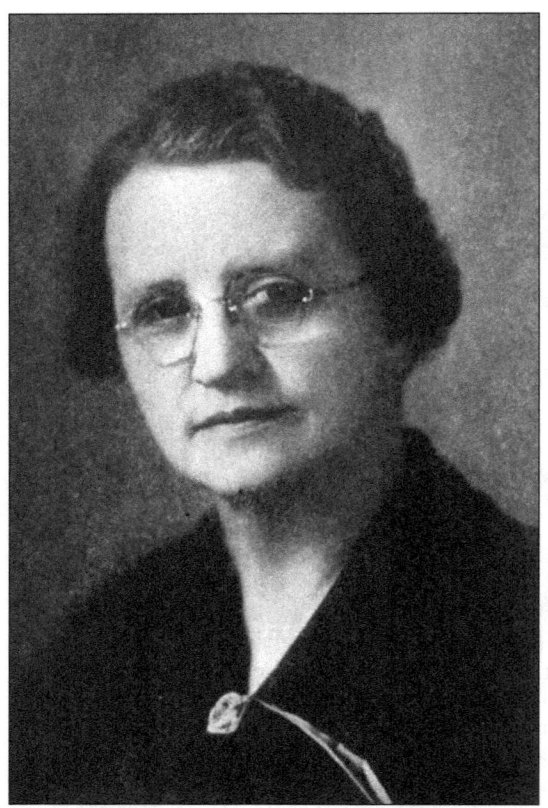

Thomas Jenkins's wife became the first female employee of the OSR. During her husband's tenure as superintendent, she served as the first matron. Along with purchasing, maintenance, and upkeep of the residences, she also oversaw hundreds of inmates who were charged with the cleaning of the residences as well as meal service to the families, guests, and guards. Her favorite duty was the planning of formal dinner parties, which brought dignitaries from around the state and region to the reformatory.

During Superintendent Jenkins's tenure, he was temporarily assigned to the Lancaster Reform School when its superintendent was abruptly fired. In his absence, C.W. Rowe (left) was appointed on a temporary basis. Rowe had risen through the ranks of the institution, starting as a guard in 1898. By 1900, he had attained the rank of captain, then disciplinarian. He was reassigned to a field office in Cleveland. Rowe came back to the OSR and was promoted by Jenkins to the position of assistant superintendent.

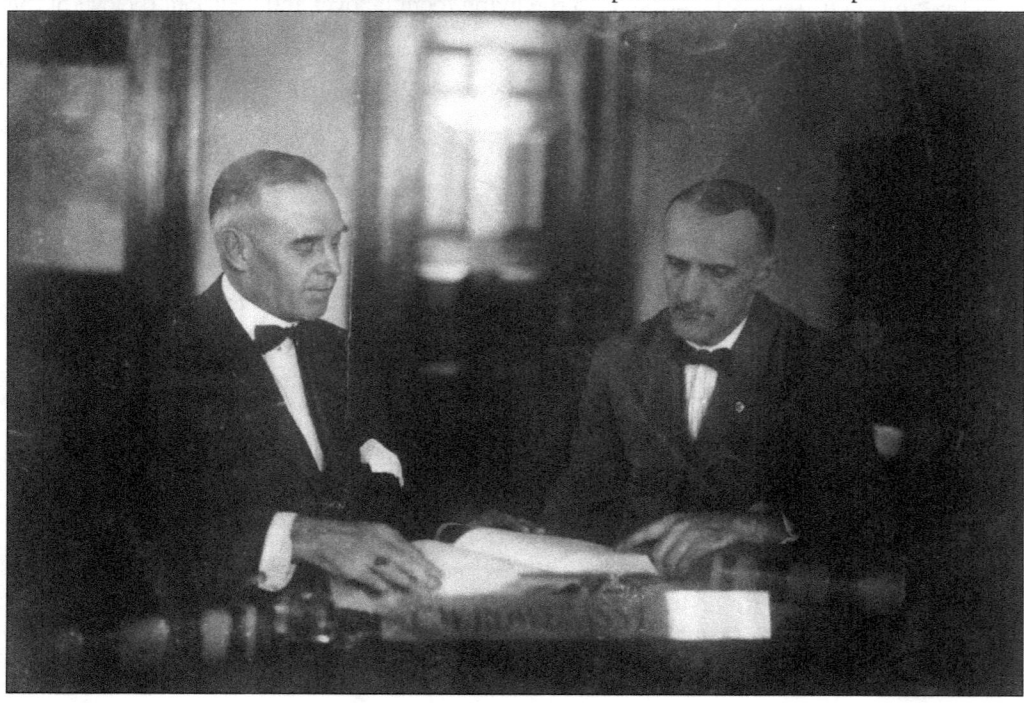

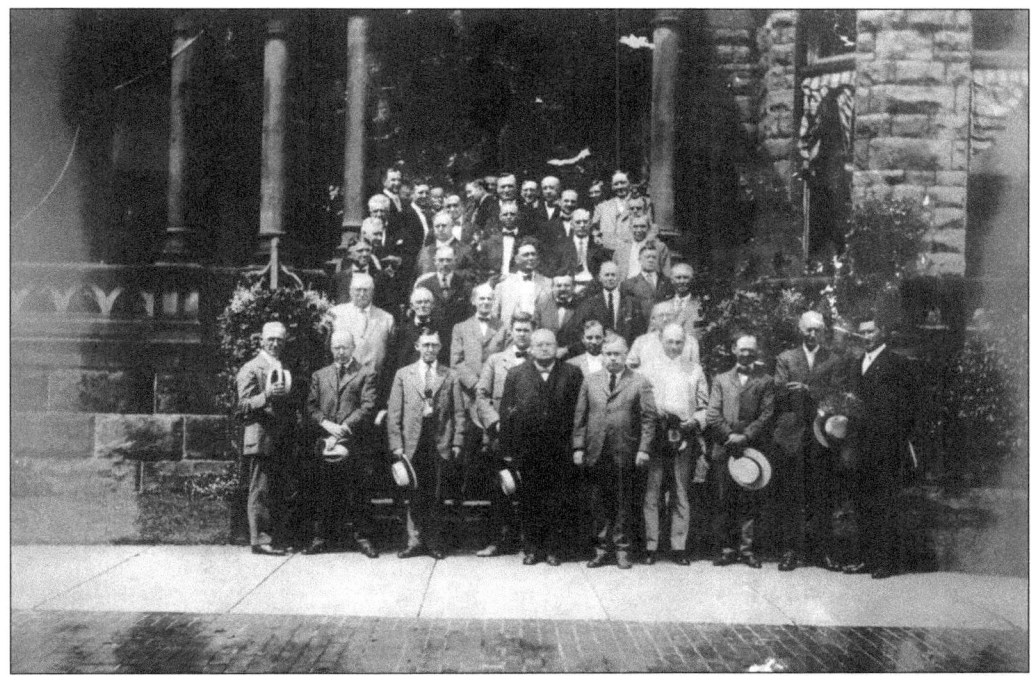

Not all employees dealing directly with inmates were guards. Throughout the history of the OSR, many civilian and non-uniformed staff worked within the walls and with the inmates. In this 1920s group photograph are administrators, department heads, and teachers both in the school and workshops. Other civilians included the prison's doctors and dentists, who were licensed in their specialty and served as civilian employees. During this time, the superintendent's wife, Mrs. Jenkins, became the first female employee at the OSR. Later, women became secretaries to administrators as well as nurses and eventually guards.

Non-uniformed employees were vital to the economic life of the reformatory. The sales and manufacturing department (pictured) was an important group. These men were charged with promoting the products made within the walls of the OSR, not only to other state institutions but to the private sector as well. The industries included the furniture factory, clothing factory, shoe factory, and printing shop. In a 1913 catalog created by this department, the reformatory was called the "University of Second Chances."

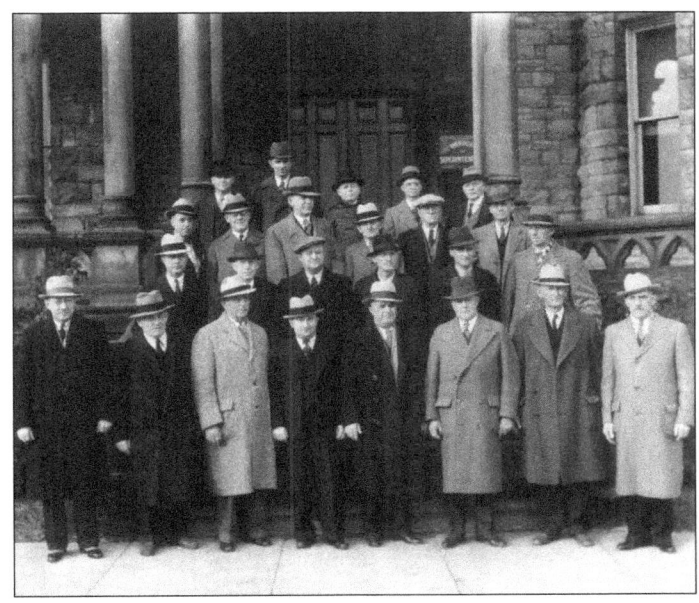

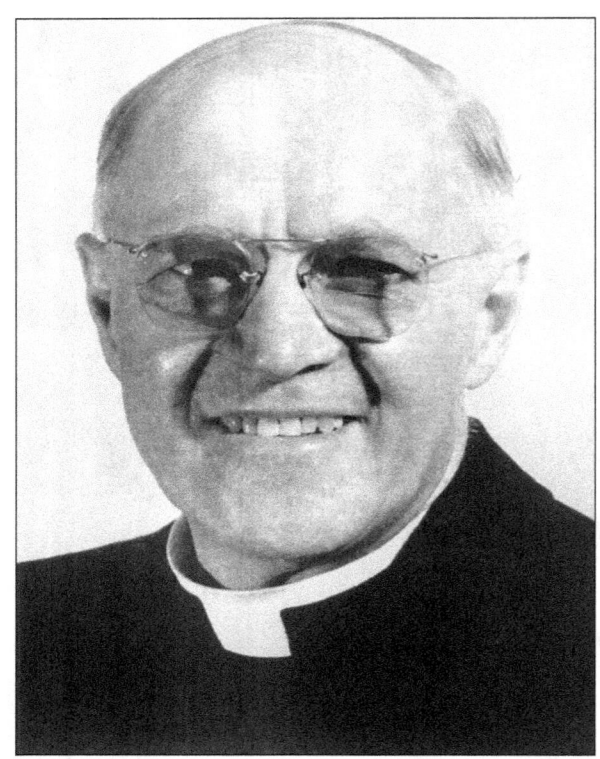

The chaplain met with each inmate sent to the prison. Along with spiritual guidance, the chaplain was charged with planning entertainment, which included movies, boxing matches, and talent shows. He was in charge of the institution's publication, the *New Day*, which chronicled the day-to-day happenings at the OSR. Along with the superintendent, the chaplain and school administrators would recommend inmates worthy of parole. On a few occasions, the chaplain and band director organized talent shows. The longest-serving chaplain was Martin Wappner, seen at left, who came to the reformatory in 1938 and served until 1960, when he was killed in a car accident on June 15. In keeping with the OSR's tradition, he conducted Protestant services and hosted clergy from other faiths as they performed services. Below, Chaplain Wappner and his wife, Elizabeth, pose in 1957 outside of their residence.

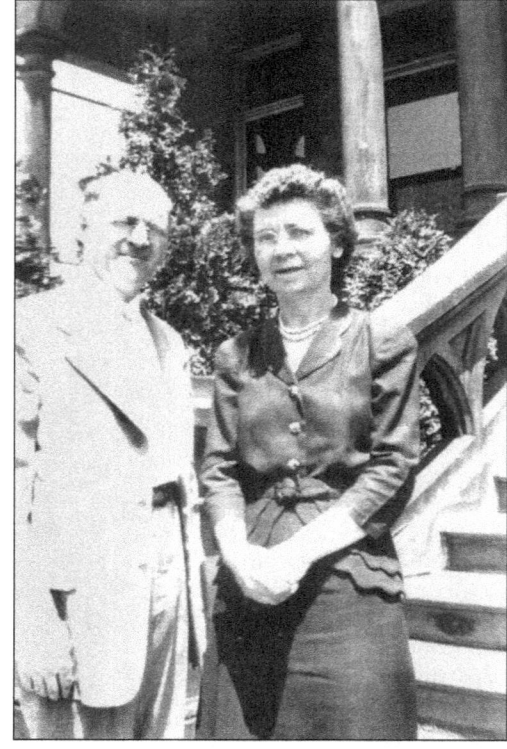

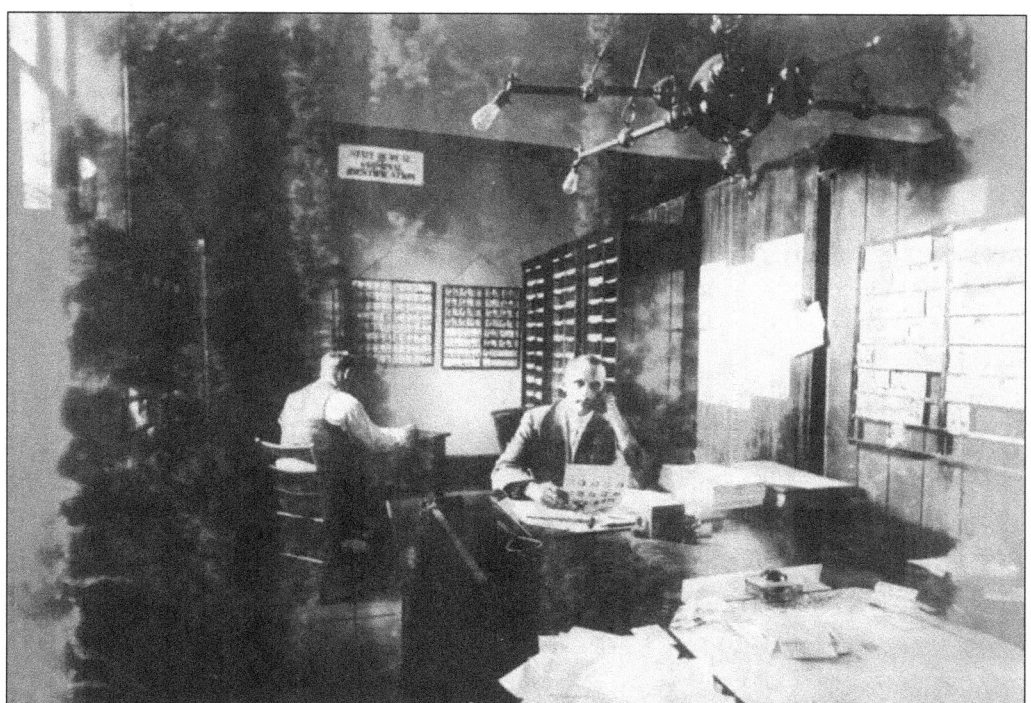

The identification department was integral not only to the reformatory but also to other law-enforcement agencies. New inmates met with the department within a day of intake. An identification department officer would meet with each inmate for an interview to gather information. The inmate would be asked about family history, aliases, criminal history, and details of the crime that brought about their incarceration. Once this information was recorded, mug shots (front and profile views) and fingerprints were taken. Included on the inmate's card were eye and hair color, height, weight, nationality, and identifying marks, scars, or tattoos. In 1933, the identification department had over 40,000 sets of prints on file, and it added over 1,200 prints to the system from incoming inmates.

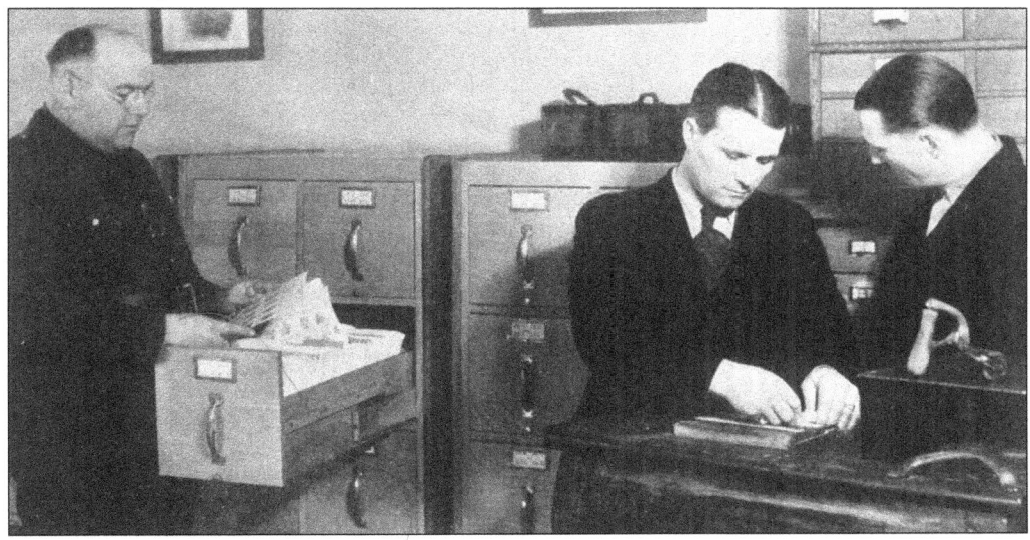

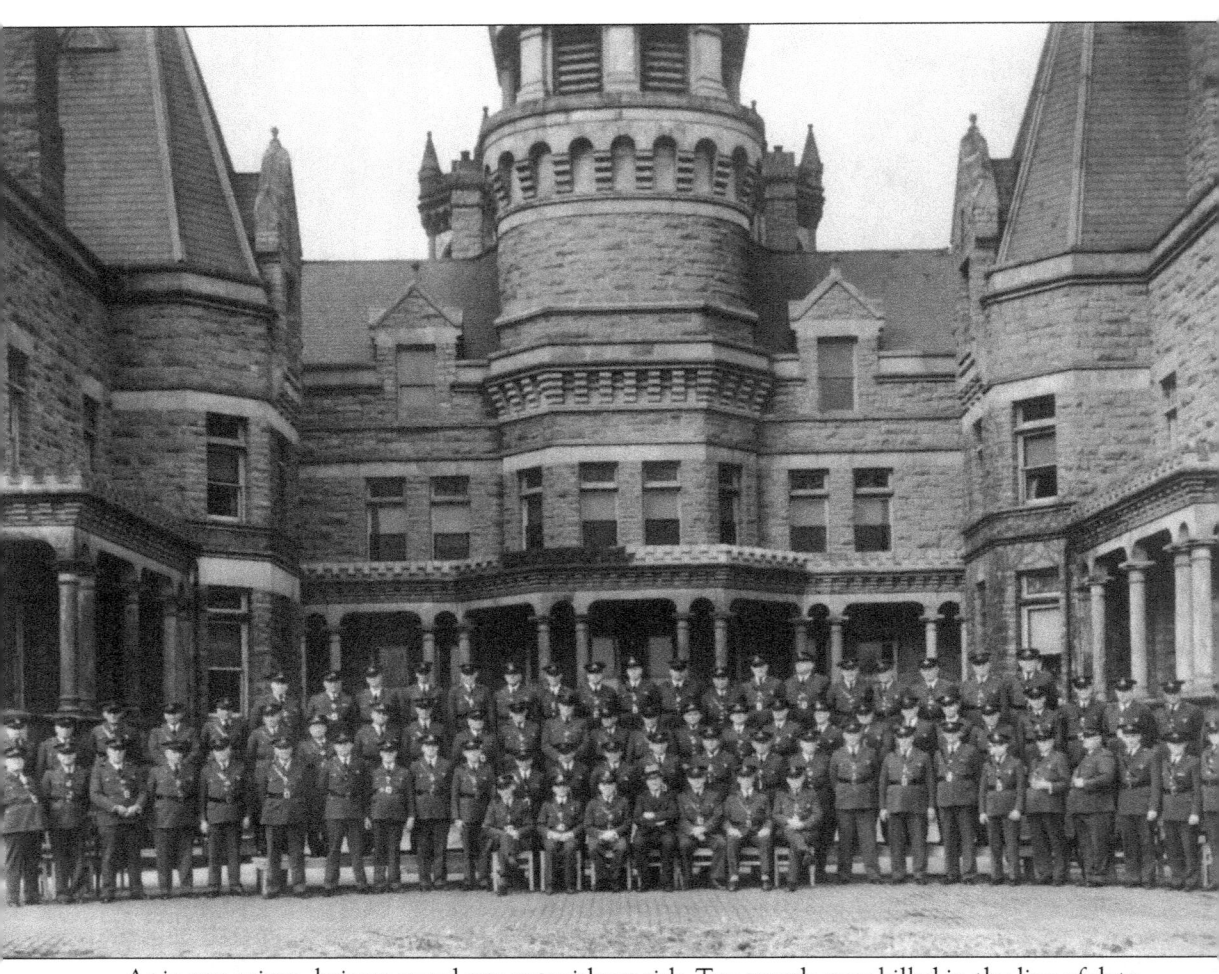

As in any prison, being a guard was not without risk. Two guards were killed in the line of duty. In 1926, Philip Orleck, an ex-convict, approached the west gate in an attempt to break out an inmate. In the process, he shot and killed Officer Urban Wilford. Orleck was later executed in the electric chair for the killing. In 1932, inmate Merrill Elza Chandler, being held in solitary, was able to break the lock on his cell and lay in wait. He bludgeoned Office Frank Hanger with a three-foot bar of welded iron as part of a plan to escape with 12 other inmates. A trustee was credited with foiling the plot and attempting to save Hanger's life. Chandler and another inmate involved were both executed on November 24, 1933. Tragically, J.E. Niebel (second row, fourth from the left), his wife, and daughter were murdered in 1948. Supt. Thomas Jenkins is also seen (seated center, first row) in this 1934 photograph of the guards.

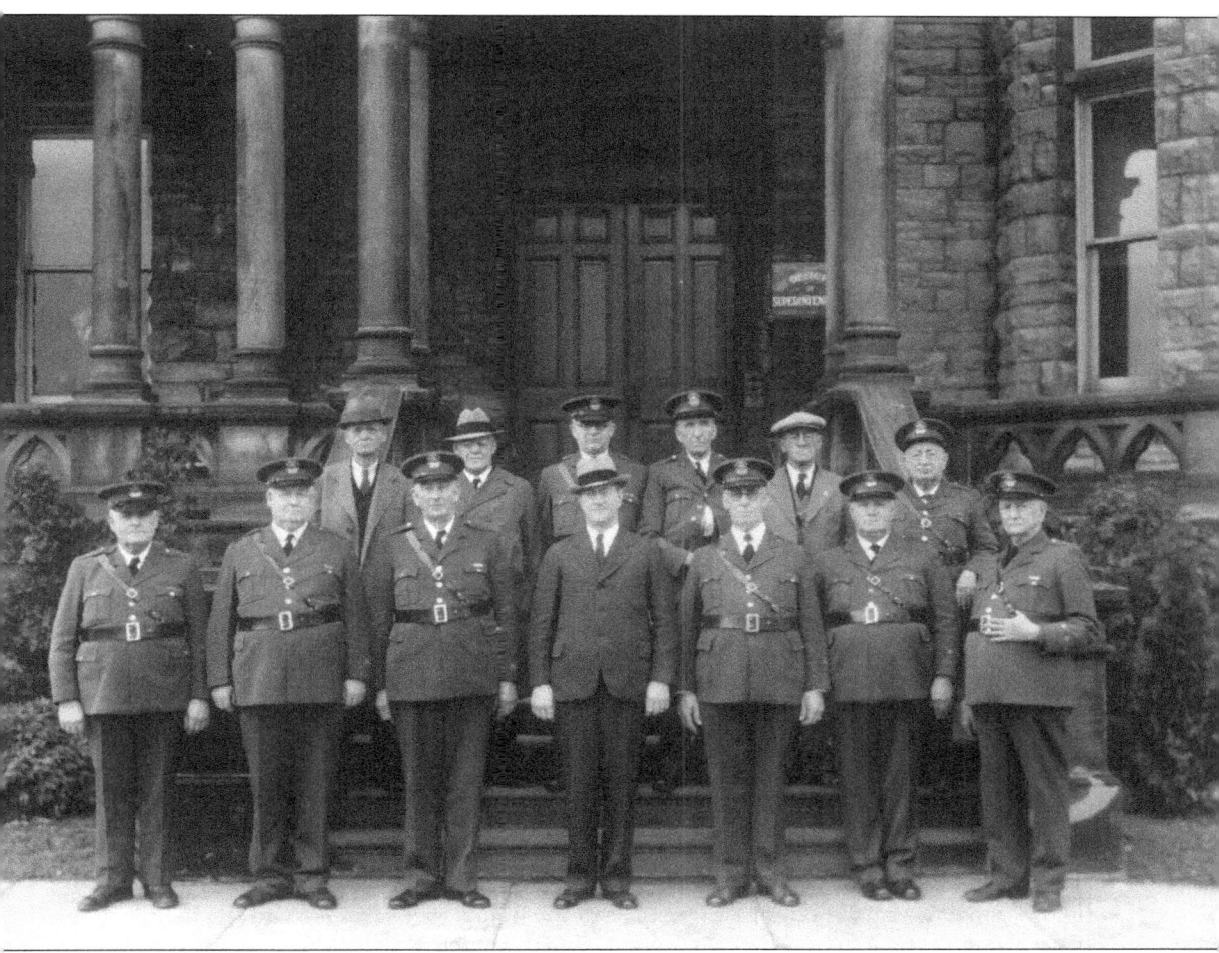

By 1934, there were 78 uniformed guards; 13 of them were considered veterans and are pictured here. They are, from left to right, (first row) William Brink, U.S. Henry, C.N. Bonnett, Supt. T.C. Jenkins, W.A. McFadden, J.C Davis, and G.E. Silcott; (second row) J.A. McClure, A. Willford, O.F. Garver, E. Aplin, A.N. Shaw, and J.H. Wierman. The collective experience of these men was 386 years. Of special interest is Bonnett, who began his work at the OSR when the building opened in 1896. He left in 1899 and then returned in 1905. By far the most experienced among these men was Silcott. In 1900, he began working as a printer of the newspaper at the reformatory, and 27 years later he became the postmaster of the institution. Silcott was 83 years old at the time of this photograph. McClure began with the reformatory in 1903 and worked as a guard/teacher, carpenter, and instructor in the furniture factory. He is 70 years old in this image.

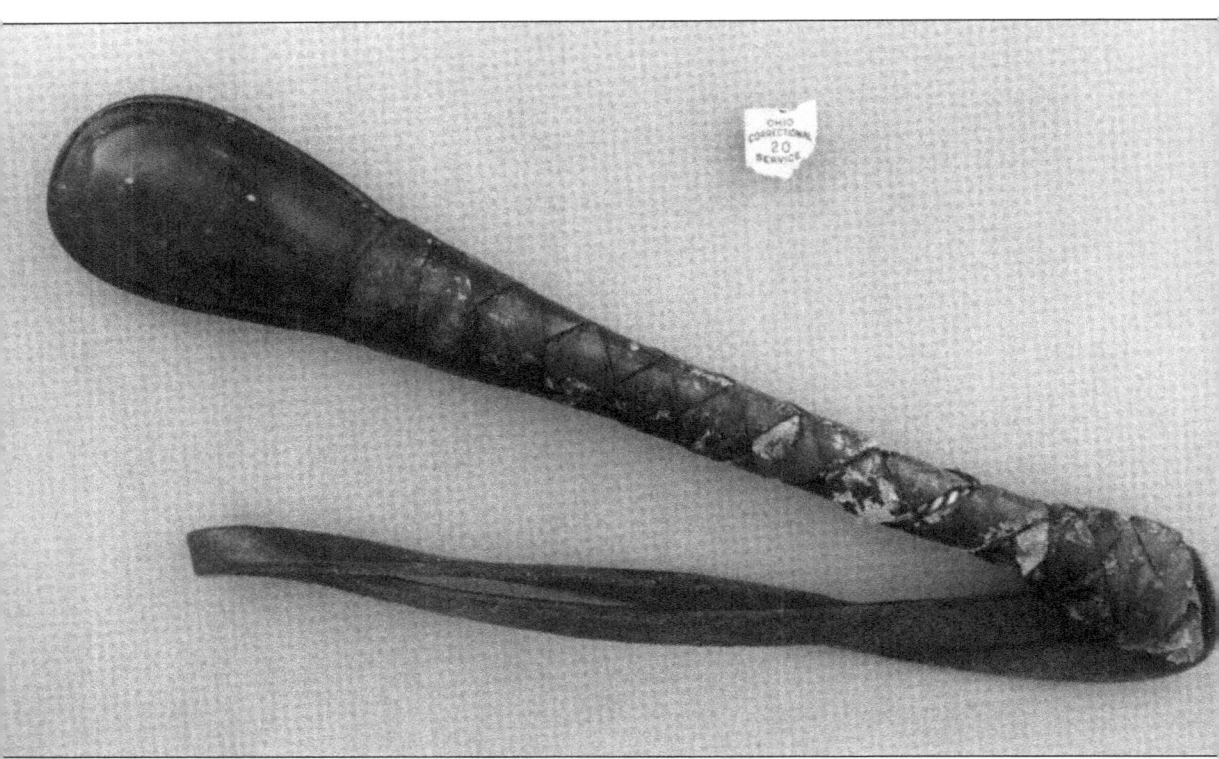

Guards were not armed with guns within the prison. They did, however, need some form of protection when dealing with defiant inmates. Over the years, guards were provided with billy clubs. The form and style changed, but the tool was intended to protect the guard and control an unruly prisoner. Shown here is a leather billy club filled with BBs. In earlier times, guards wielded canes. By the 1960s, the billy club had become longer, more solid, and rigid. The club was used not only to direct and confront inmates, but in the dining hall when a guard felt the inmates had had enough time to eat, he would simply tap on their table with his club. The inmates would then stop eating.

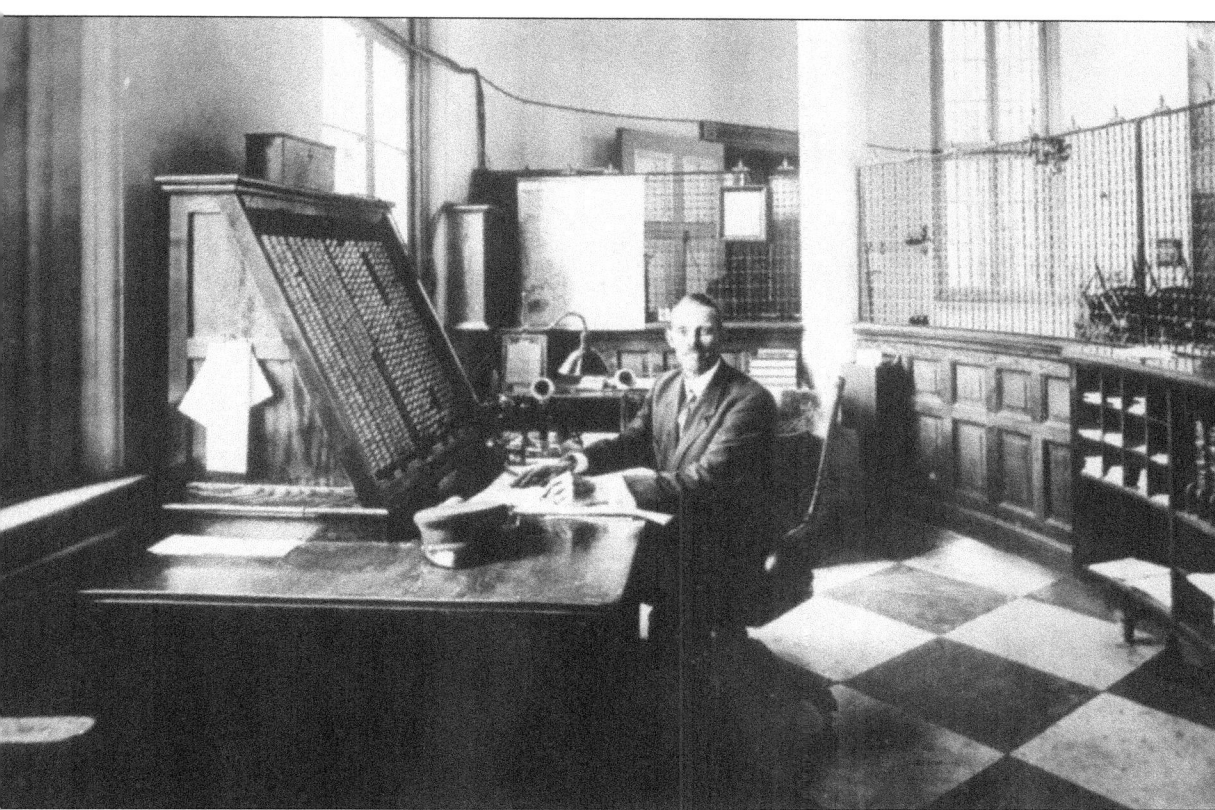

The captain's cage was located in the central guard room. According to a 1934 report to the state, within the cage were the keys to all master keys to cell blocks and all dormitories. The cage also monitored the movements of prisoners through the institution. Each inmate was represented by cards. One card identified their assigned cell, and others represented the movement of the inmate from one room to another. Behind the cage was the armory, where a large variety of weapons and ammunition was stored. As technology improved, the captain's cage became the communications hub as well as a security center. The locks into and out of the CGR could be controlled from the captain's cage. The cage also connected administrators and guards to one another through a switchboard.

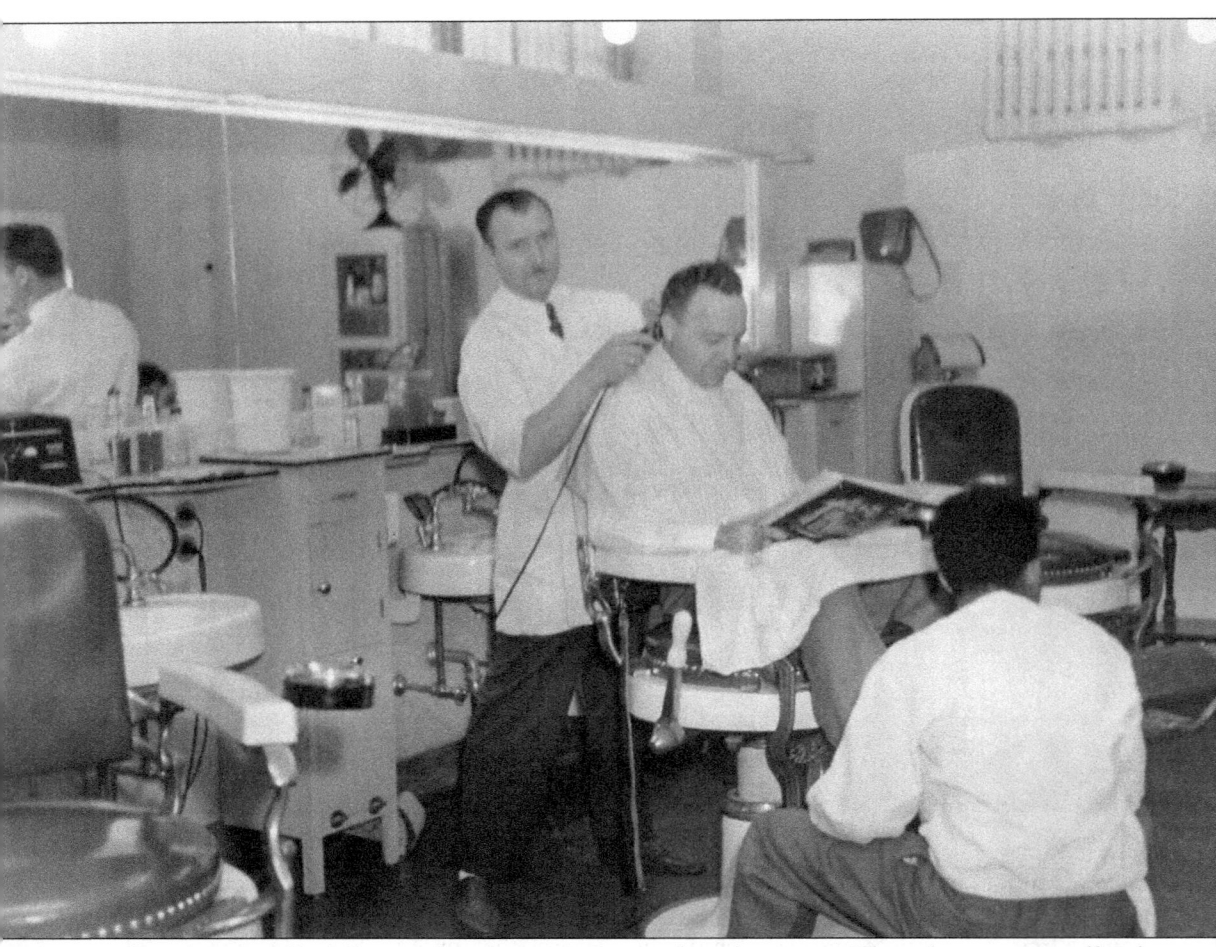

Guards were afforded special accommodations within the prison. Their dining room offered much better fare than that served to inmates. Another special accommodation for guards was their barbershop. Initially, one was set up for training and use by inmates, but eventually the OSR opened one for guards and their families. Trustee inmates worked in the guards' shop; as always, these inmates were highly trusted and exhibited good behavior. The training program provided a skill for inmates that could be applied to life after prison, either with an established barbershop or for self-employment. By 1977, the training program was at risk of closing, as the OSR could not find an instructor who met the licensing requirements and who would work for the salary established by the state.

Unmarried guards could rent bunks in rooms within the administrative wing. Shortly after prison construction started, Robert J. Hancock, the son of OSR contractor Robert G. Hancock, built a tract of 10 houses directly across from the reformatory known as Hancock Heights. Initially, workmen lived in the houses, but they were later rented to guards and their families. The homes' proximity to the prison meant that the guards, if necessary, could be at the reformatory in a matter of minutes. These two-bedroom homes, built in the late 1890s, are still standing and are privately owned. In addition, two of them have been donated to the reformatory through a land bank and are currently being restored, in part through the help and cooperation of a neighboring prison. (Both courtesy of Scott Sukel.)

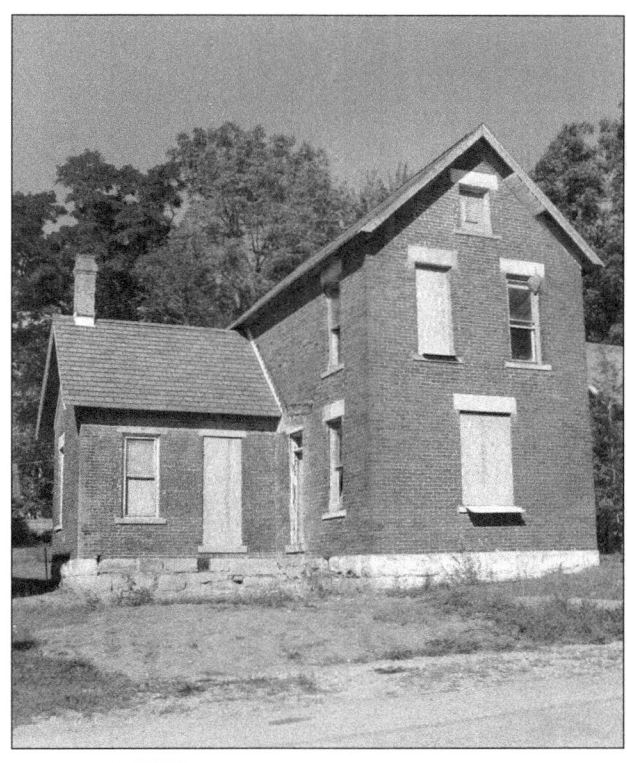

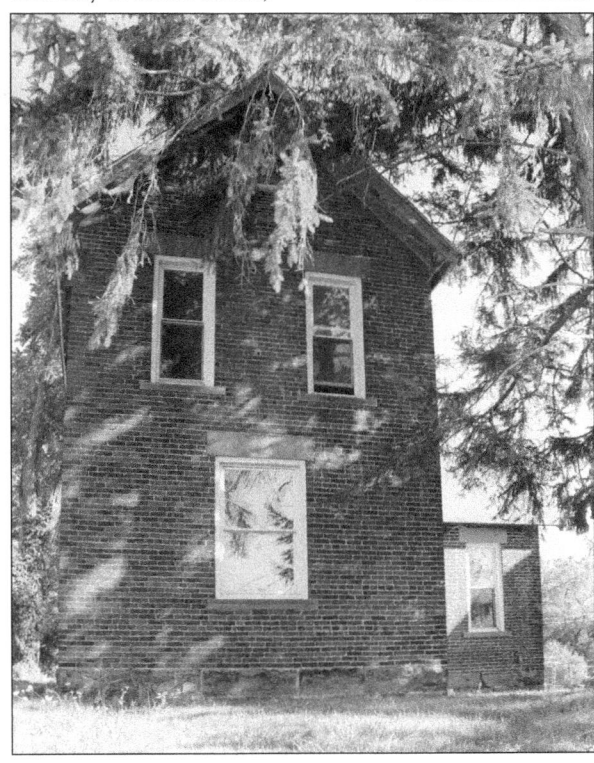

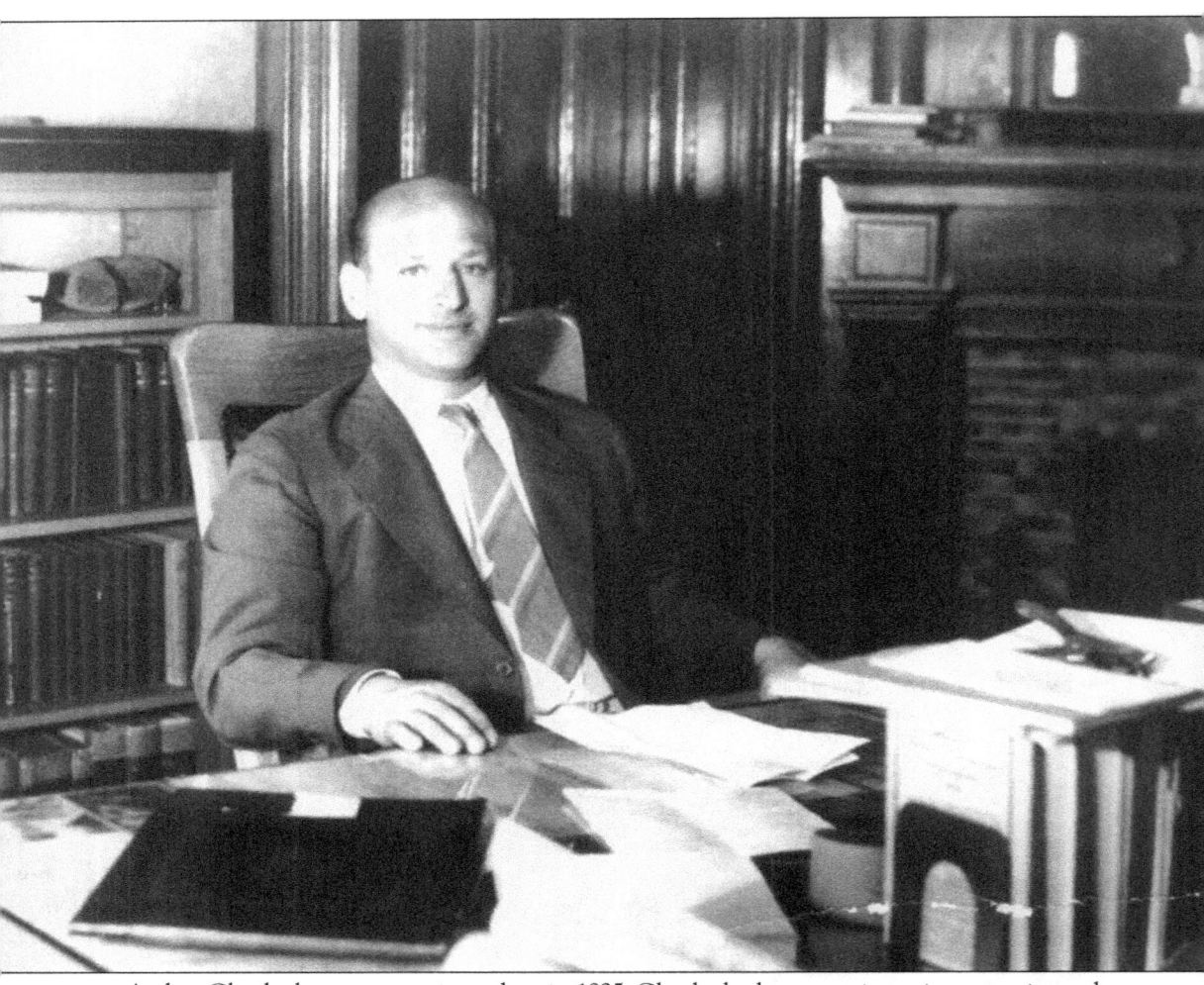

Arthur Glattke became superintendent in 1935. Glattke had no experience in corrections when he was appointed. His experience as a teacher and coach was seen as an asset for the OSR's core mission of training, education, and rehabilitation of young offenders. Tremendous growth occurred during his tenure. Improvements in training opportunities and treatment evolved from his appointment until his death in 1959. Glattke oversaw the construction of a new dining hall and kitchen in 1938 and a new hospital in 1950. He continued to bring the most innovative equipment for inmate training programs. Glattke went on to become a leader not only at the OSR but throughout the state as president of the Warden's Association of America and the Ohio Prison and Parole Association. Between 1949 and 1954, Glattke was acting division chief of the state division of corrections.

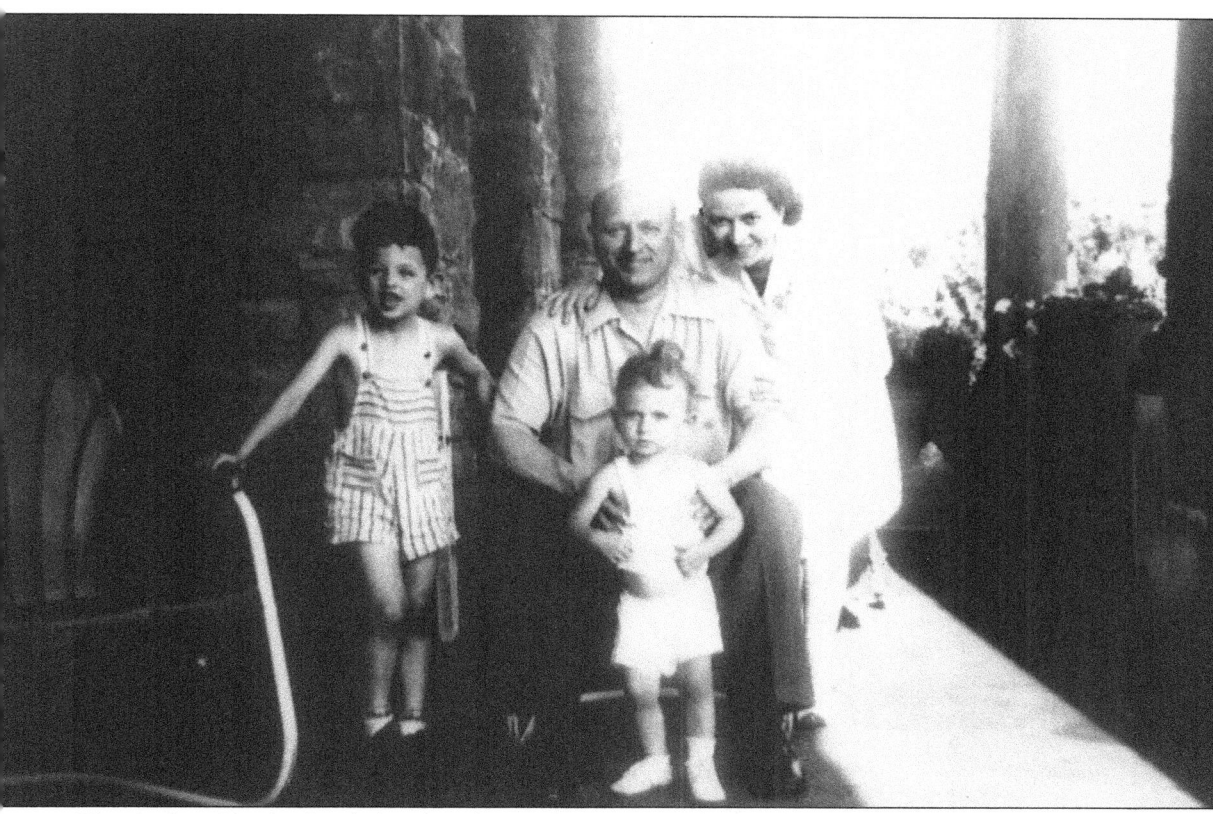

The Arthur Glattke family lived in the warden's quarters longer than any other family. Arthur was appointed to the position in 1935, and he and Helen married shortly after and moved in. Their two boys, born during Glattke's tenure as superintendent, had happy childhoods that offered experiences both common and uncommon to other children. They had friends visit for ice-skating and dinner with the family. Sadly, Helen died after a tragic accident in November 1950, when a gun fell off a closet shelf and a bullet discharged and struck her. Warden Glattke and their sons continued to live there until he died of a heart attack while at his desk on February 10, 1959. Glattke headed the prison during some of its most important growth, as well as its transition from its original, reform-minded intent to its later housing of more violent offenders.

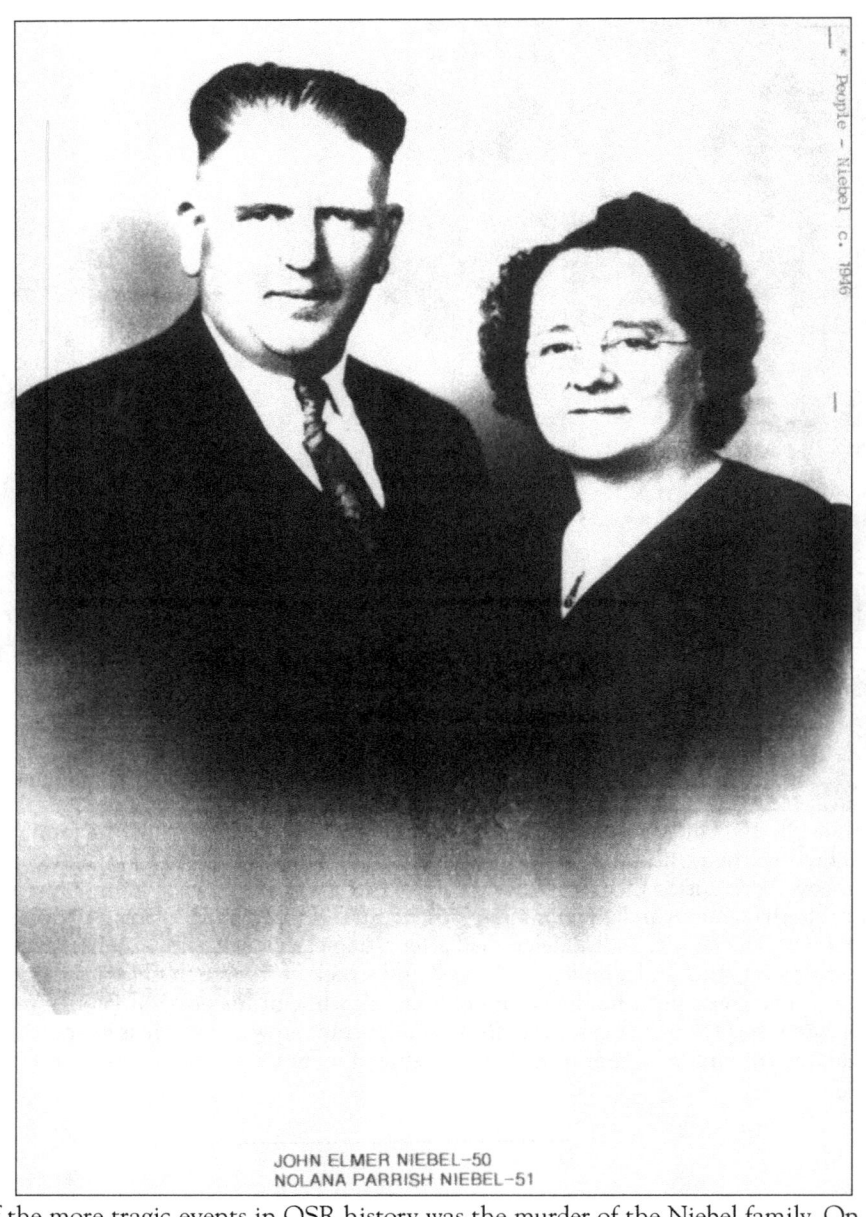

JOHN ELMER NIEBEL–50
NOLANA PARRISH NIEBEL–51

One of the more tragic events in OSR history was the murder of the Niebel family. On July 21, 1948, John Niebel, superintendent of the farm, along with his wife, Nolana, and their 22-year-old daughter Phyllis, were found in a neighboring field. All three had been shot to death. Within a day, two suspects had been named, and the largest statewide manhunt had begun. On July 23, Robert Daniels and John West had been found, but not before they killed two other people. In a shoot-out with police, West was killed and Daniels was captured. Their killing spree started on July 9, with the murder of two men in Franklin County. Initially, Daniels pled not guilty by reason of insanity, but on July 30 he changed his plea to guilty. He was executed on January 3, 1949. Daniels confessed that he and West, former inmates, had returned to the area to kill a guard, "Red" Harris, but could not find him. The two happened upon the Niebel home and, having a grudge against Niebel as well, decided to kill him and his family.

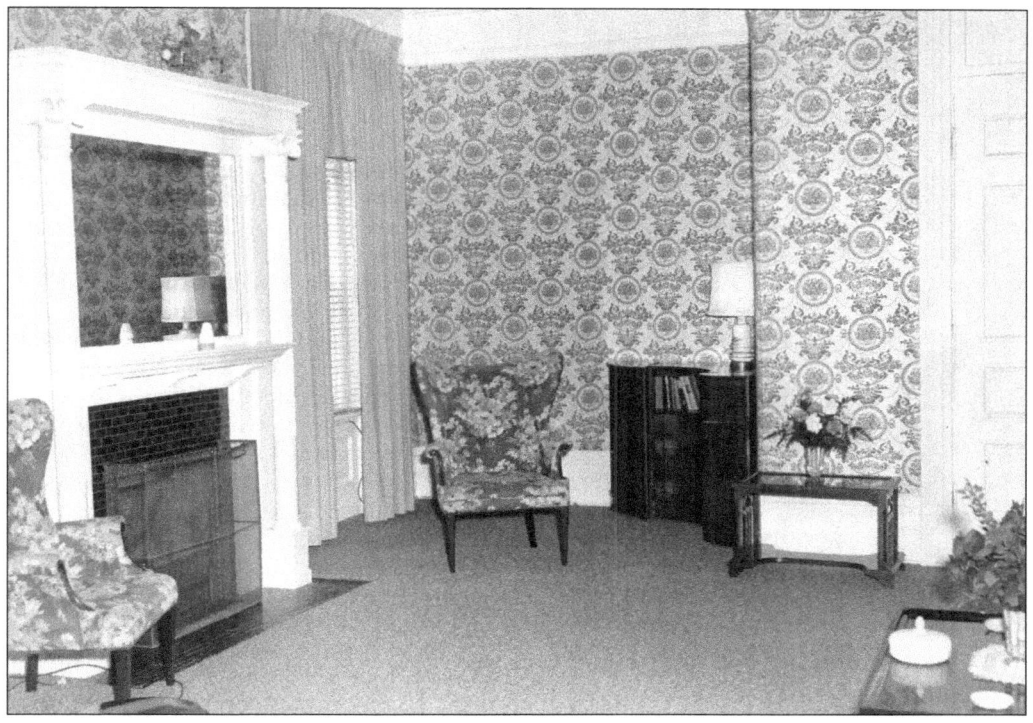

During the years that administration officials lived on the grounds, the residences were finely appointed. The living quarters hosted officials and visitors from around the state, region, and nation as they came to visit the families or observe the prison's operation. Because of the important status of the warden, assistant warden, and chaplain not only within the prison but within the greater Mansfield community, it was deemed appropriate that the residences have fine furnishings. Children of the administrators were taken into account when rooms were decorated, including wallpaper reflecting their ages. Some boys' rooms, for example, had wallpaper featuring trains. Shown here are the living room (above) and bedroom (below) of the warden's residence in the 1950s. By the 1960s, administrators chose to live off of the prison grounds. Private residences were purchased for their use while in the employ of the OSR.

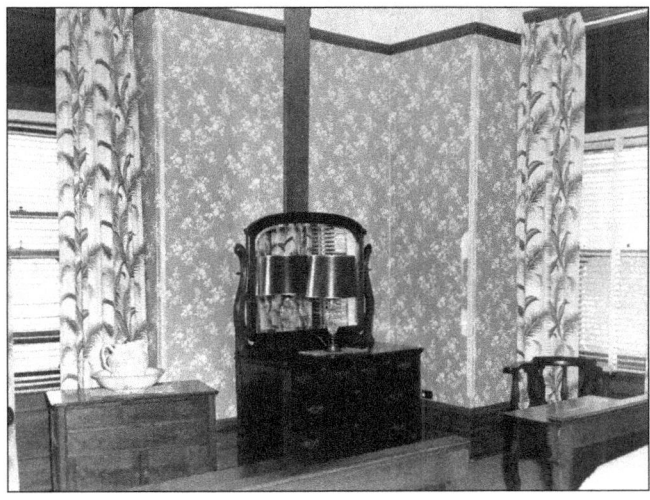

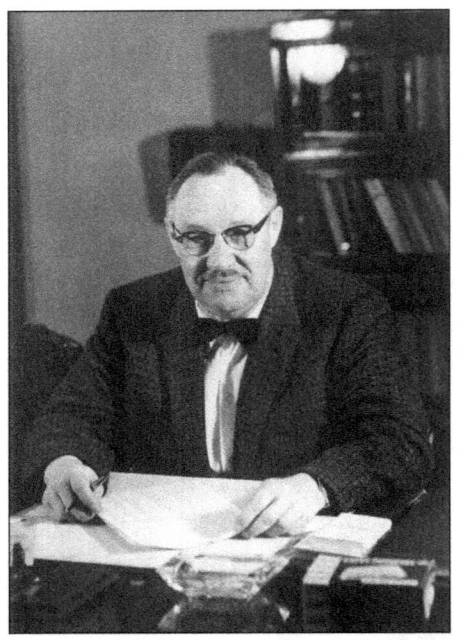

During his short tenure as superintendent (1959–1963), George Allarding left his mark. Like many of his predecessors, Allarding worked as a teacher at the OSR. In 1932, he became assistant superintendent under Arthur Glattke. Continuing the work and policies of Glattke, Allarding credited careful screening, the threat of added prison time, and the loss of trustee status for a low escape rate by inmates assigned to work outside the prison proper. In 1959, Allarding reported that two percent of the nearly 700 inmates working at honor farms had attempted escapes. Allarding also reinstituted measures that promoted minimum standards of reading and writing for inmates. Below, Allarding (left) and captain of the guards Ike Webb (center) talk with guards and an inmate in the yard.

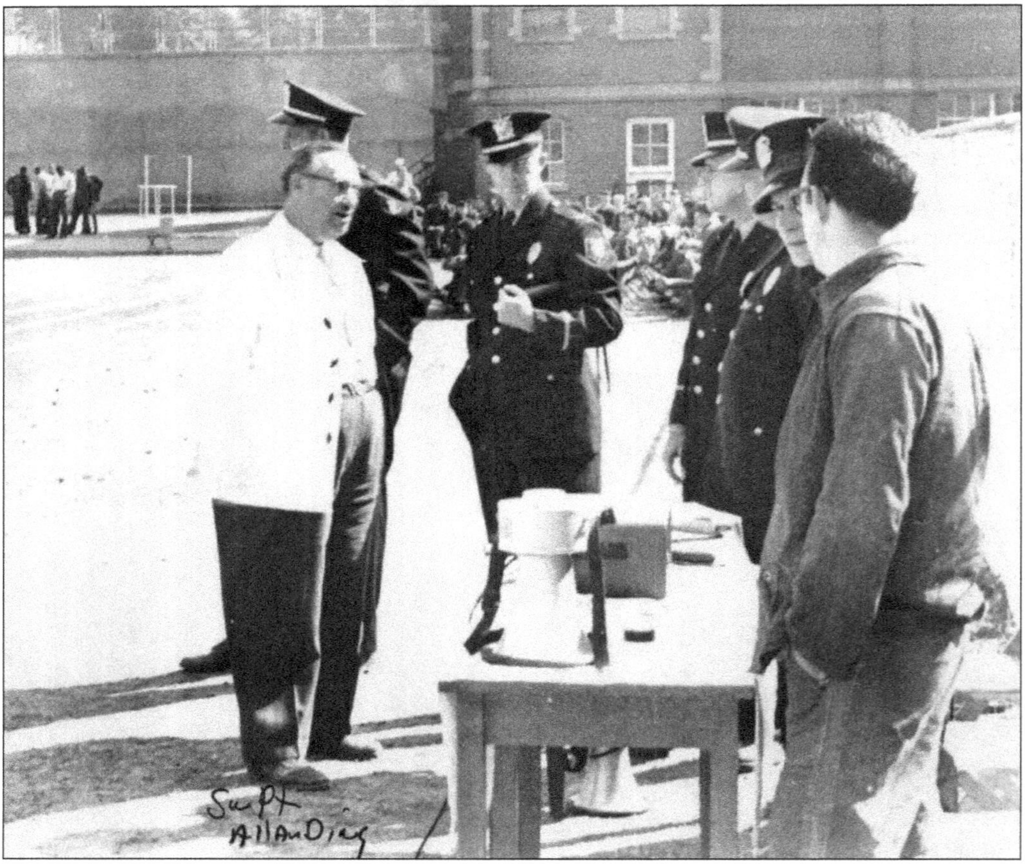

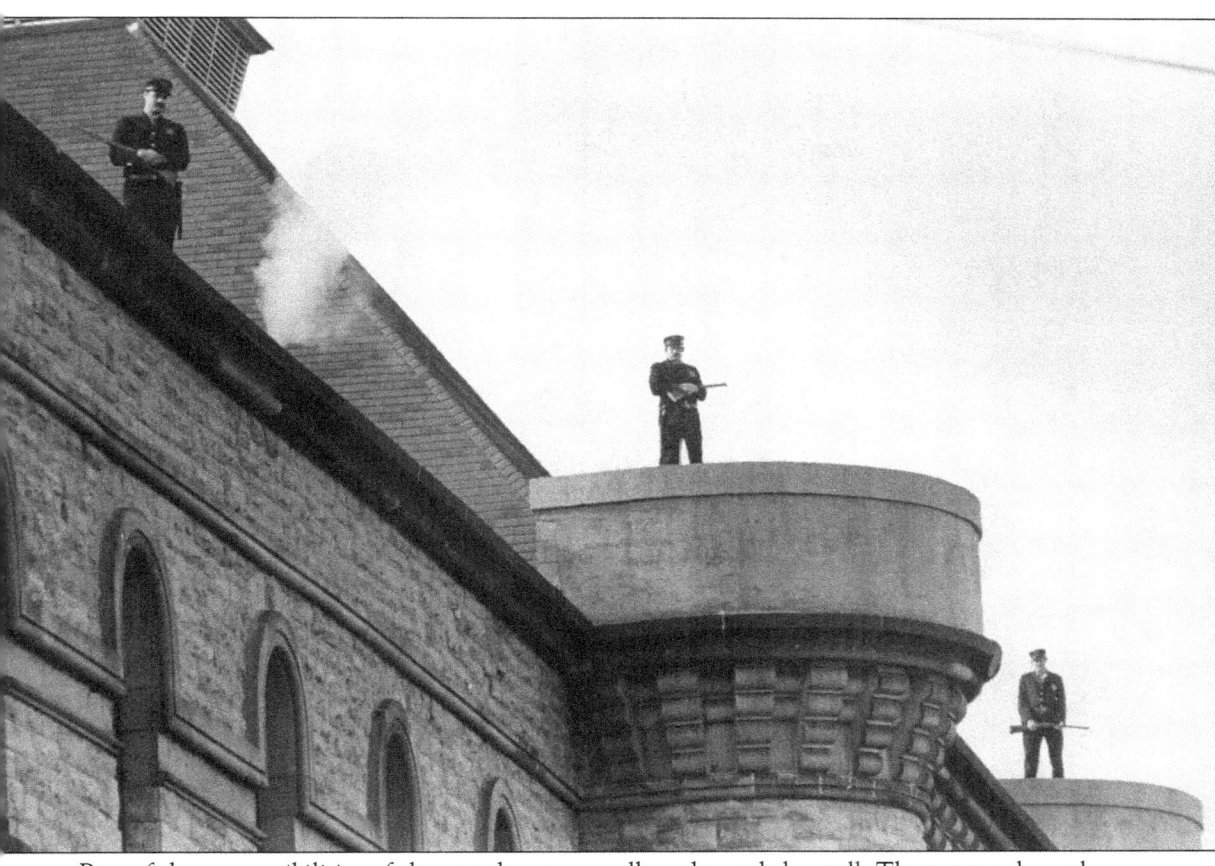

Part of the responsibilities of the guards was to walk and guard the wall. These were the only guards permitted to carry guns. Each guard was armed with a rifle and was trained to shoot at prisoners attempting to scale the wall or work their way through a gate. On the corner of each side of the wall was a tower. Guards assigned to this area were required to watch the wall and the yard during their eight-hour shift. Water and timber for the wood-burning stove were sent up to the guards by rope from the ground. Contact with the guard cage was extremely limited until inter-prison communications were set up. The captain of the guard would call the tower at least once each shift. If the guard did not answer, the captain made his way to the tower.

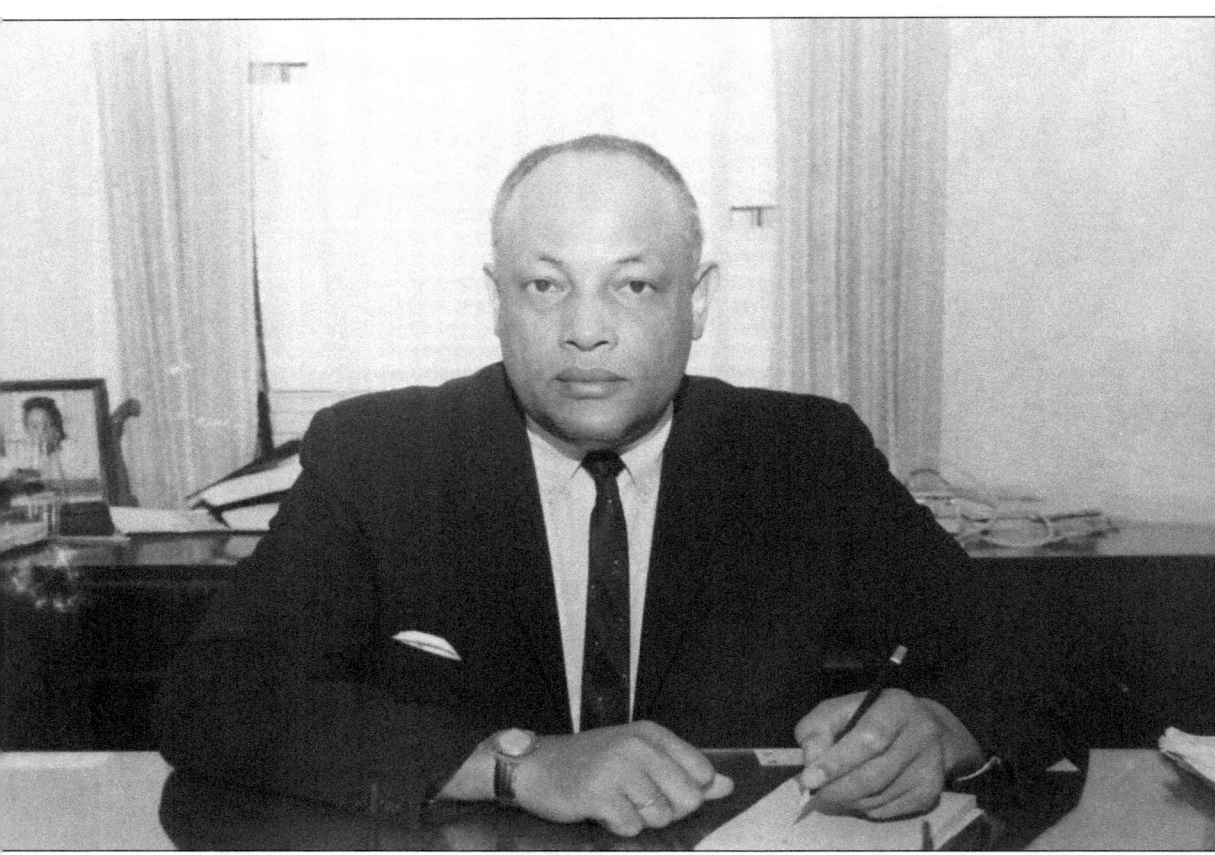

Bennett Cooper was named superintendent of the OSR in 1966 and held that position until 1970. At the time, he was the first African American superintendent in the state as well as in the country. His tenure was marked by important changes within the institution. Soon after his appointment, Cooper began plans to offer college courses to inmates through Ashland College. He was an advocate for giving inmates the skills necessary for success upon their release. Another major change was the desegregation of the cell blocks and the dining hall. Upon Cooper's promotion, he ordered the guards to ensure that seating in the dining hall was integrated, even though some guards were unsure of the consequences. He then eliminated the "white only" and "negro only" ranges in the cell blocks.

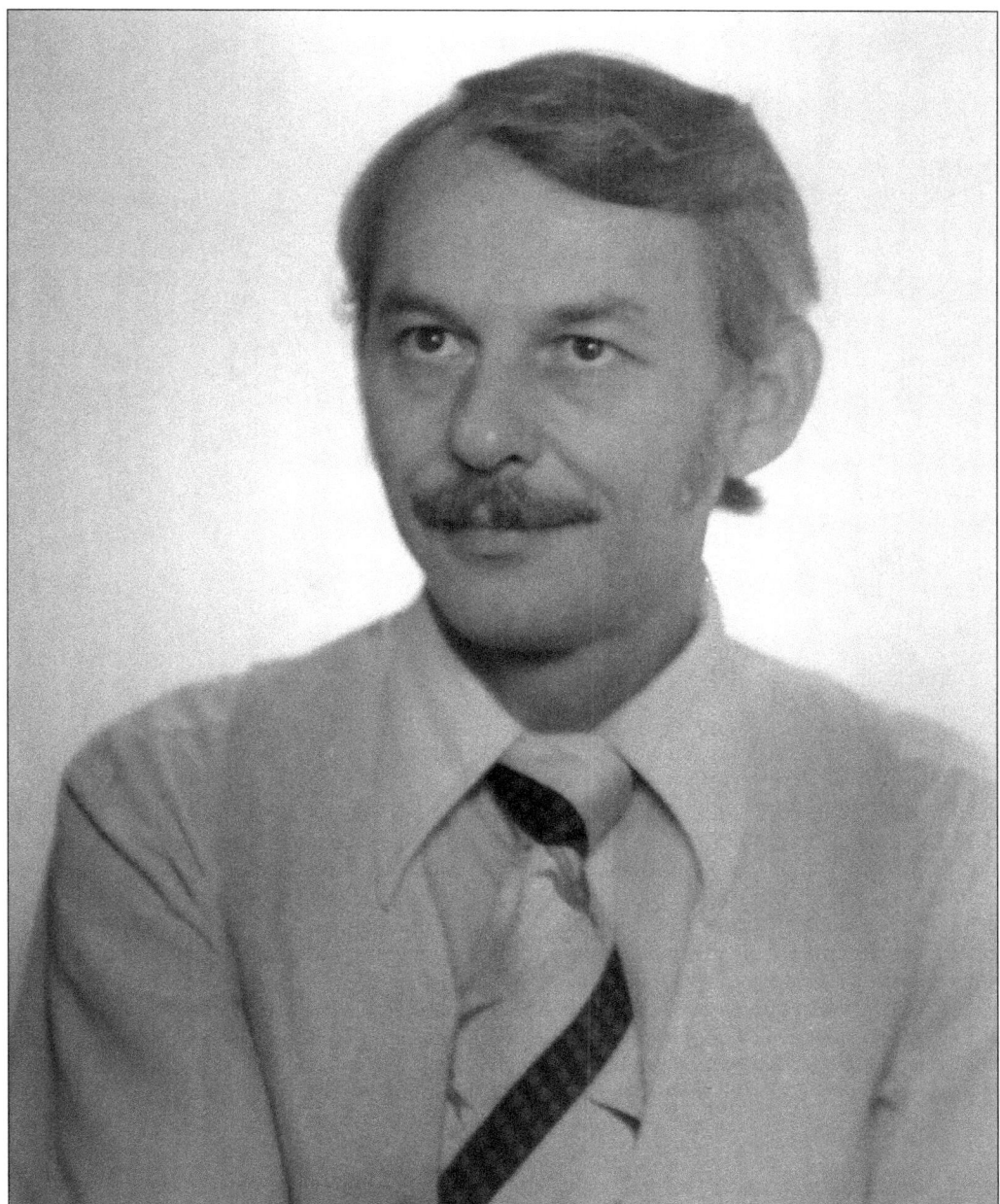

In 1975, a number of inmates escaped from the Grafton farm. As a result, Supt. Robert White was removed, and Frank Gray was appointed to the top post at the OSR in August. At 40, Gray was the youngest man appointed to that position. He came to the post with a background in psychology and education like many of his predecessors. During his eight years as superintendent, Gray oversaw a $200,000 project to repair and repaint deteriorating walls throughout the building. In October 1975, and again in 1982, he faced labor problems as the guards participated in "sick-out" days due to stressful job conditions, a result of being understaffed. Finally, it was under Gray's watch that the first women were hired as corrections officers working directly with inmates rather than as support personnel.

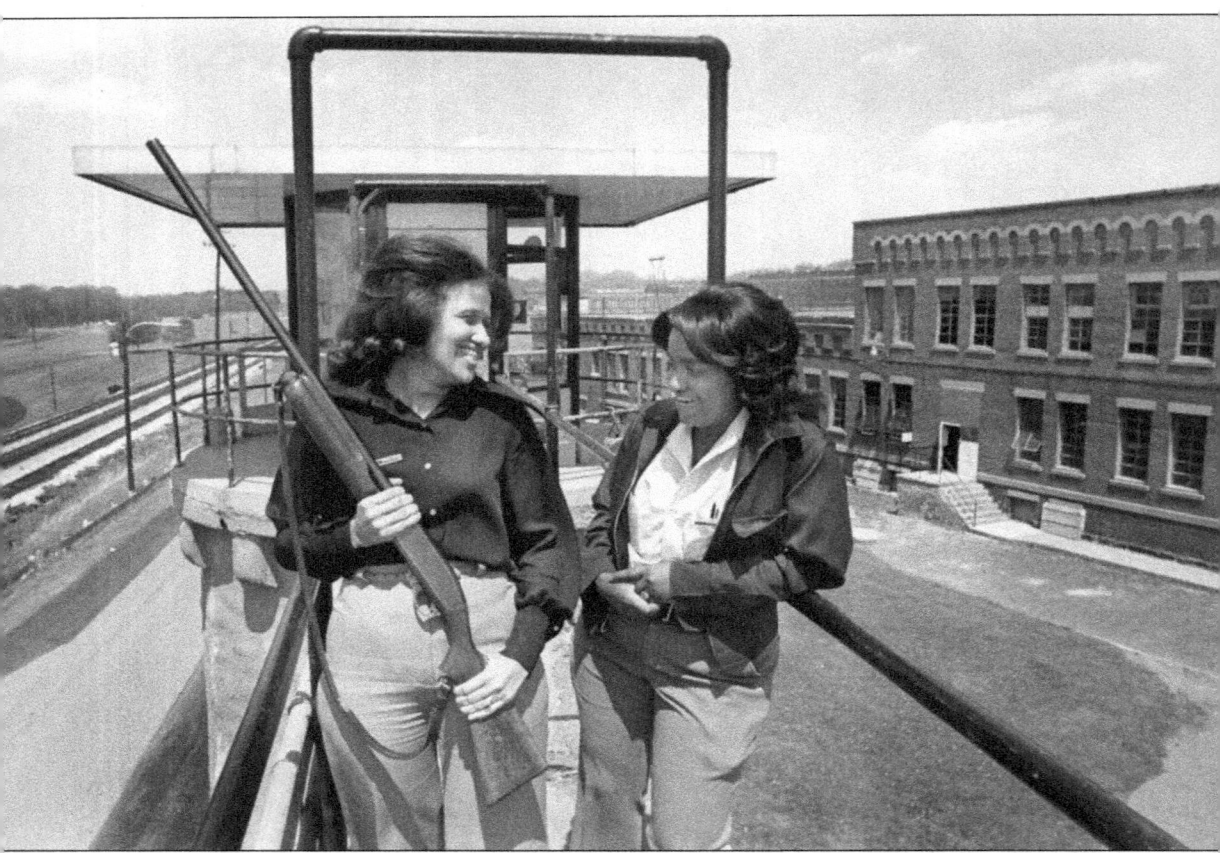

The implementation of Title IX of the United States Education Amendments of 1972 made it possible for women to move into the area of corrections. The Ohio State Reformatory employed female "corrections officers" prior to the new law, but they worked outside the cell blocks and did not go through the same training as male officers did. In 1976, two women, Rita and Mary Shoulders, became the first trained officers to work side by side with their male counterparts. As with anything new, some of the male officers were less than pleased to have women among their ranks. The new hires were charged with the same responsibilities for prisoners as all other guards. Rita (left) was assigned to work in the commissary to supervise the inmate clerks, and Mary (right) was assigned to the "Six South" tier of the east cell block. Both earned $4.24 per hour when they started their tenure at the OSR. (Courtesy of Jeff Sprang/*Mansfield News Journal*.)

Three

Preparing for a Better Life

Work and Training

The reformatory movement had two essential missions. Not only should the young inmates learn a trade to take them into a productive post-prison life, but education was equally vital to their success. Through the years, the Ohio State Reformatory administration encouraged inmates to attain academic levels that, prior to incarceration, had eluded them. By the time of the OSR's closing, inmates had an opportunity to receive a high school diploma and to take advantage of coursework available from a local college. Initially, the trades were part of what the state called "contract labor." Business owners could contract with the prison to have inmates produce their products, which would then be sold on the open market. In 1912, state law prohibited the use of such labor, as it took jobs away from the public sector. At this time, the law provided for what was called "state use system" of inmate labor. In essence, this system required that items made within the prison be sold only to institutions that operated using tax dollars. The items produced by the reformatory, then, were only available to state institutions, state departments, city and county institutions and departments, and public schools. In 1910, the Ohio Department of Corrections required all state institutions to buy from the reformatory unless the OSR certified that items were not available from Mansfield's prison. The shops included furniture, clothing, shoe, printing, and machine factories. Along with a large farm, the reformatory was self-sufficient by producing more of its own needs than buying from outside. The farm, kitchen, butchery, cannery, and hospital created opportunities for inmates to learn trades and to contribute to the profit and self-sufficiency of the prison.

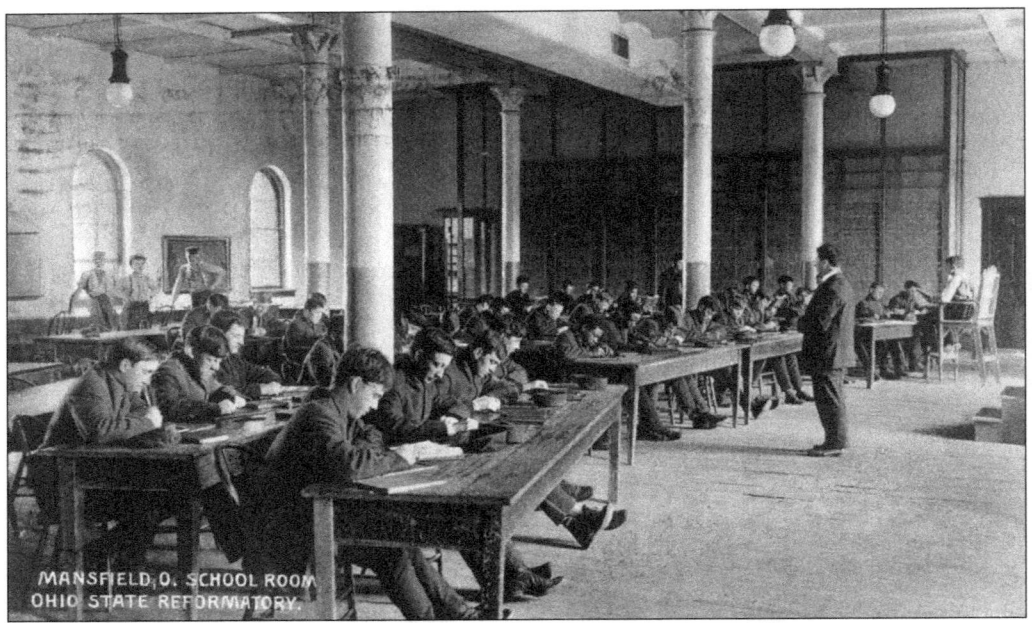

From its earliest days, the Ohio State Reformatory promoted education as an important part of rehabilitation of inmates. Incoming prisoners were required to know how to read, write, and have basic math skills. Once that was accomplished, inmates could choose to continue or move on to other types of training. The need for space increased, and classroom space was added as the prison population grew. Classrooms were added in the diagonal when the east cell block was constructed. Among the information gathered when an inmate was brought into the facility was his level of education. Inmates were assigned to the classrooms depending on their abilities. Many of the workshops required a certain level of skills, so incentives were added for inmates to learn what they needed to know in order to excel in the training programs.

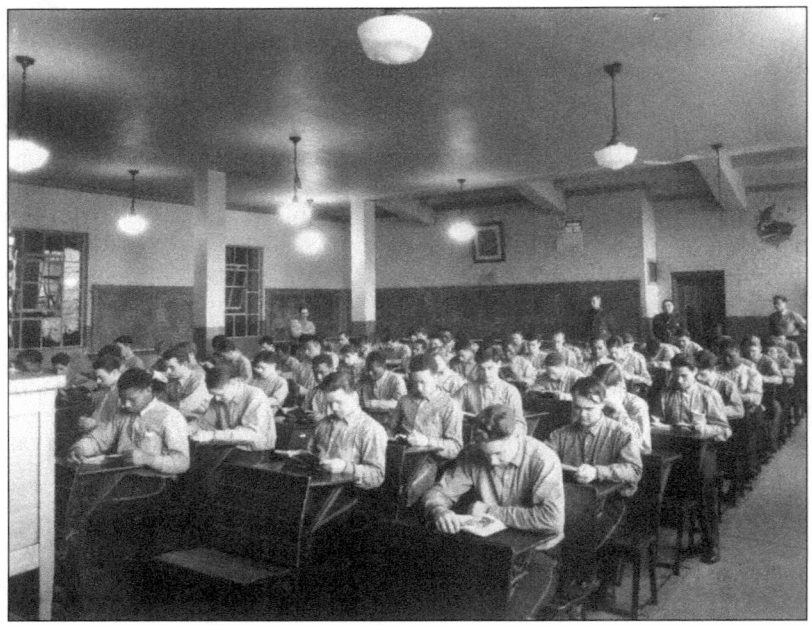

The emphasis on formal education continued and expanded throughout the existence of the institution. During his tenure as assistant and then superintendent, Bennett Cooper placed a high value on the education of inmates. Fields High School was constructed within the reformatory's walls in early 1962 at a cost of $225,000. It was the first accredited school within a penal institution in Ohio. The school employed 22 teachers as well as administrators. The OSR employed four psychologists and a dozen social workers who were available to all inmates. About 200 young offenders who attended Fields School were housed in E-Dorm. Aside from attending classes, they were isolated from older prisoners. The first graduating class of 1965 had 47 graduates. At right, Bruce North, a math teacher, takes a break outside Fields School in 1971. (Courtesy of Jeff Sprang.)

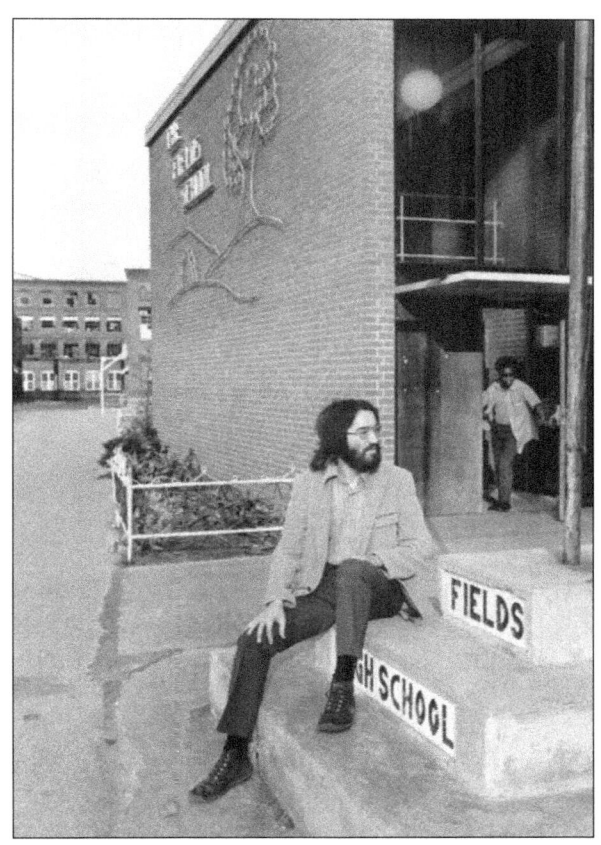

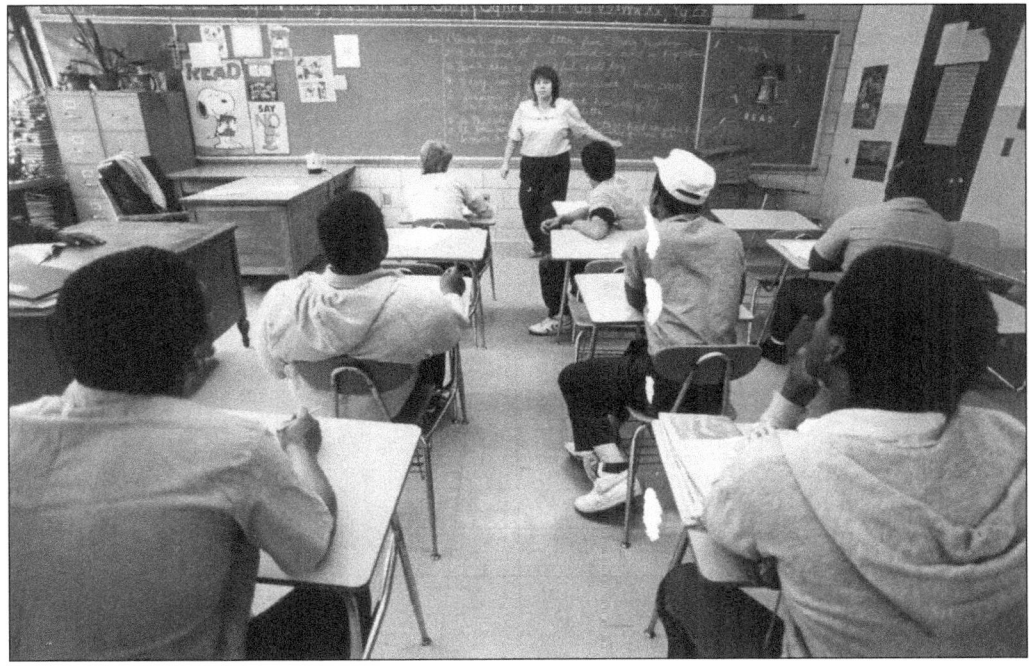

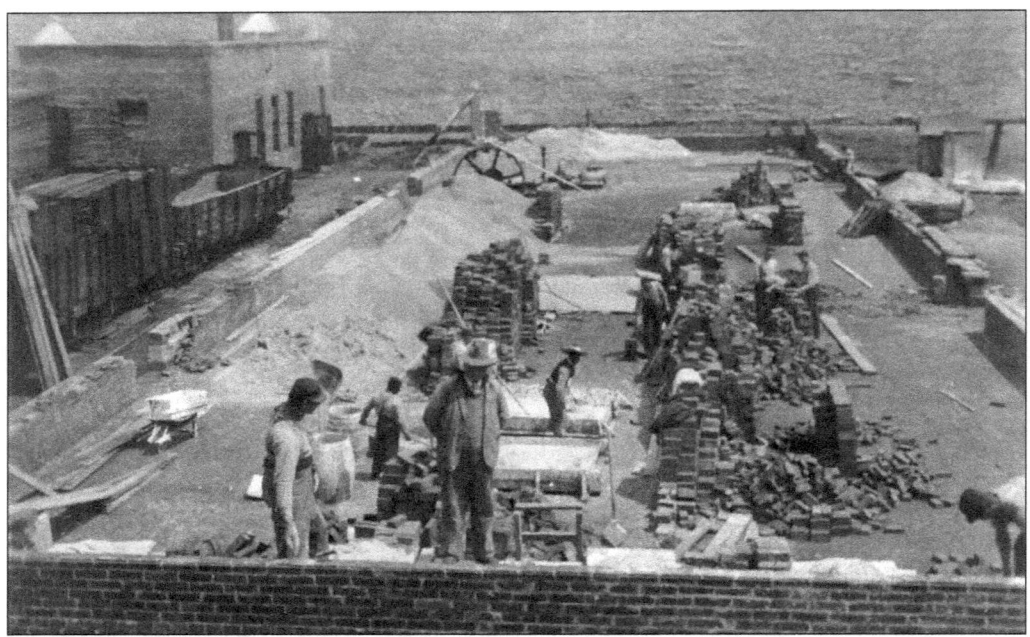

As with the construction of many of the early buildings and outbuildings, inmates were used as free labor. This also served as training for the men, with the aim that they would be able to acquire gainful employment upon their release. In the early-1900s photograph above, inmates are building the furniture factory. Before the law was changed, the building was operated by the Bromwell Brush & Wire Goods Company using inmates as labor. The image below most likely shows the operation of the Bromwell factory. The prison was paid for their labor, and the company made a tidy profit because of the low wages. When this practice was outlawed, the prison took over the factory. The trade continued as inmates worked on construction of a number of other buildings on the grounds.

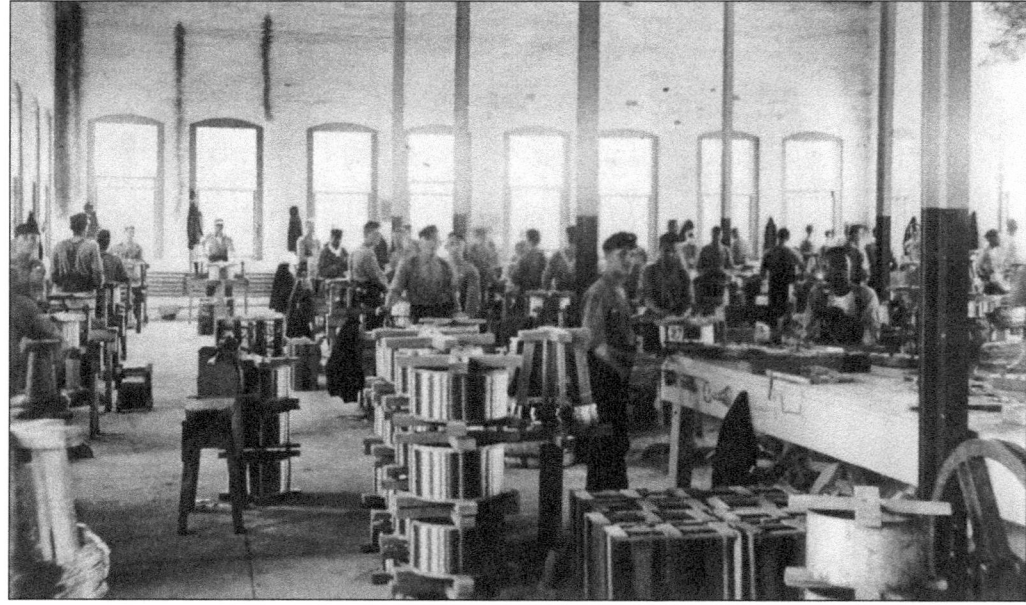

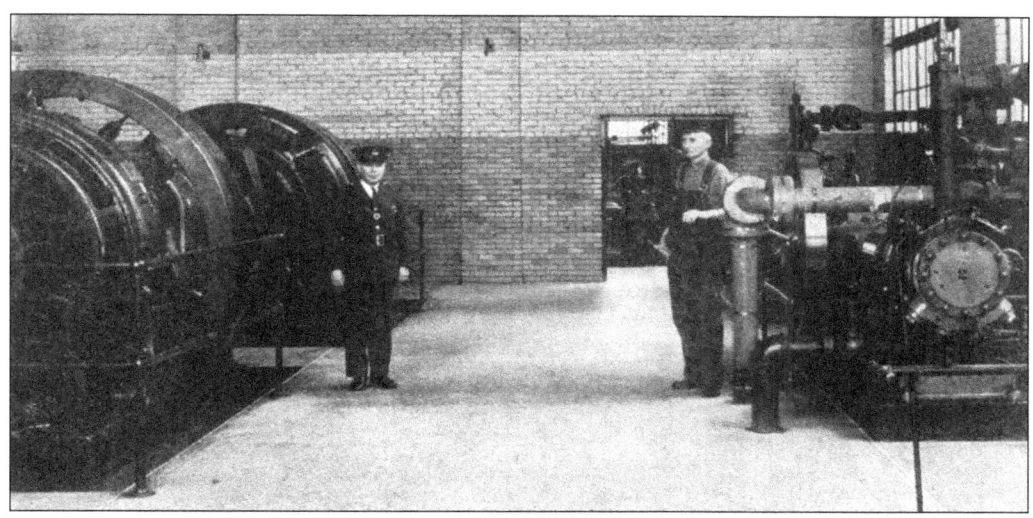

The power plant provided enough energy to run a town of over 3,000 people. Within the reformatory, the power plant ran the tailor shop, shoe shop, furniture shop, wood shop, main building, farms, and dormitories. In the 1920s, the plant generated 110 kilowatts an hour of illumination. By contrast, the average house at the time would use 10 kilowatts a month. It also pumped all the water used in the prison. Water was provided by 10 wells on the property, one of which was located at the barn. The plant pumped between 350,000 and 450,000 gallons of water daily to the main building and 100,000 gallons to the farm and dairy barn. Along with the inmates and their guards, the plant had six full-time employees.

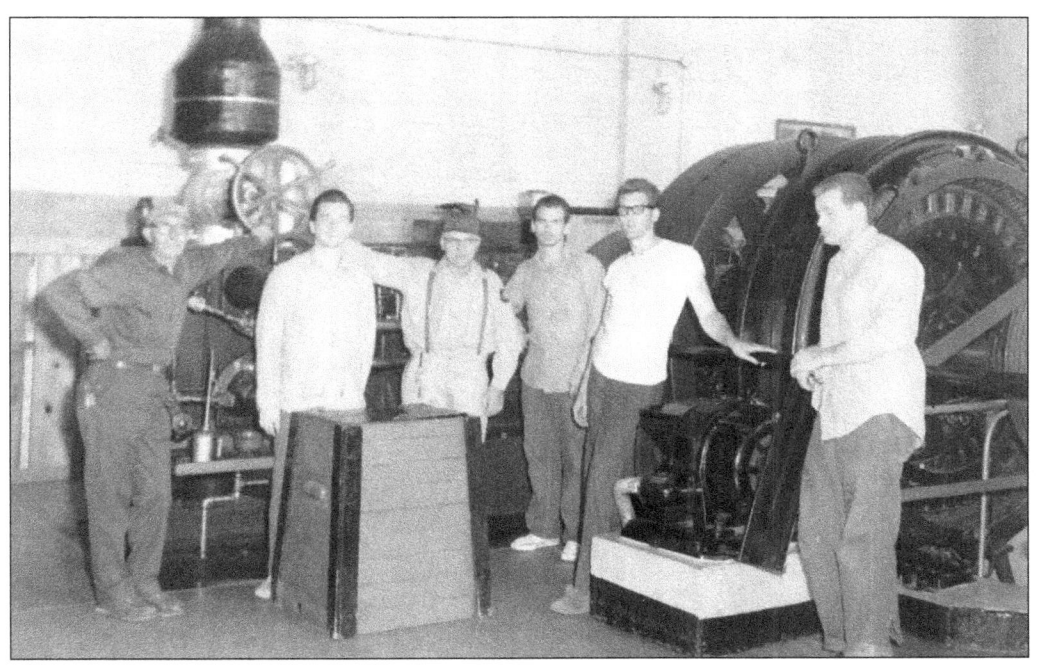

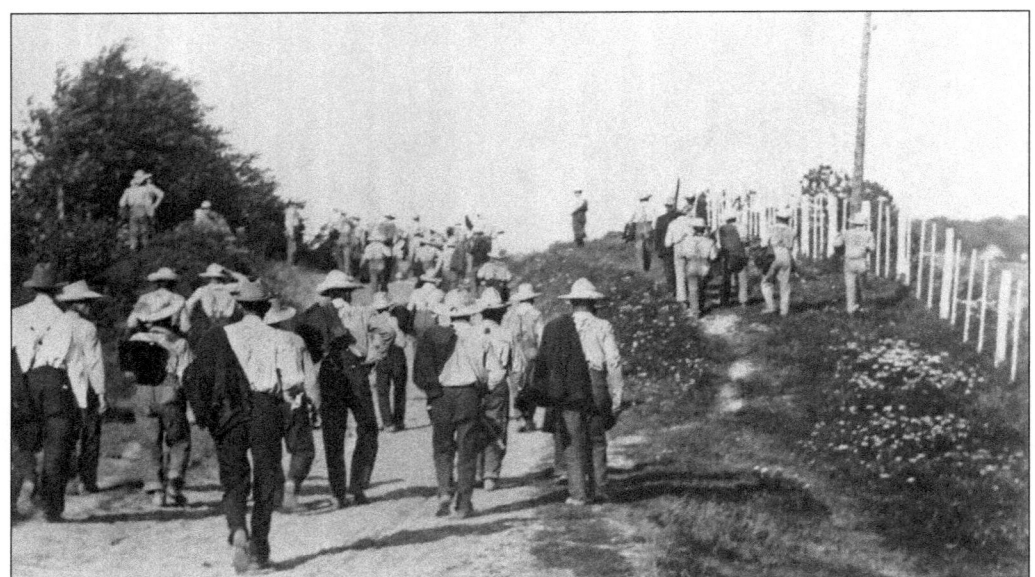

At one point, the OSR took over and displaced an entire village. According to a May 27, 1910, article in the *Orrville Courier*, the board of managers appropriated 100 acres of land that made up the small village of Spring Grove. By this time, 600 acres had been purchased, leaving the village completely surrounded by reformatory land. The village was to be relocated to an area closer to the town of Mansfield. As the need grew to produce more food, so did land acquisition. By 1948, the reformatory farm consisted of 1,600 acres between the Mansfield, Grafton, Camp Perry, Mt. Vernon, Osborne, and Sandusky sites, with inmates being housed at those locations as trustees. These farms lent themselves to lower security and experienced a higher degree of inmates walking away.

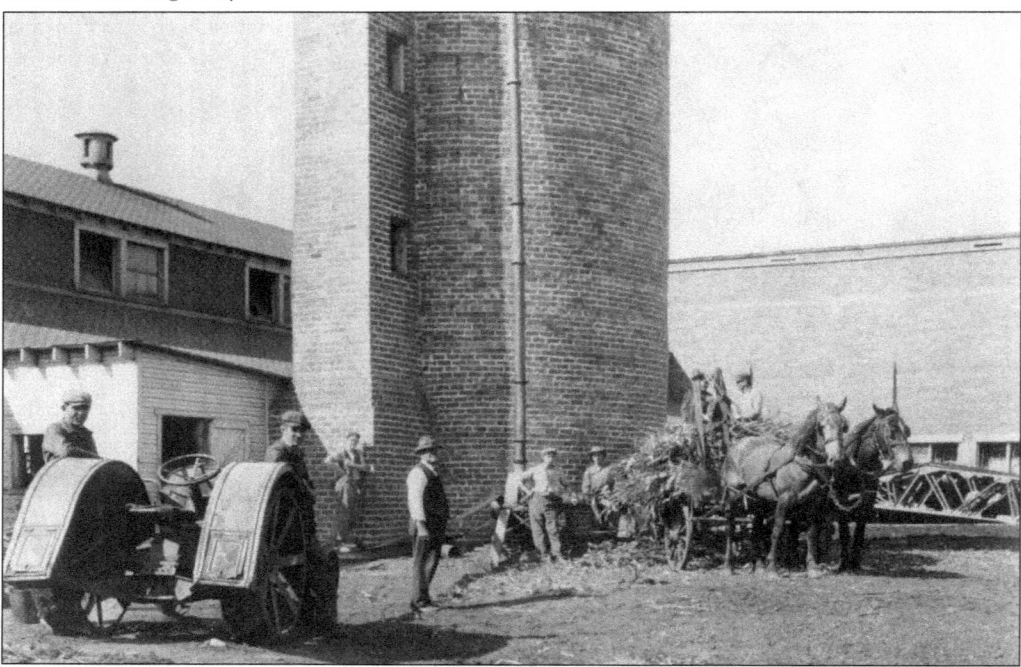

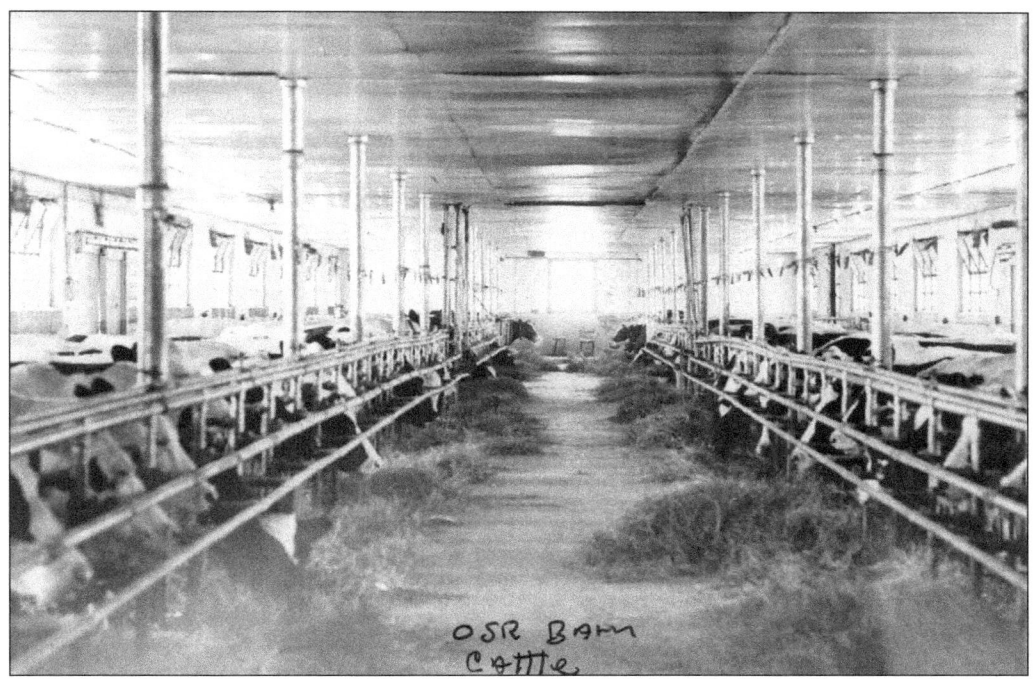

According to Winthrop Ruggles's April 20, 1949, *Mansfield News Journal* article, the 1948 farm operations at the reformatory produced $230,000 worth of food on its 900 acres of tillable land and at its dairy and poultry farms—the equivalent of $2.3 million in 2015. This output provided most of the needs of the reformatory sustenance department. Along with grain, 481,000 pounds of tomatoes, as well as peas, sweet corn, horseradish, strawberries, beans, and carrots were produced by a truck-growing project. Beyond dairy and poultry, the reformatory operated a large pig farm of 600 to 700 swine that provided pork for the needs of the kitchen. Conservation was also key to maintaining the fertility of the land. Throughout its existence, the farm operators took care to keep the land healthy.

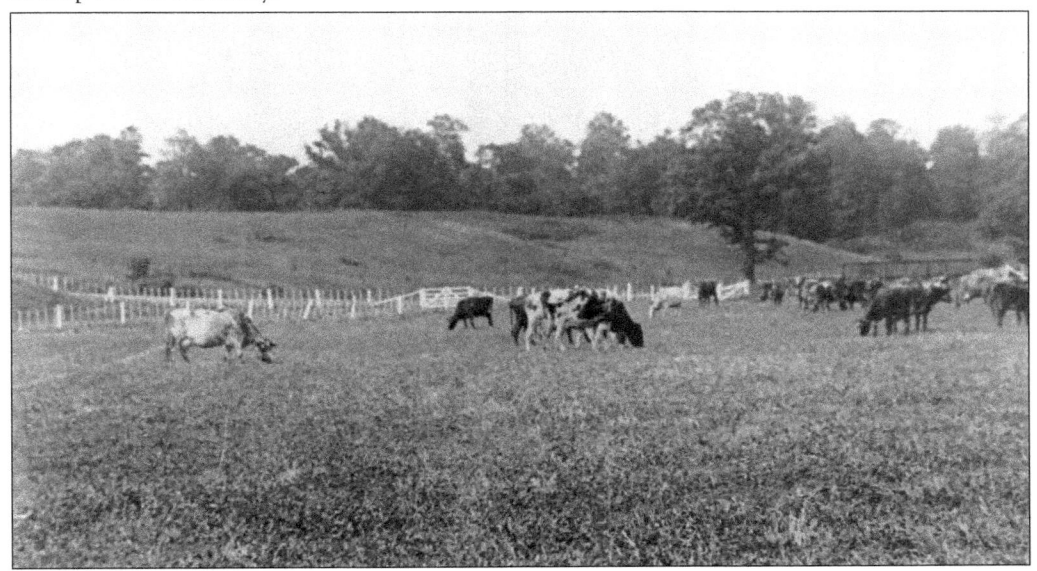

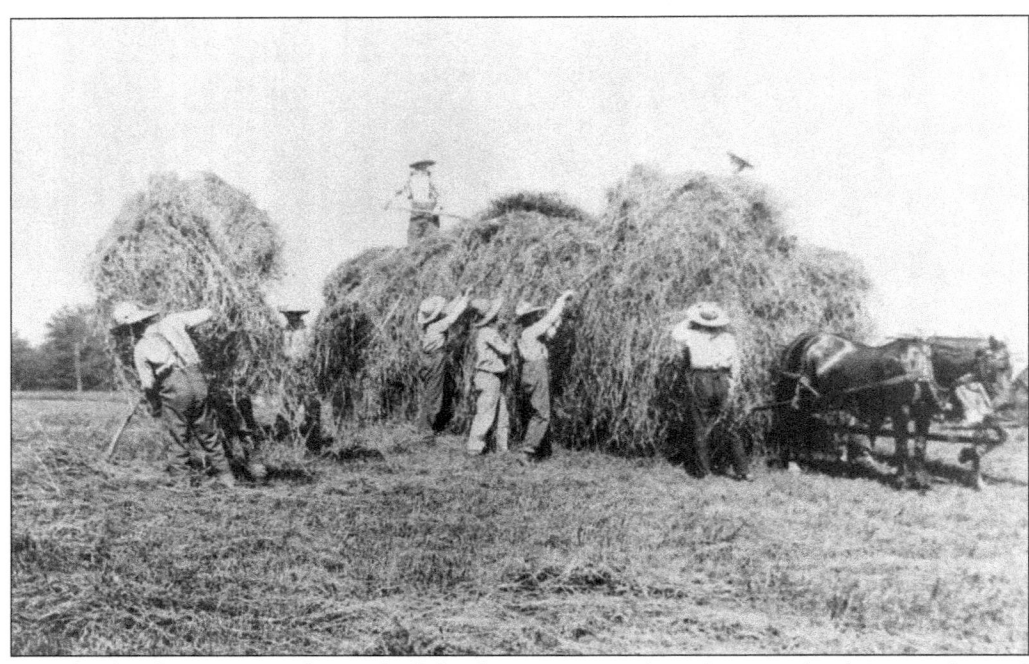

In order for the inmates who worked the farm to get to their duties early, they were housed outside the cell blocks in J-Dorm. In 1917, ten years after the building opened and the farm was started, the reformatory had 330 acres of farmland growing a variety of crops, including wheat, rye, oats, and barley, as well as hay and potatoes. A dairy barn, hog barn, and poultry buildings also contributed to the reformatory's food supply. Fruit orchards and additional crops were grown, harvested, and canned using cans made in the tin shop. Starting out with only horsepower, the farm evolved as technology progressed, and its efficiency increased when, by 1949, the farm gradually replaced the horse with trucks and tractors. As the need to be self-sustaining grew, so did the farm operation.

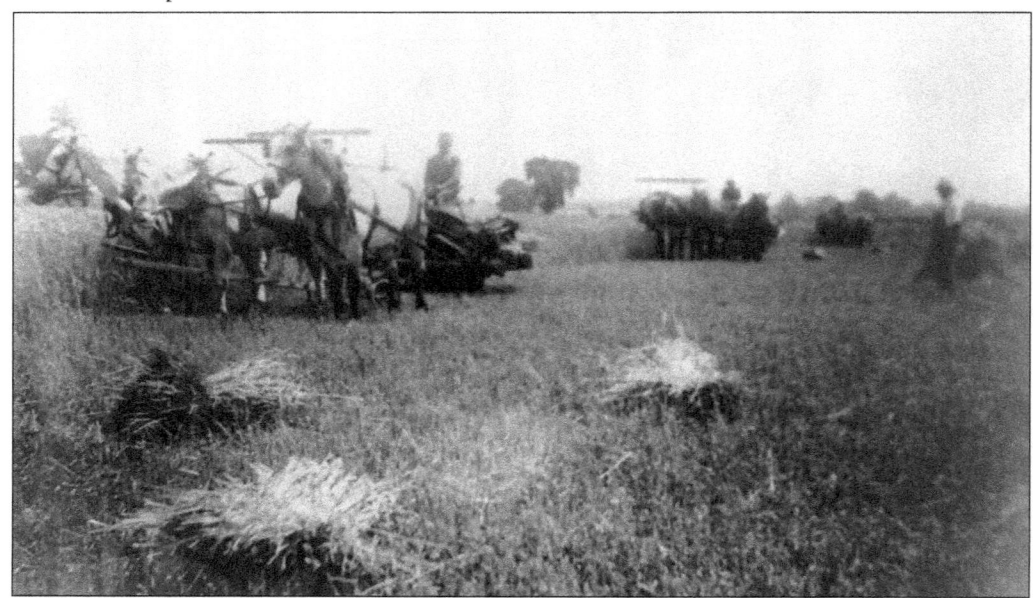

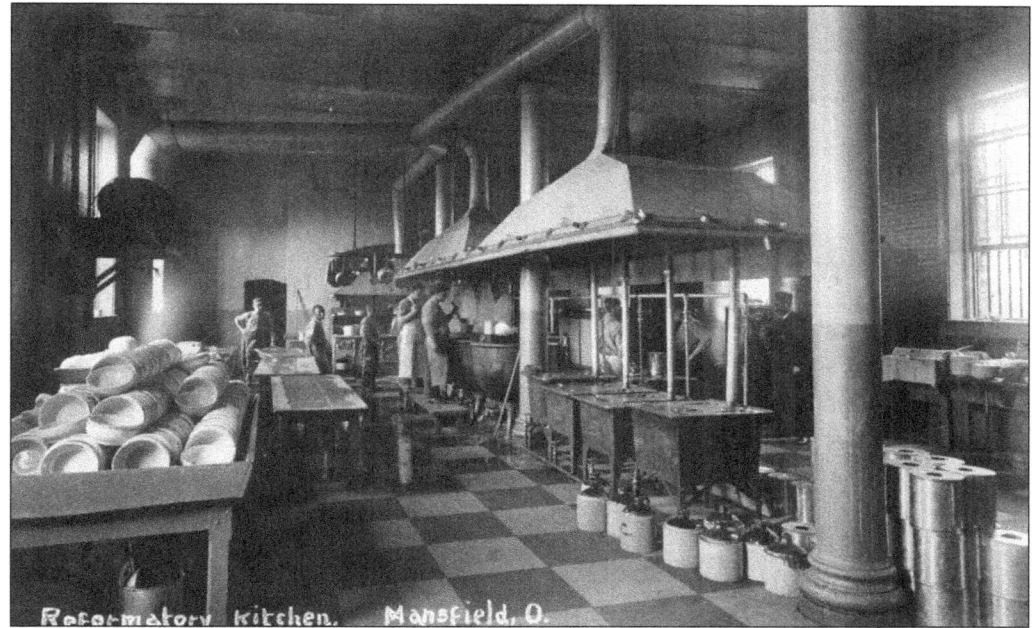

Food preparation in the prison was a massive undertaking. Along with the kitchen and bakery, the subsistence department included the canning department, paring room, creamery, butcher shop, and granary. In 1934, there were 1,700 to 2,200 inmates fed at each meal. The tables were set and the food placed on the plates before inmates were marched into the dining room. As soon as the dishes were cleared, preparations began for the next meal. A report in 1934 stated that in February of that year the bakery made 1,200 loaves of bread and 5,000 buns daily. Since so much food was grown and raised on the reformatory grounds, the cost of each meal per person was slightly over 4.5¢.

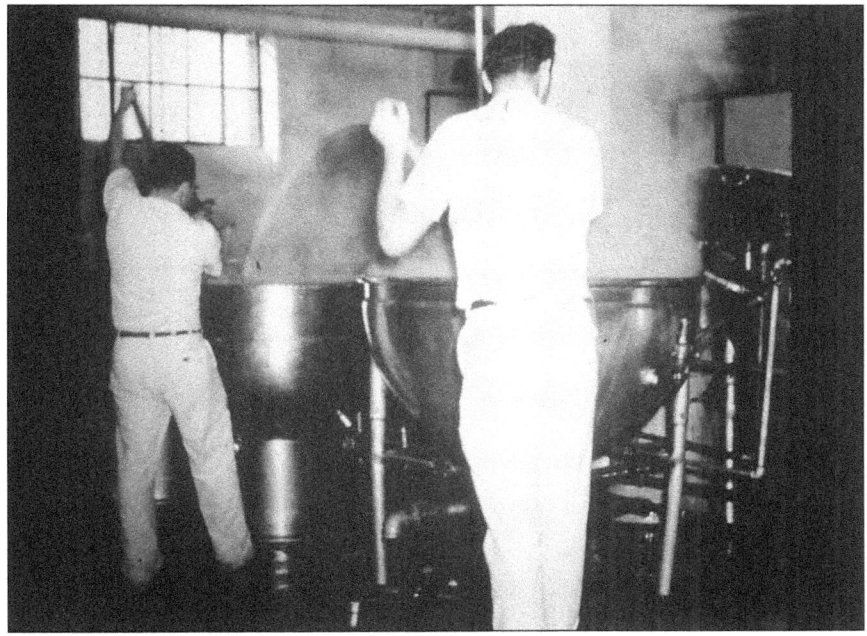

Meals for prisoners were sufficient but plain. Inmates were fed three meals a day Monday through Friday. On weekends, however, they had two meals per day. Shown here is a portion of a July 4, 1897, report on the day's menu. The menu shows that only lettuce was grown on the farm and not included in the cost-per-meal total. The total spent on food for inmate meals was $28.28; feeding 309 inmates on this day cost 9¢ per person. The reformatory had been open for about nine months at this time and had not yet started the farm operations in full. By 1934, a total of 2,100 men were fed at a cost of slightly over 4.5¢ per meal.

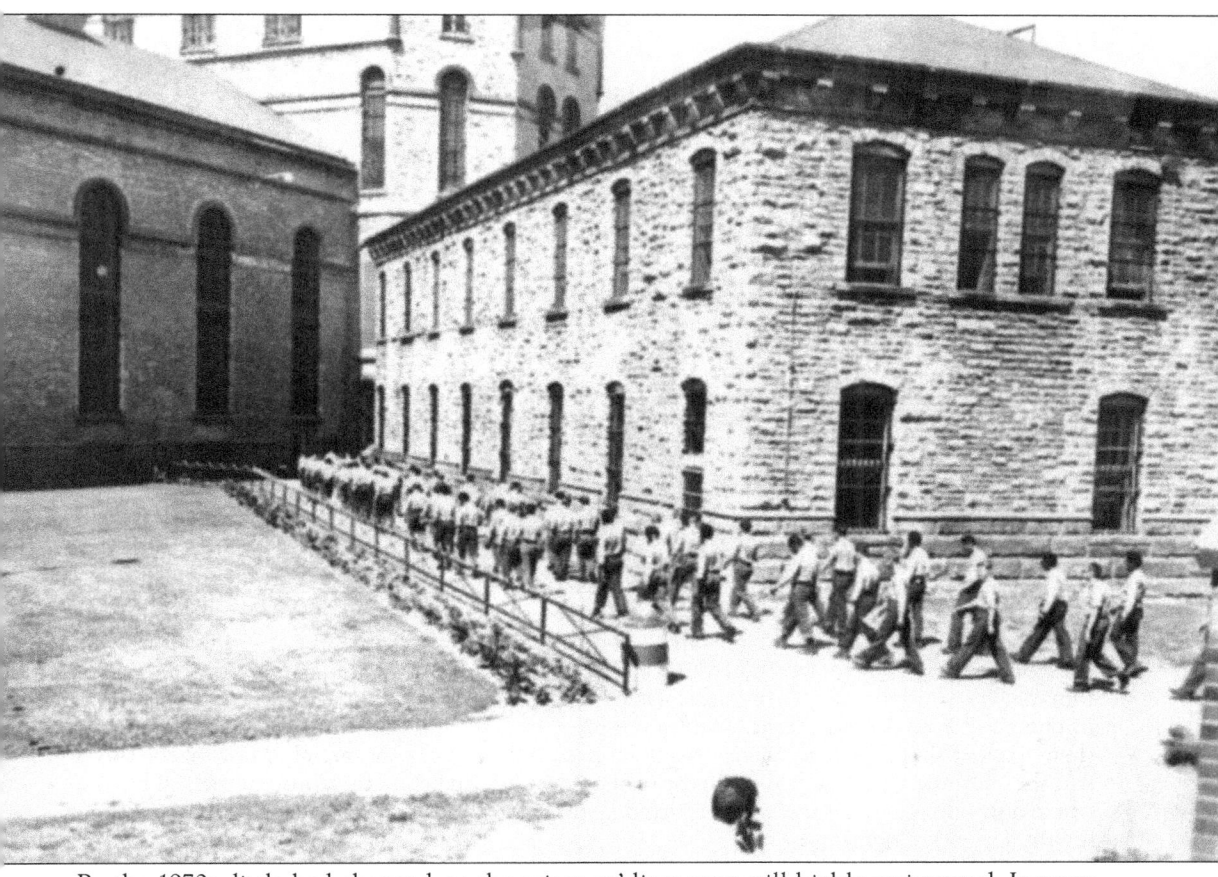

By the 1970s, little had changed, as the prisoners' lives were still highly regimented. Inmates were required to be in their cells several times daily for head counts. When the men arose in the morning, they would stand outside their cells to be counted. They would be marched in lockstep to the dining hall for breakfast and at noon were returned to their cells for another count before returning to work. The men returned to their cells at the end of the day for one final head count. During the day, inmates could travel from one place to another unescorted only if they had a pass. Typically, inmates would be given a pass to go to the infirmary, dentist, or barber. The passes were checked and recorded as they moved through the prison.

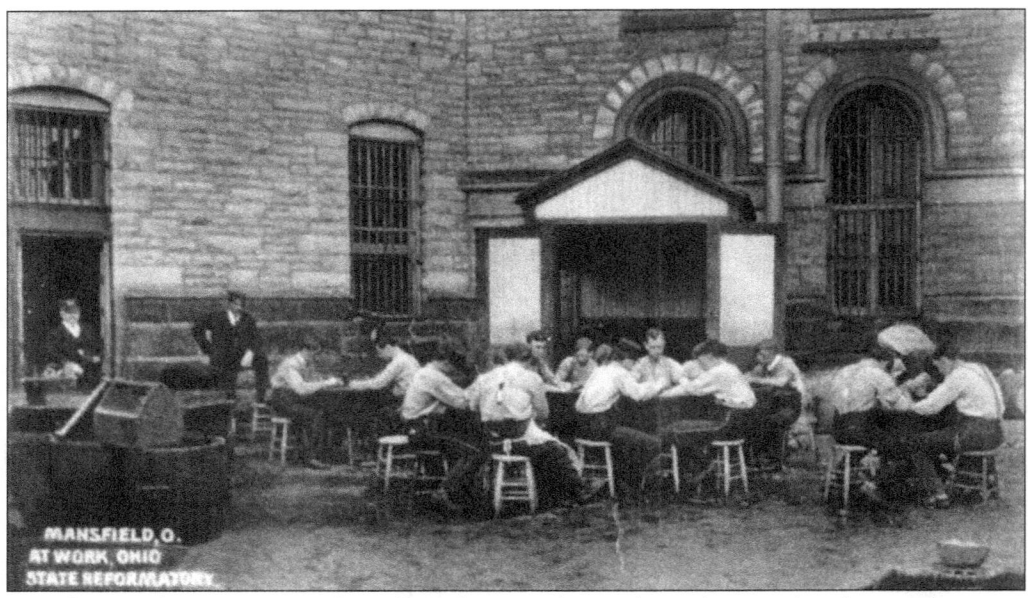

Guards at work assignments often allowed minimal special privileges and took special interest in post-release work for the inmates in their charge. Above, a guard oversees inmates as they work outside in the warm weather. Many guards would contact potential employers on behalf of inmates who showed particular promise with their skills and motivation. As shown below, guards in charge of a work assignment would often meet inmates in the dining hall and accompany them to their shop, allowing them to walk more casually rather than march. Many of the shops had showers, and guards would allow the inmates to wash up before returning to the cell blocks, where only one shower a week was permitted. One inmate reported that a guard intervened when he was accused of fighting.

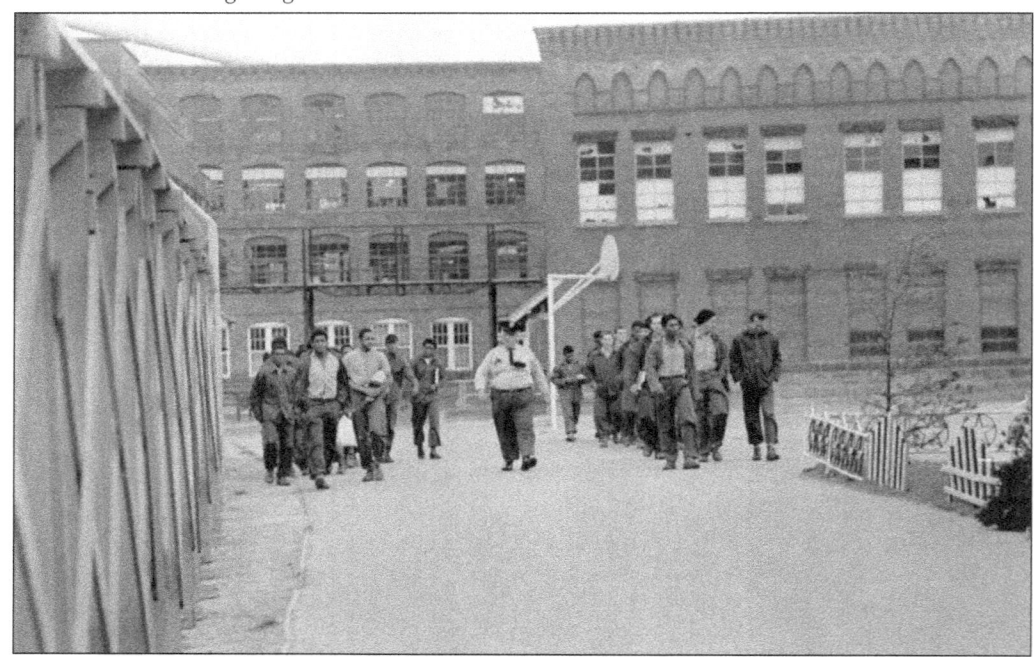

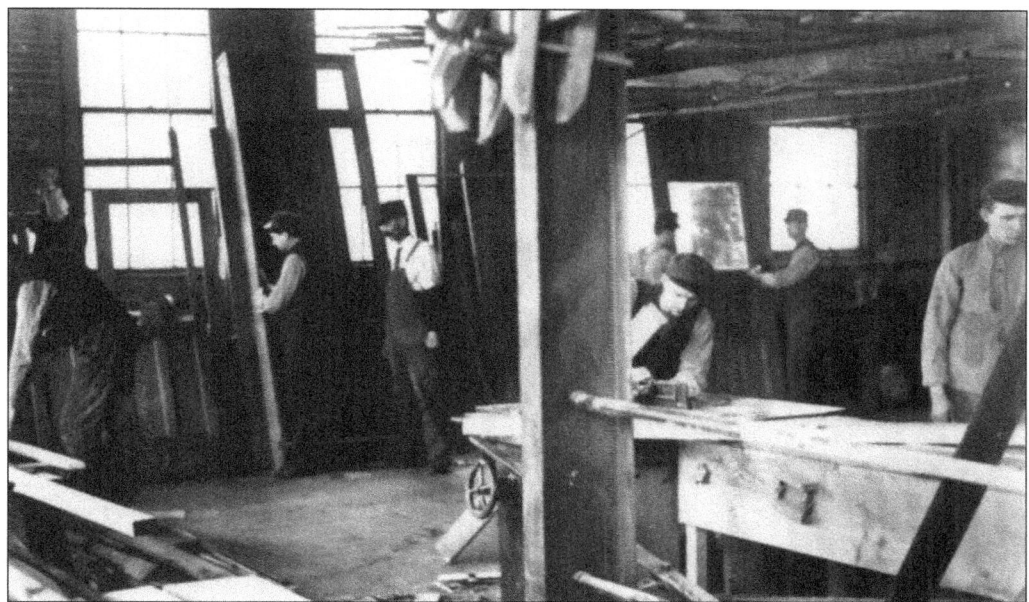

The furniture factory produced items, starting with milling the wood. Raw wood was delivered to the reformatory by rail and brought in through the gate on the west side of the yard. The process involved air-drying lumber for 90 days before being kiln-dried until it reached the proper moisture content. In the early 1930s, between 600,000 and 700,000 feet of lumber were used each year. The factory used plain and quarter-sawed white oak, birch, figured red gum, poplar, and mahogany. Each year, 100,000 feet of pine was used in the manufacture of shipping crates. These crates were used to transport finished products in other departments, like the shoe and broom factories. Running at full capacity, the furniture factory employed up to 500 men.

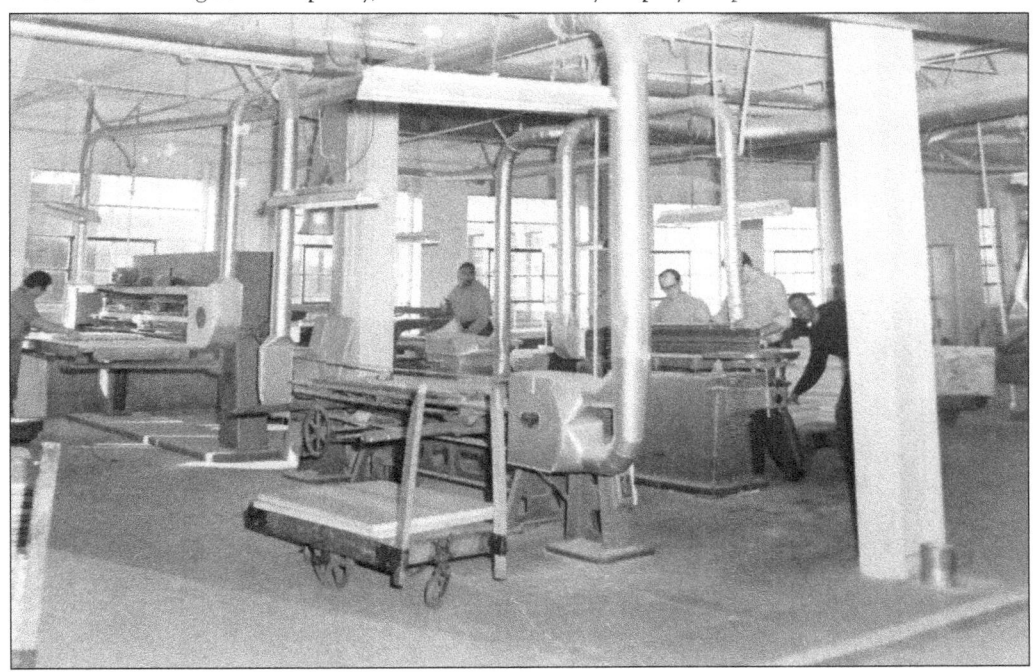

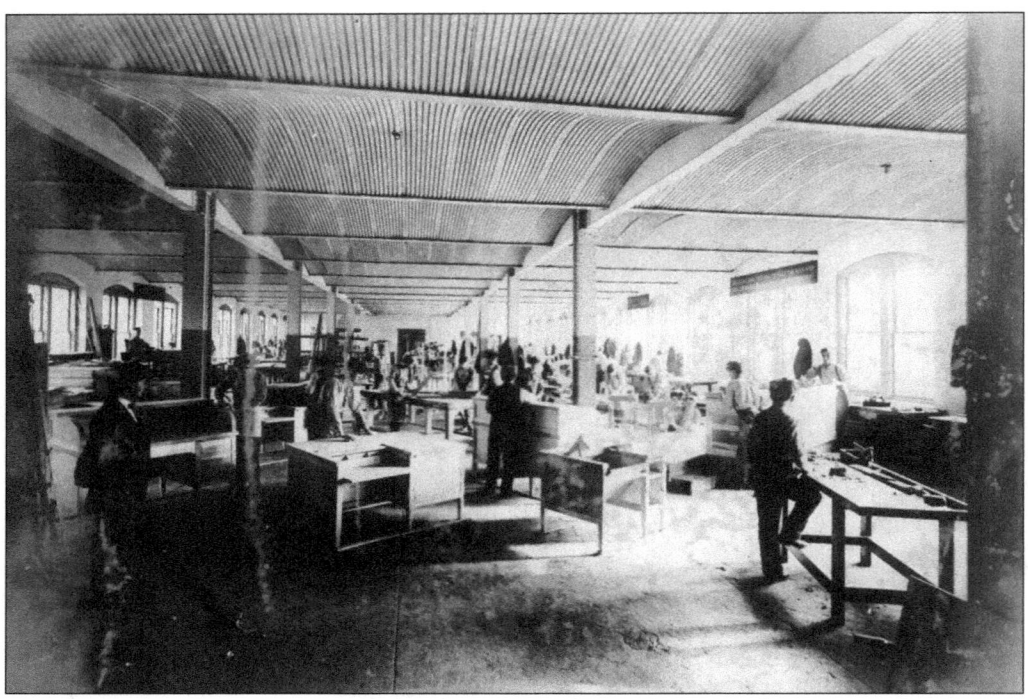

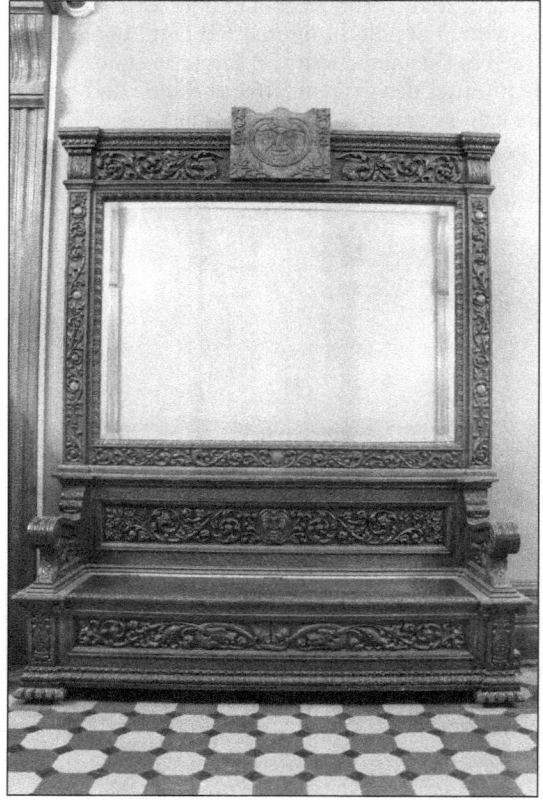

Opened in 1912, the furniture factory created pieces ranging from the ornate to the utilitarian. After lumber was milled, it was sent to the machine shop and then to the finishing shop, where it was assembled, sanded, and finished with stain and then sprayed with waterproof lacquer. Furniture used throughout the prison and administrative wing was built in the factory. At one time, the furniture was constructed for the governor's office and other state offices in Columbus. The factory also manufactured furniture for other public offices, courthouses, county homes, state institutions, and schools. The factory produced more mundane items as well, such as school desks and small tables for cells. Some items are still in use today, and others are on display in the OSR museum.

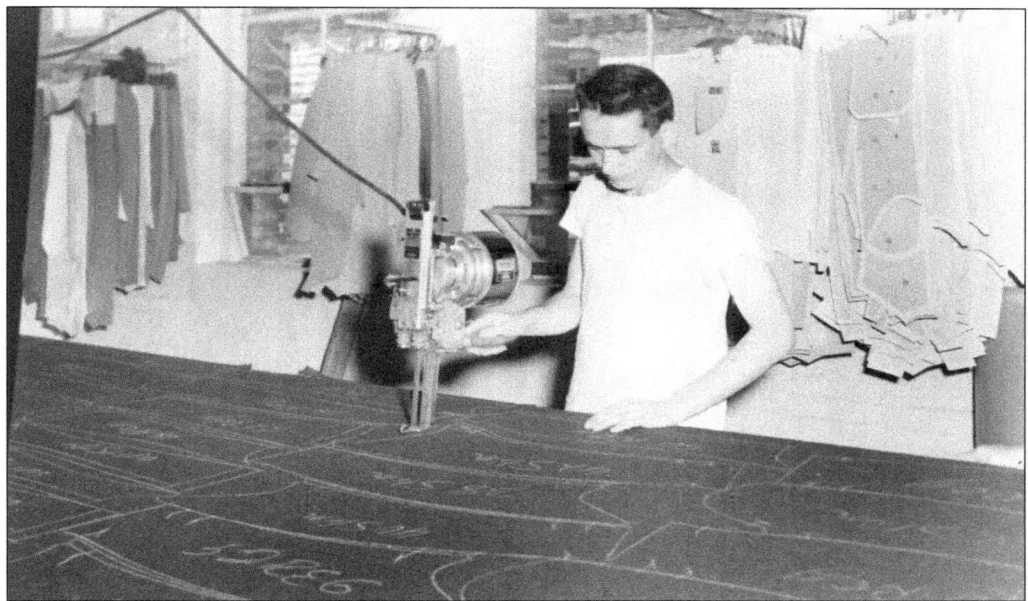

The tailor shop was one of the main industries at the reformatory. In one year, it used 35,000 yards of wool and 60,000 yards of cotton in the production of inmate uniforms, officers' uniforms, caps, shirts, and suits for boys in county children's homes throughout the state. Suits made in the shop were used in all Ohio state hospitals for patients and for the reformatory to give to paroled inmates. Suits were also made as a burial garment for inmates who died within the prison walls. The tailor shop made upwards of 5,000 of these suits per year. Two- and three-piece suits were made, with a three-piece suit selling for $7. In 1934, the tailor shop had 85 sewing machines, along with special machines for cutting buttonholes, two cutting machines, and steam-pressing equipment.

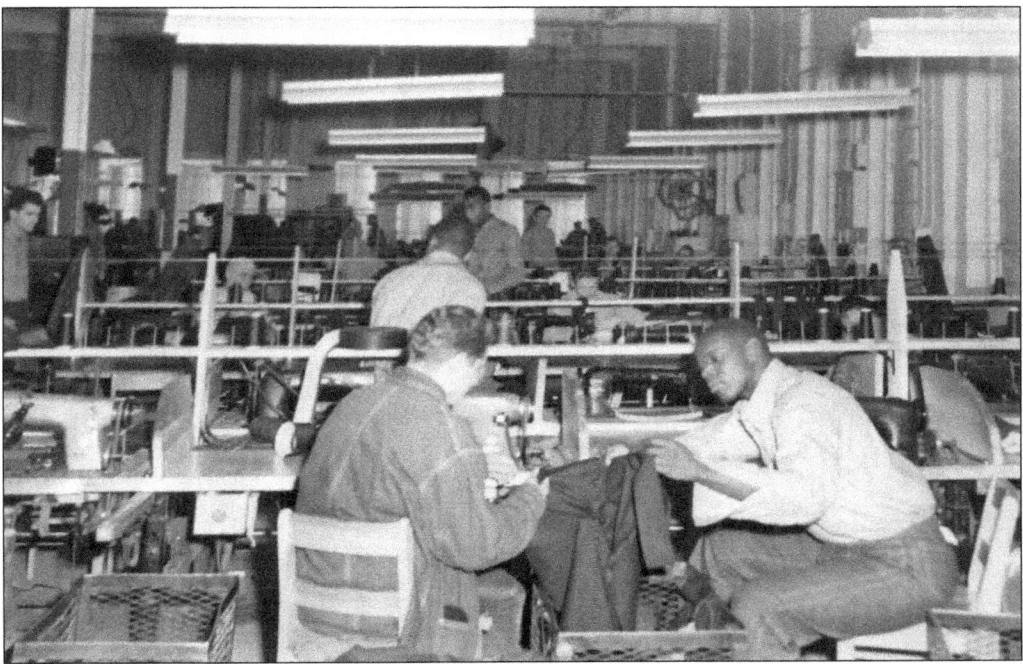

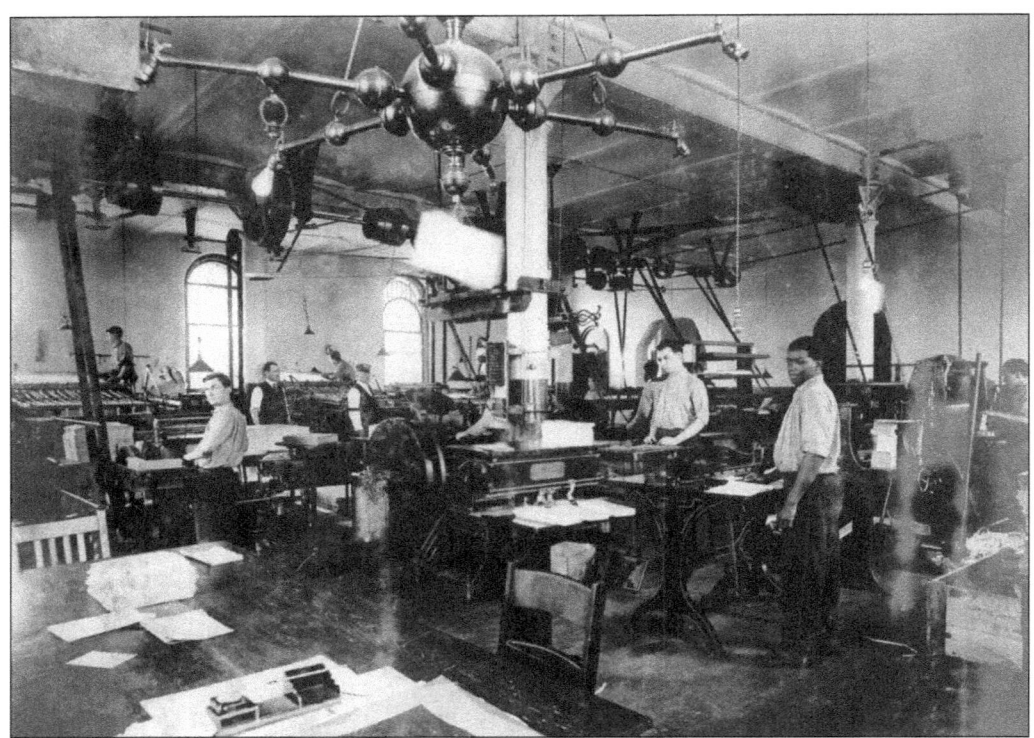

The printing shop was responsible not only for the production of print materials for the OSR, but it was busy with projects across the state. As part of the manufacturing and sales division, the shop's work was printed and sent out to other state institutions. Much of its work came from Ohio colleges and universities. These institutions would order catalogs and bulletins, ranging in length from 36 to 250 pages; orders ranged from 250 to 10,000 copies. In 1934, it was reported that each year the print shop used 200,000 pounds of book stock. Printing had the potential to be a very successful trade for the inmates. They learned to work with modern printing equipment, as well as typesetting, proofing, and composing. Upon release, an inmate would qualify to become an apprentice with the Typographical Union.

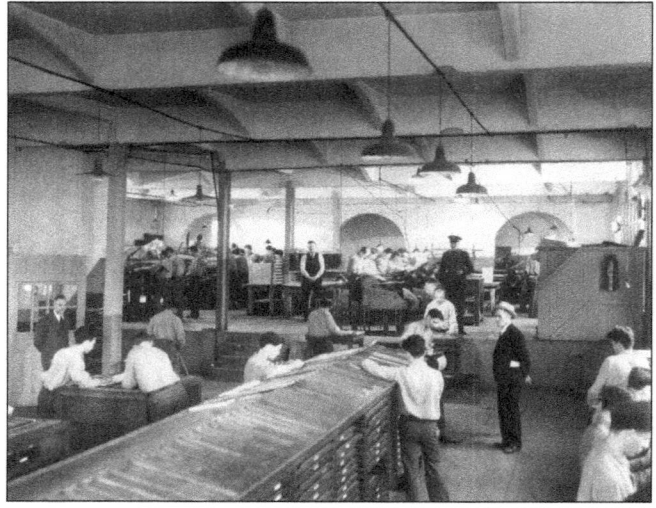

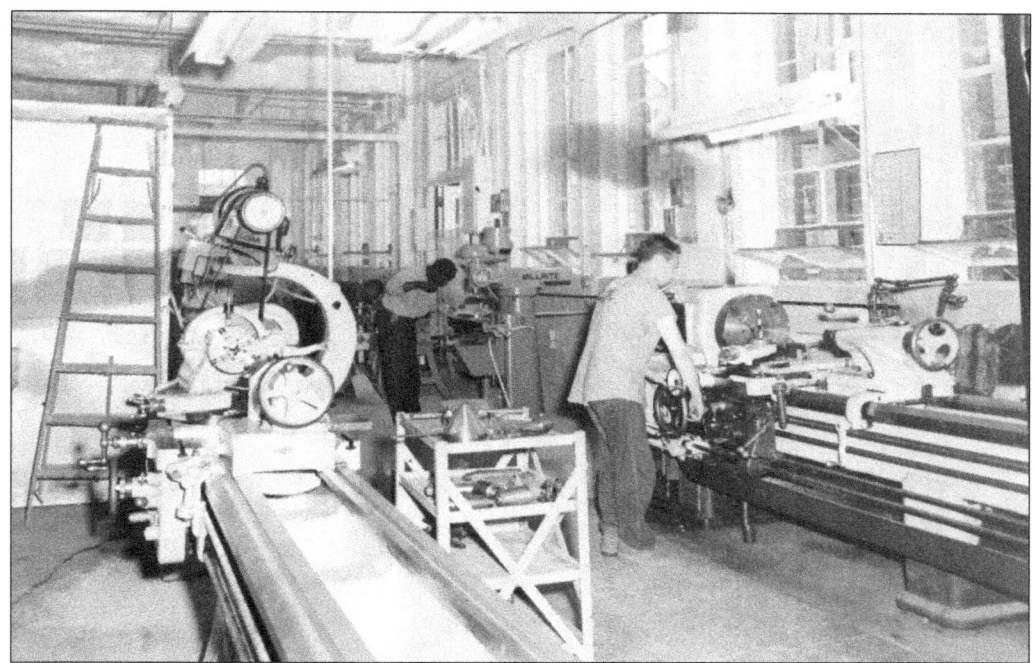

Precision machining and welding were among the over 30 trade programs that provided inmates with marketable skills. At full capacity, the machine shop employed 75 inmates. They were responsible for machining parts used throughout the prison as well as at other state institutions. Tubes used in the shop were formed into frames for beds for the prison hospital. Frames and adjustable backrests were sold to state-operated hospitals. The machine shop manufactured all the steel frames used for cots in the cells. In 1931, the machine department sold 2,700 beds to outside institutions, including state-run nursing homes and orphanages. The inmate machinists also made parts that were used in other shops within the prison. Prison-trained welders were used throughout the building as equipment and training programs were upgraded.

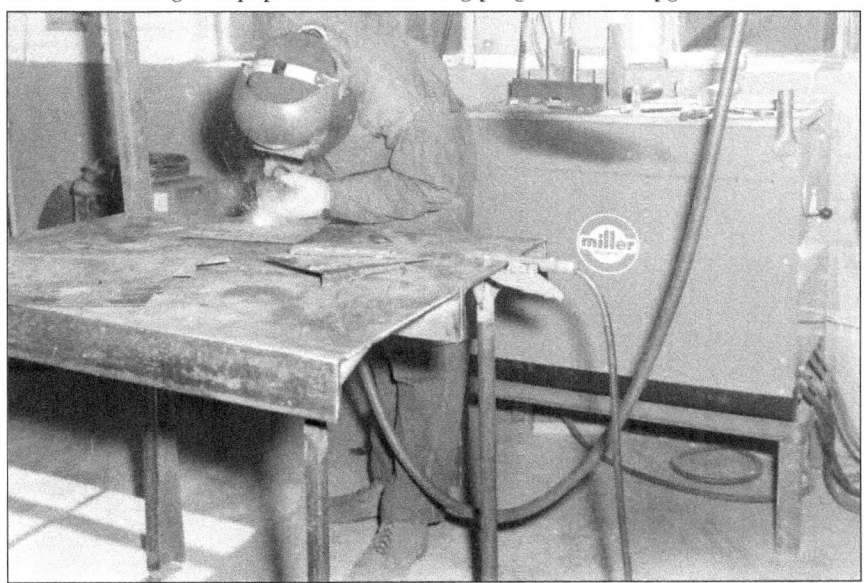

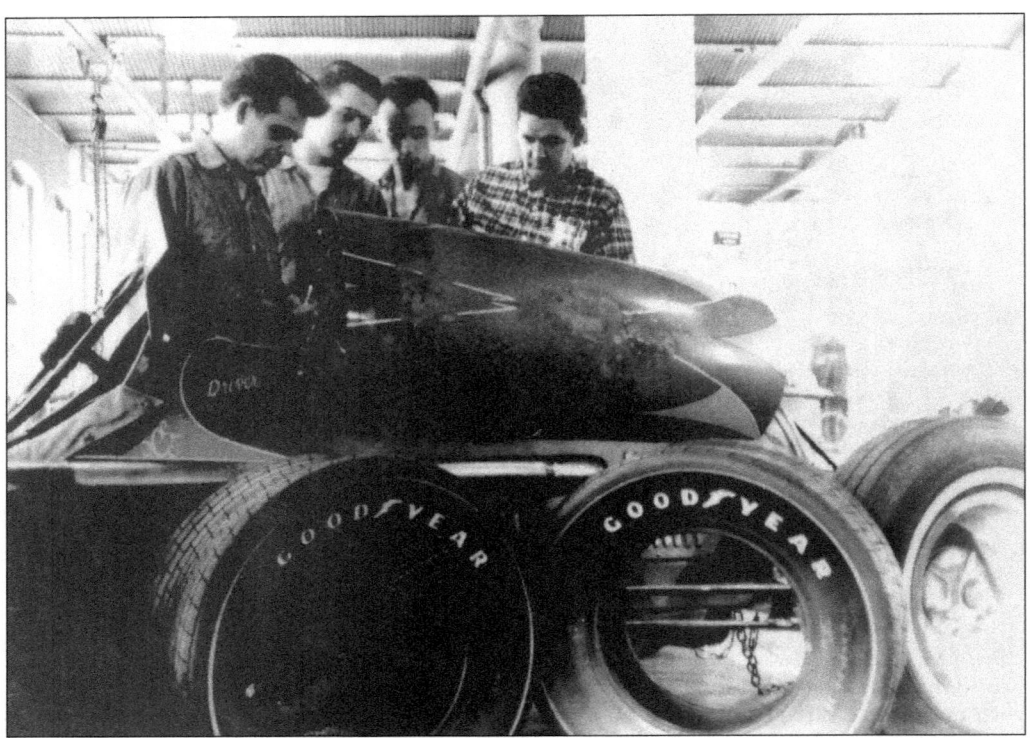

Jerry Campbell began work at the reformatory in 1962 as a corrections officer. In 1965, after approaching Supt. Bernard Barton, he became auto-tech instructor and formed the Penal Racing Association (PRA). The PRA met each Friday afternoon for updates on plans and shared interests in race cars. As the average sentence at the OSR was 18 months, most inmate PRA members could learn only the most rudimentary aspects of auto mechanics. The parole board recognized a significant change in attitude of inmates involved in the program and took that into consideration when an inmate came up for release. Membership in PRA and the mechanics class was very selective. Officer Campbell went out of his way to find employment for inmates that showed talent. Above, Campbell (right) instructs three inmate/students. Below, Campbell poses next to the race car with trophies. (Courtesy of the Campbell family.)

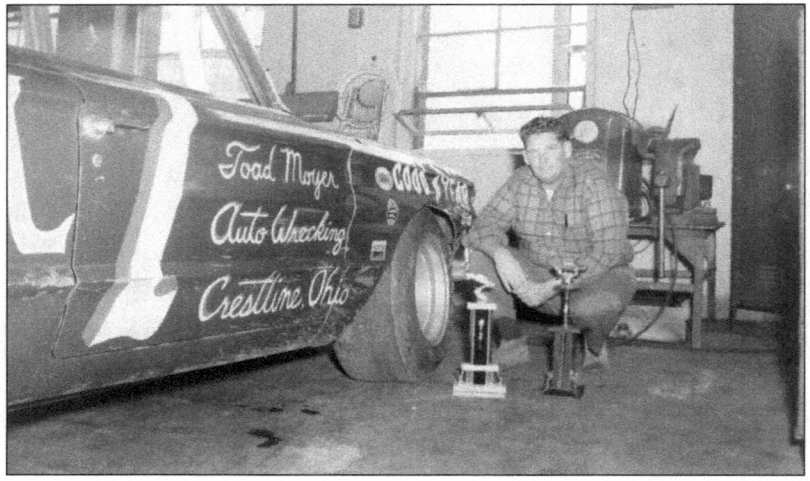

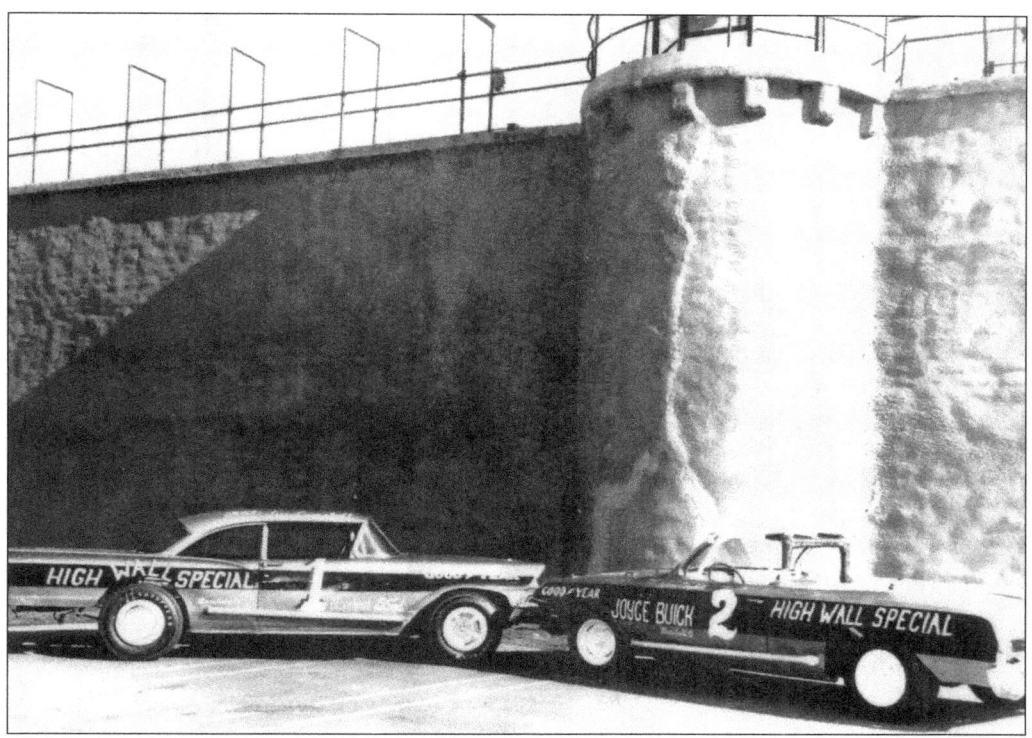

Taking the auto mechanics class and PRA to the next level, Officer Jerry Campbell acquired the body of a Ford Thunderbird. He then approached the Ford Motor Company for engines; other major companies contributed materials and equipment. Thus was born the High Wall Special. Not all the work was done inside the walls though. Campbell was the driver, and he selected two inmates each racing season as his pit crew to accompany him to local races. The crew members, though unguarded, never attempted an escape. That did not stop other inmates, however, from using the coming and going of the car for escape attempts. In September 1975, two inmates were able to hide in the truck transporting the race car, but they were soon recaptured. Below, two inmate pit-crew members pose next to the race car. (Both courtesy of the Campbell family.)

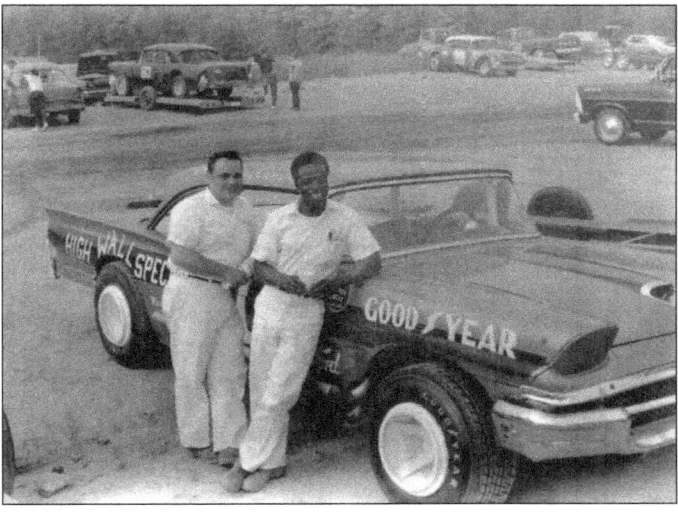

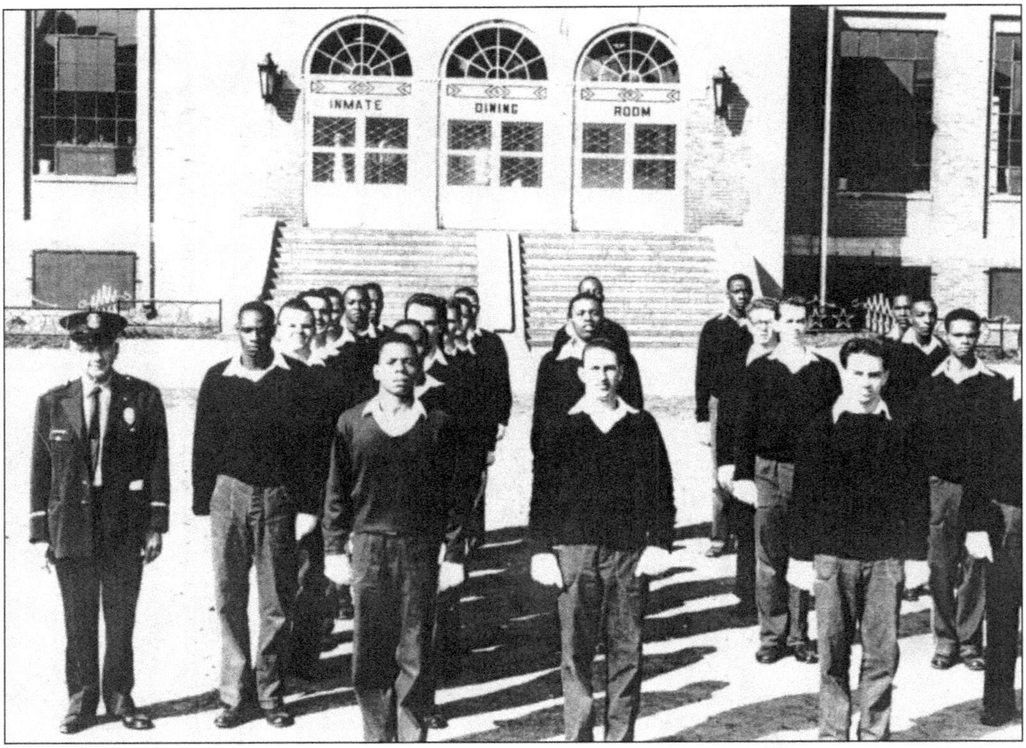

Among the training programs available to inmates was the barber school. Upon achieving a level of skill, inmates worked on not just other inmates, but on guards and members of the public. Later, guards were provided barber services in a separate area by an instructor and highly trusted inmates. Qualified inmate barbers were assigned to honor farms, the hospital, E-Dorm, and J-Dorm. In 1968, prison rules required that each inmate receive two haircuts a month, translating into 5,000 haircuts in the barbershop each month. Above, guard/instructor Clifford Moore (far left) taught at the OSR for 27 years. The photograph below depicts the barbershop in 1971. (Below, courtesy of Jeff Sprang.)

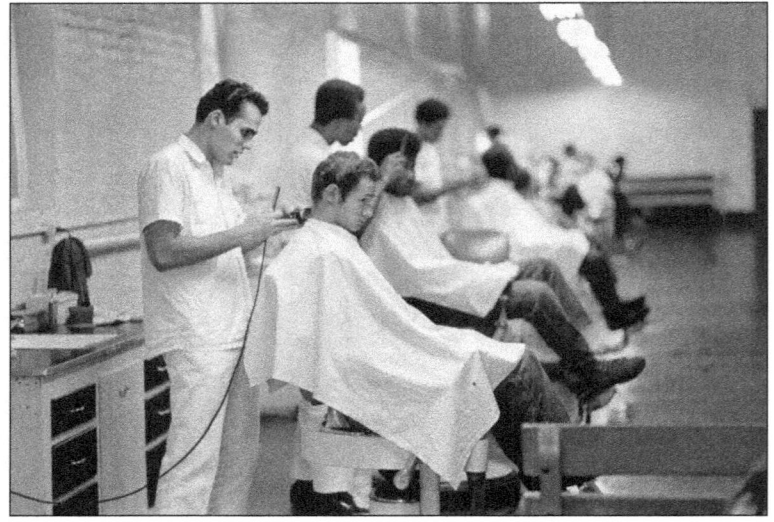

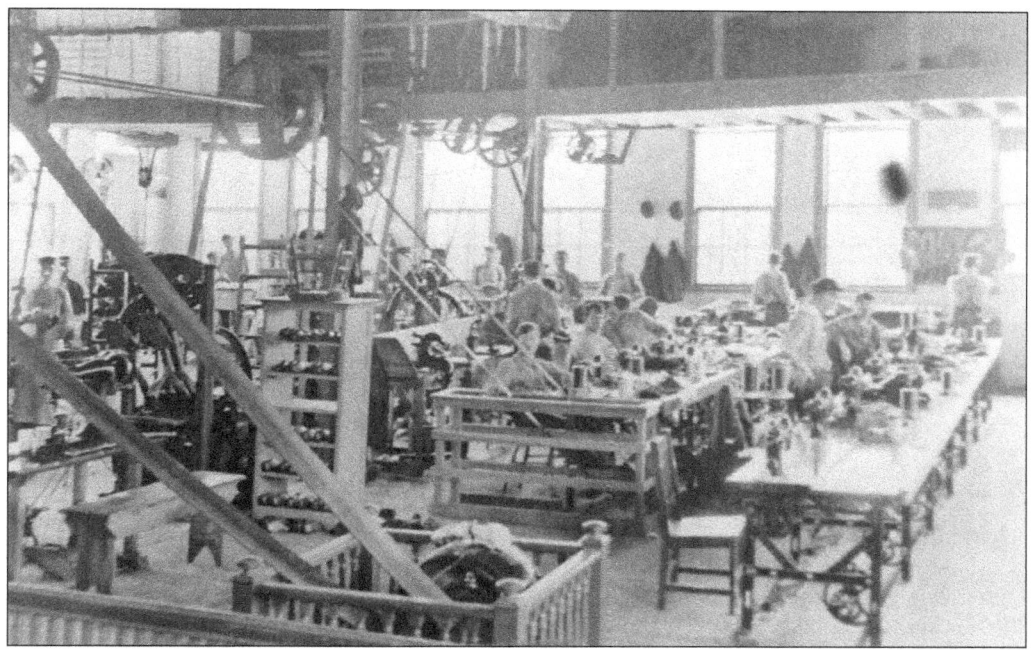

The shoe shop was one of the major industries in the manufacturing department. In a 1933 report to the state, the OSR reported that in 1931 the shop made over 49,140 pairs of shoes. Of that, 36,737 were for men and boys and 12,301 were for women, misses, and children. Public institutions bought shoes at a cost of from $1 to $2.10. It was reported that sales that year amounted to $117,000. The shop produced 57 styles of shoes in all sizes. The shoes were more utilitarian than fashionable, as they were produced for state institutions rather than the general public. In 1933, the OSR consistently employed 120 inmates for the numerous machines. In 1965, the shoe factory was moved to the Ohio Pen, and the 120 inmates were reassigned to other factories.

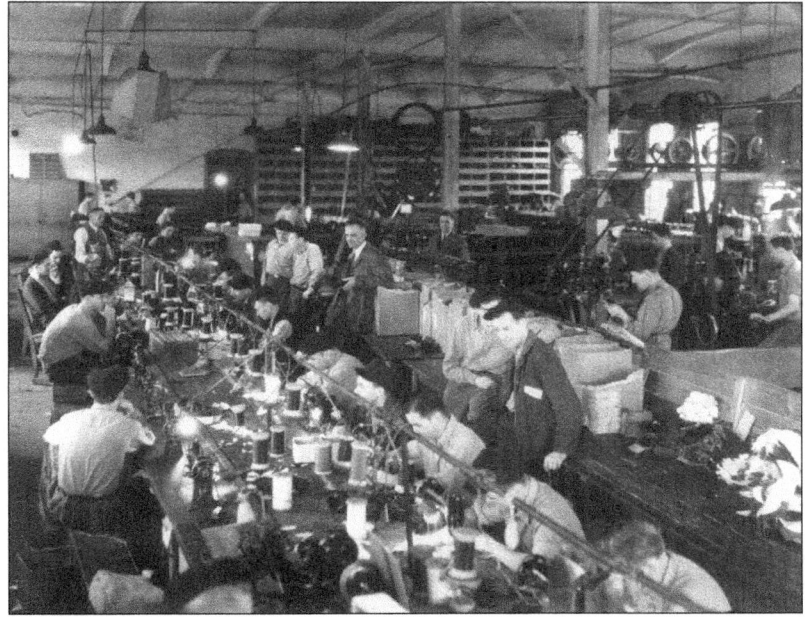

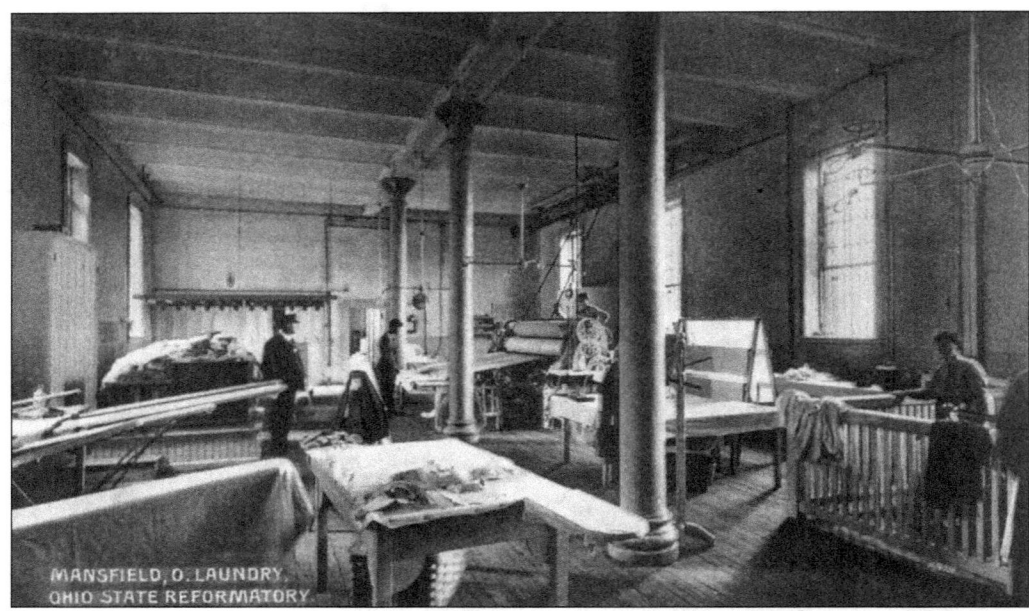

Little is known about the reformatory's laundry. It was reported in 1934 that the facility employed 72 inmates. A huge amount of laundry was generated each day, with the facility handling 45,000 pieces each week. By the 1970s, many protective-custody inmates were employed in the laundry. Many of these men were in danger of being harmed by other inmates because of certain circumstances, including crimes against children, being homosexual, or being informants. These inmates could not safely work or be housed with the general population. Their cells were located on the third tier of the northeast block. Inmates' uniforms were washed, dried, and returned to the inmate. The clothing was identified by the last name or inmate number attached to the shirt. Some inmates paid laundry workers a "quarter" (a pack of cigarettes) to iron their clothes.

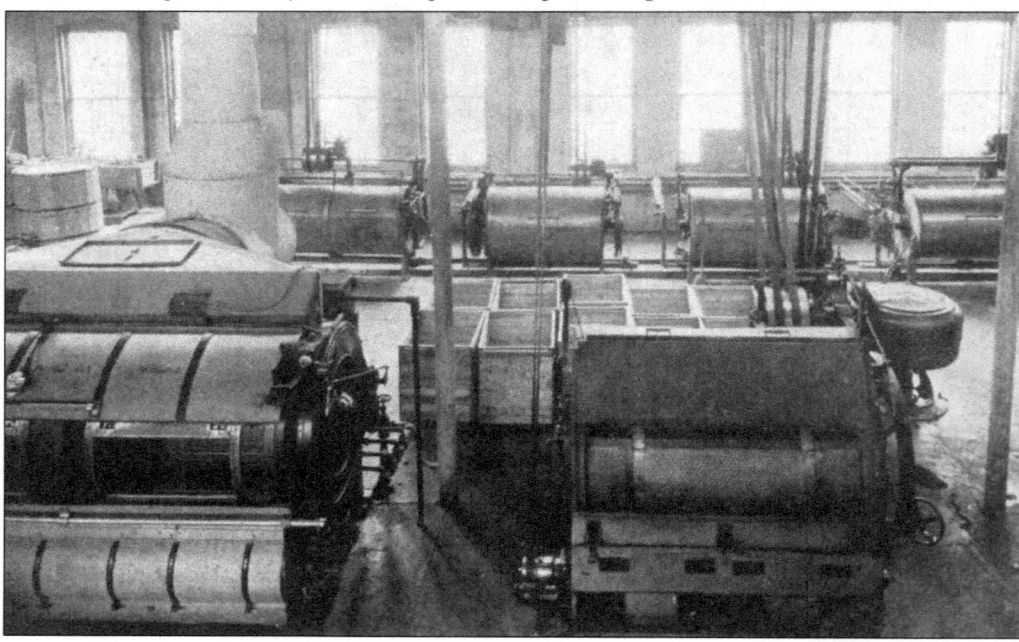

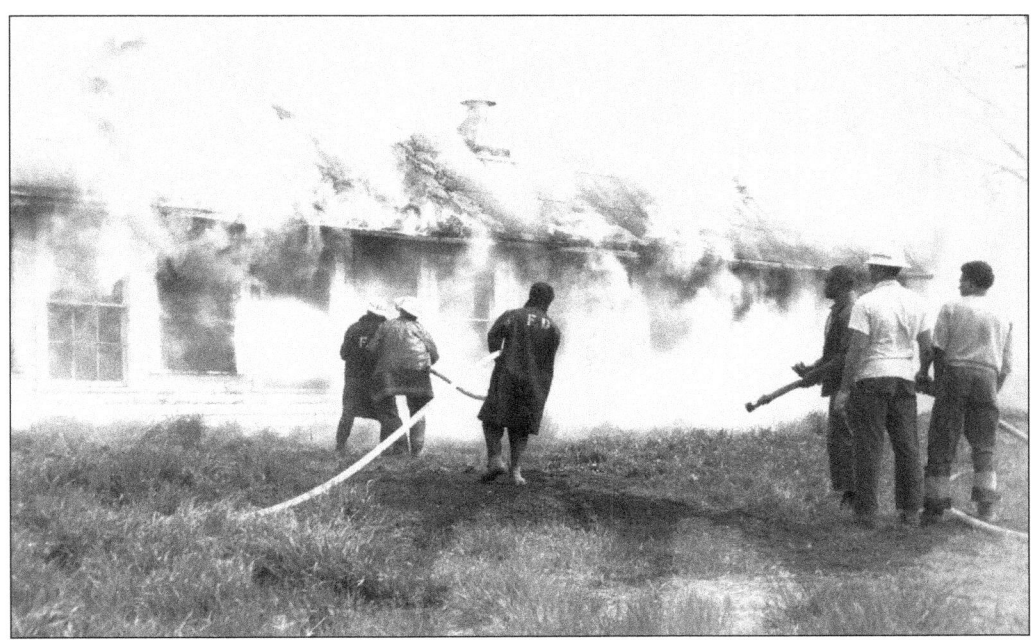

Throughout its history, several fires occurred at the prison. The *Mansfield News Journal* reported on November 25, 1938, that a fire broke out in the shower room, where 100 straw-filled mattresses caught on fire. The local fire department responded, and 50 trustees formed a bucket brigade to help. The fire filled the east cell block with smoke, but the blaze was contained to the shower. The blaze was blamed on spontaneous combustion. In September 1974, the *News Journal* reported that two fires were set in two days by inmates. A larger fire destroyed the barn at the reformatory farm. To reduce loss from blazes, the OSR formed and trained a group of inmates to be the first responders in the event of fire.

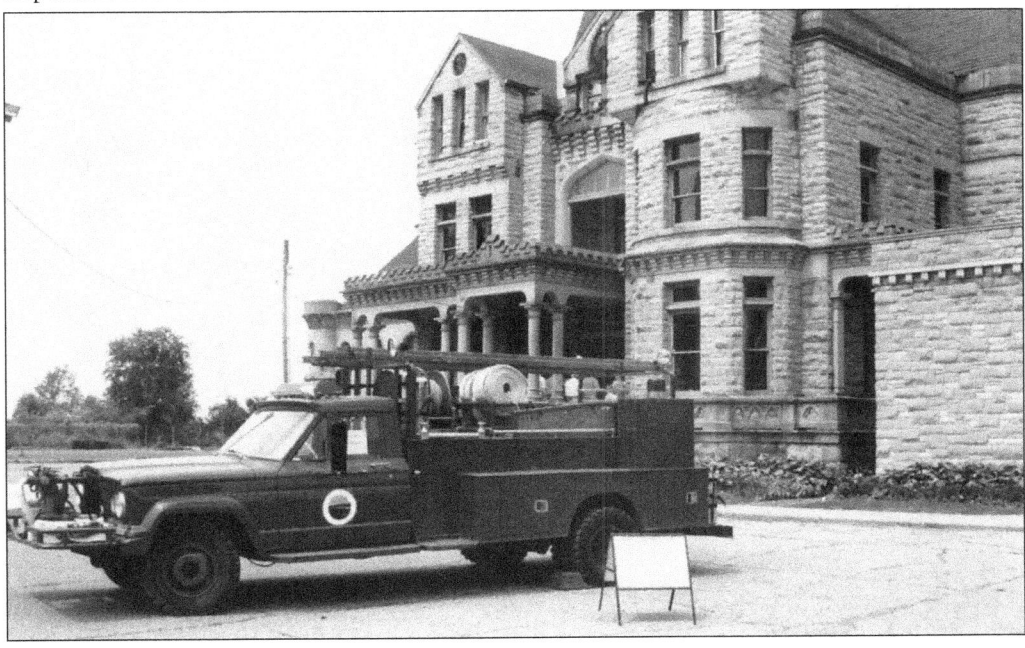

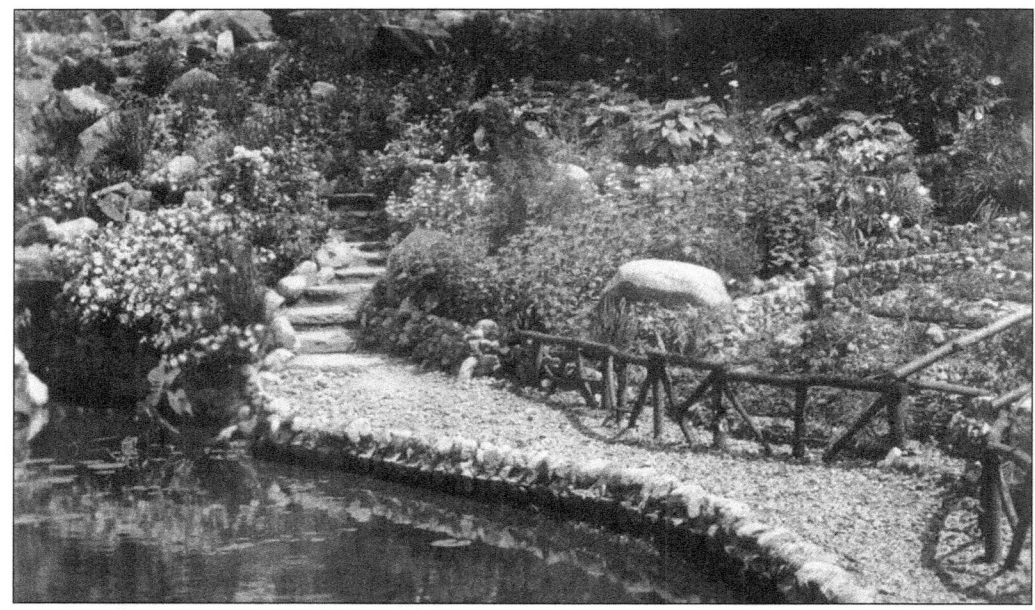

Inmate Ermil "Frenchy" Belaneco had been convicted for the murder of his girlfriend. He believed that he deserved a pardon, as he felt he had done nothing wrong. He passed up his first parole hearing. In the 1930s, Belaneco approached Supt. T.C. Jenkins with an idea. He was interested in landscaping the front gardens of the reformatory grounds. Without formal training, he created an elaborate rock garden around the pond on the southwest side of the front yard. The garden became a popular tourist attraction. He continued his work, creating other beautiful gardens. Belaneco never did get a pardon. When he next came up for parole, he decided to appear before the board and was released. He remained in the Mansfield community as a sought-after landscaper for well-to-do families.

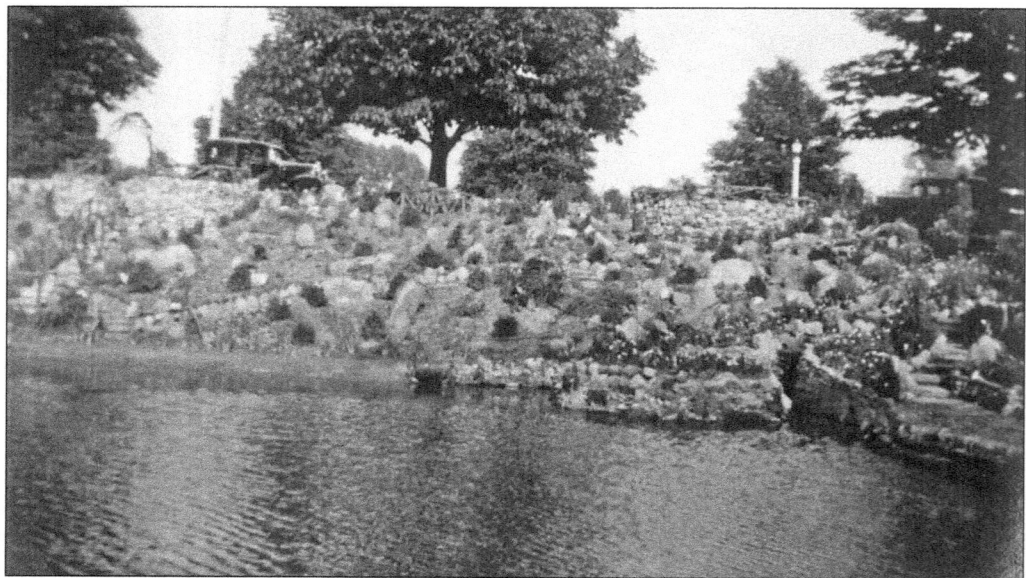

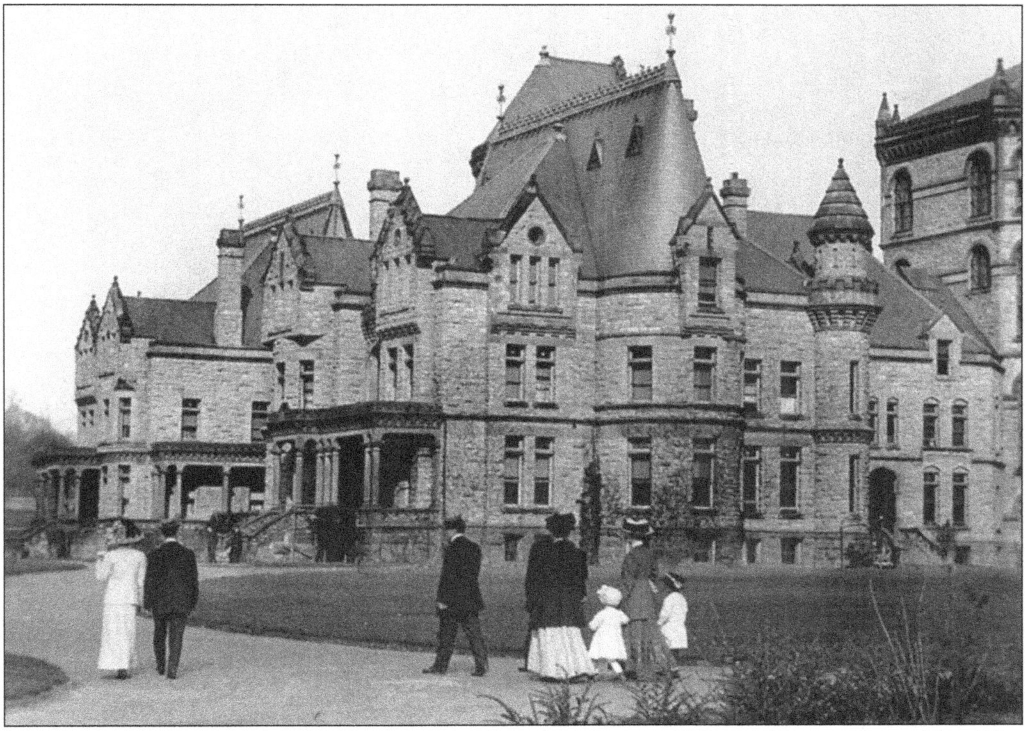

Another important group that was essential to the success of the OSR was the public. The administration was keen to maintain the goodwill of Mansfield's citizens. During planning for the reformatory, officials rallied the support of the public, describing the economic advantages of the institution. They also promoted the grounds as a park-like area that would be available to the public. Upon its opening, the Ohio State Reformatory was an attraction for members of the Mansfield community. A trolley stop was added to the line to bring citizens to the grounds. Although not permitted on the front grounds on weekends, landscaping and maintenance was done by inmates as part of their work assignments on weekdays. The OSR band would occasionally perform on Sunday afternoons.

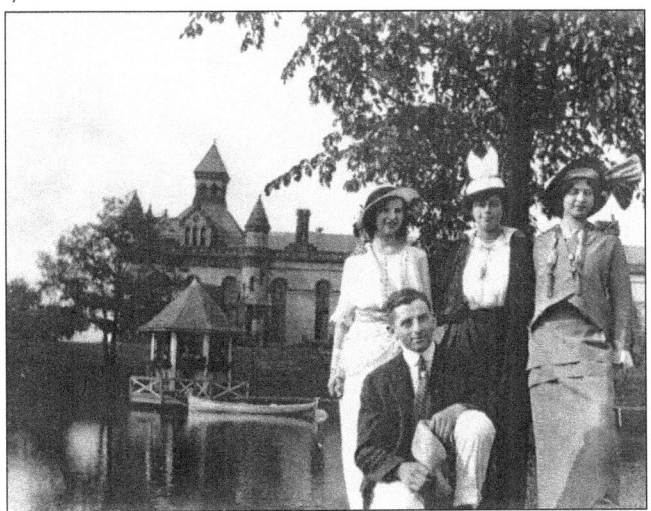

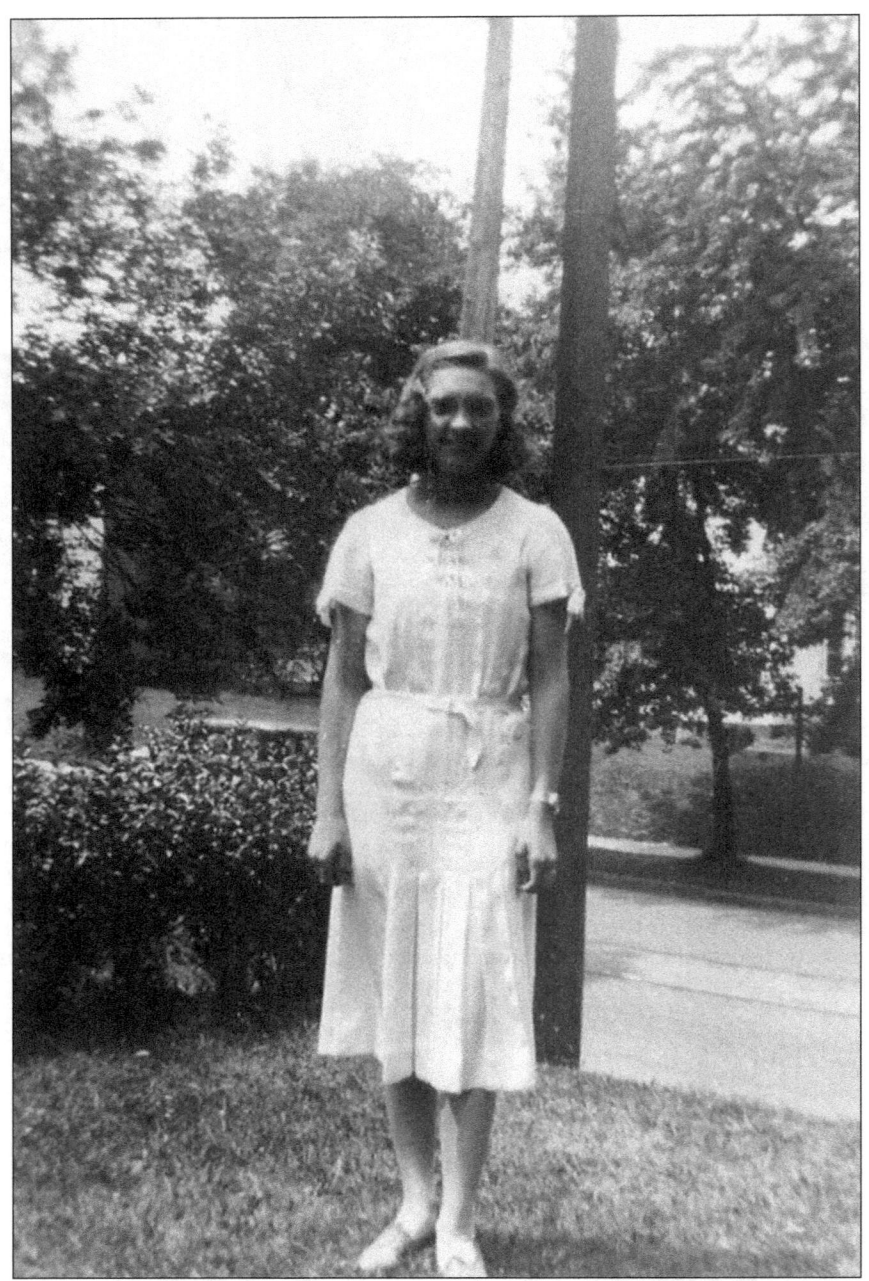
Sylvia Fritz and her family would frequently pack a picnic basket and walk to the grounds to play games and visit with others on the front yard. She became friends with Mary, the daughter of assistant superintendent O.F. Garver. Fritz visited the residence and had dinner with the family. As was customary, the trustees to the residence would make sure that her milk glass was always full. It was not the only time Fritz spent time at the OSR though. As a member of the Fritz Sisters Ensemble, a string and piano group, she and her sisters would be asked to perform when the warden had dinner parties in the residence. Sylvia went on to become a volunteer at the reformatory when it opened for tours in 1995. (Courtesy of the Martin family.)

Four
Behind the Walls
Fun and Games

Though work, training, and education took much of the inmates' time, other activities were available. Recreation took many forms and made inmates' lives as full as possible. Religion was a focus of rehabilitation. The chaplain worked with inmates to develop and distribute a prison newspaper and to plan movies and entertainment opportunities for other inmates. Sports teams competed both inside and outside the walls. The prison band played at ceremonies within the OSR and at numerous community events. Inmates interested in art had opportunities to create a variety of styles and techniques. Many of these opportunities also provided skills that prisoners could use after their release. Inmates also took advantage of their ingenuity to make life more comfortable while confined to their cells.

Some inmates, however, used their down time to pursue less than positive pursuits. Escape was always on their minds, and weapons, whether for protection or harm and retribution, were always a concern of the guards. Walkaways from the farm were not uncommon, and escapes were attempted from the prison itself. When it happened, the security of the prison, guards, and other inmates was at risk. When found, the inmates involved were placed in higher-security custody or in solitary confinement for a period of time. Inmates, then, had opportunities to pursue activities that could enrich their lives and invest in activities that would make their time behind bars more tolerable, or they could use that time for more nefarious purposes.

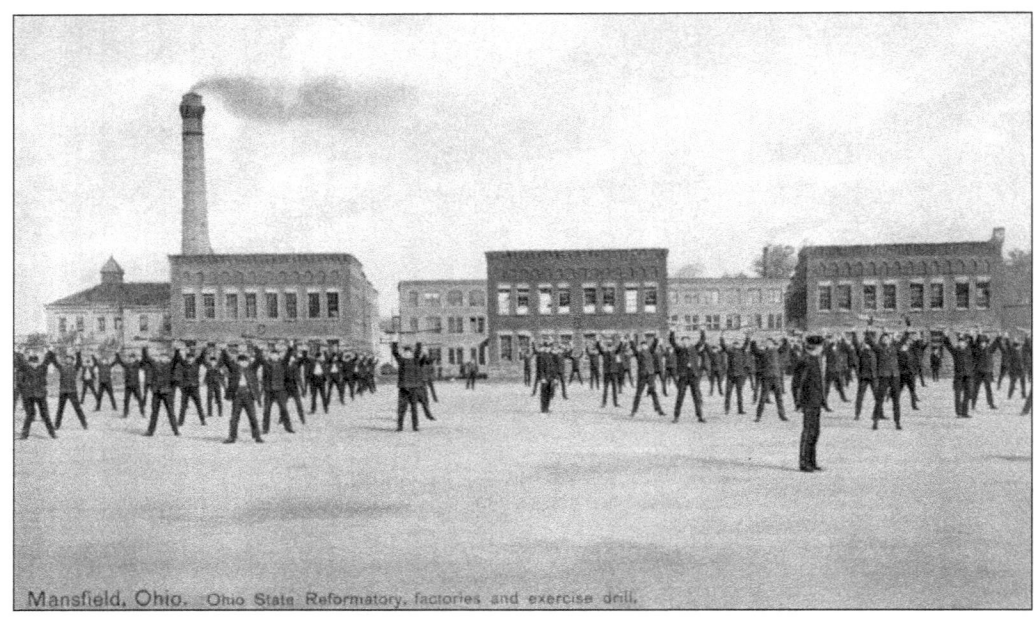

From the earliest days of the Ohio State Reformatory, inmate discipline and order was a high priority. To that end, prisoners were required to march in step when moving several times daily. In the morning and again in the evening, they were marched to the yard behind the cell blocks and stood at attention for review by guards and the raising or lowering of the flag. Above, inmates stand for review. Below, prisoners exercise with "weapons" as the band plays.

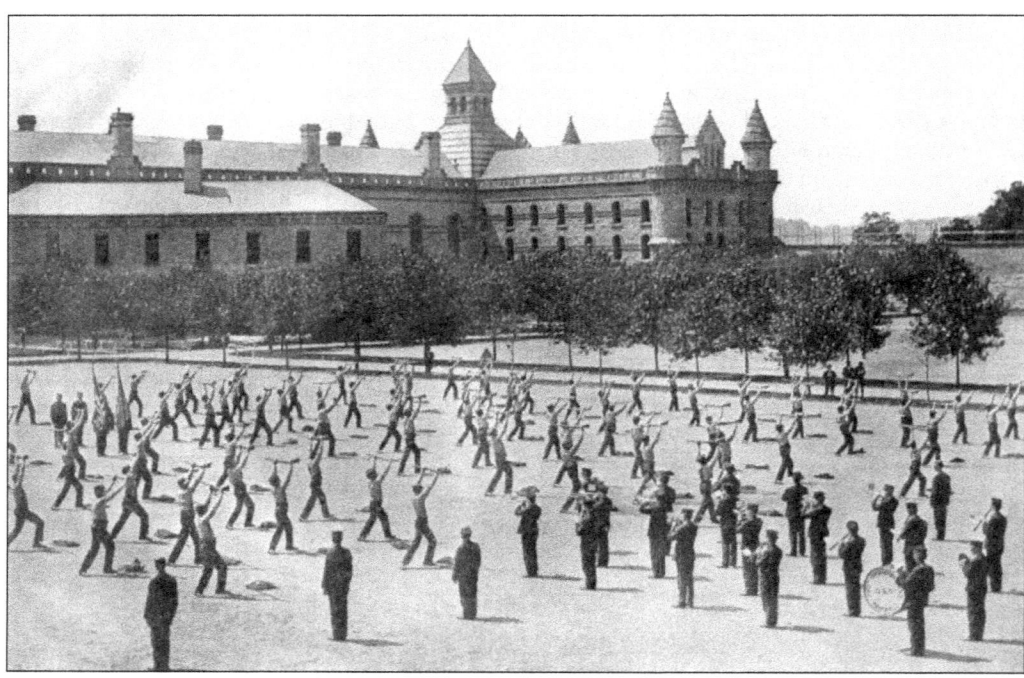

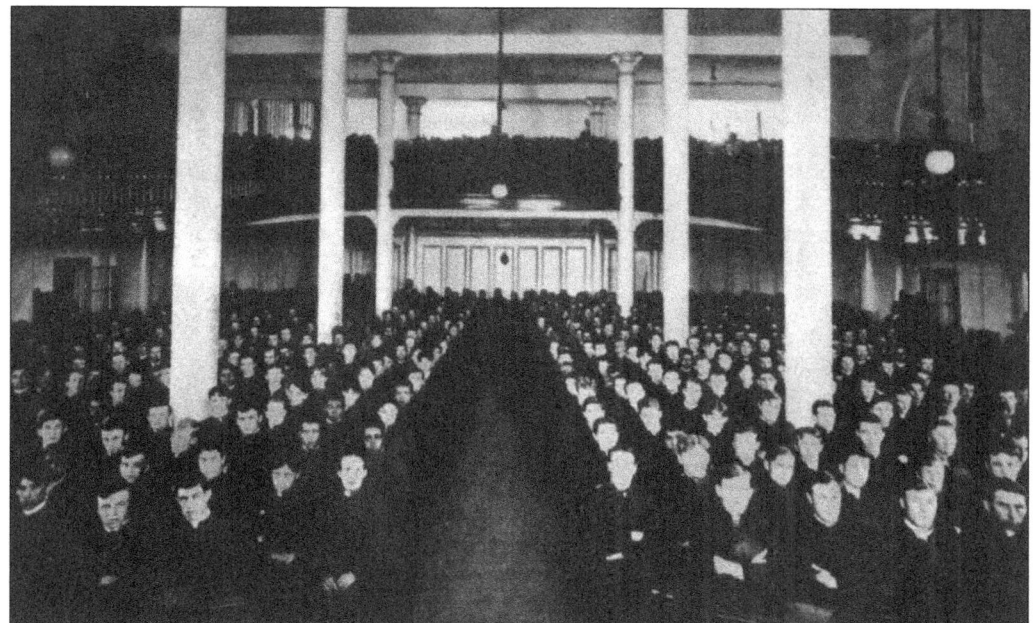

The chapel was integral to the prison's mission of reformation. A new chapel, built and dedicated in 1928, also served as an auditorium, with classrooms located beneath it. In a 1934 report to the state, the chapel was called the "Heart of the Prison." Each Sunday, two Protestant services were performed by the prison chaplain, who also arranged for services each week to accommodate prisoners of other faiths. All inmates were required to attend one of these services. Throughout the year, other services were considered optional, and attendance was voluntary. By the mid-1900s, attendance at services was voluntary. Going to church gave inmates the opportunity to be out of their cells. Chaplains and administrators were encouraged when many inmates chose to attend. (Below, courtesy of Jeff Sprang/*Mansfield News Journal*.)

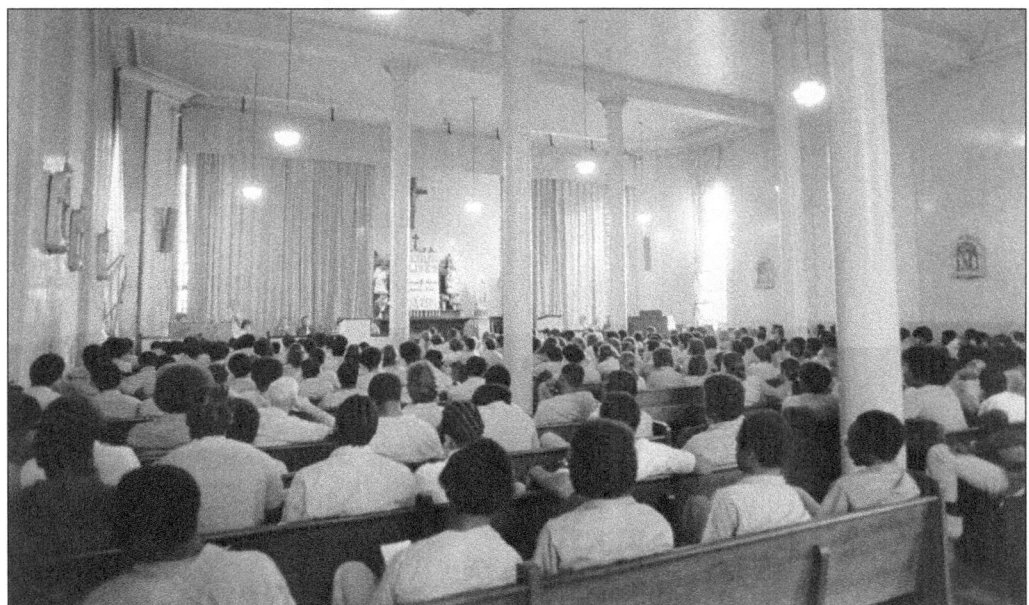

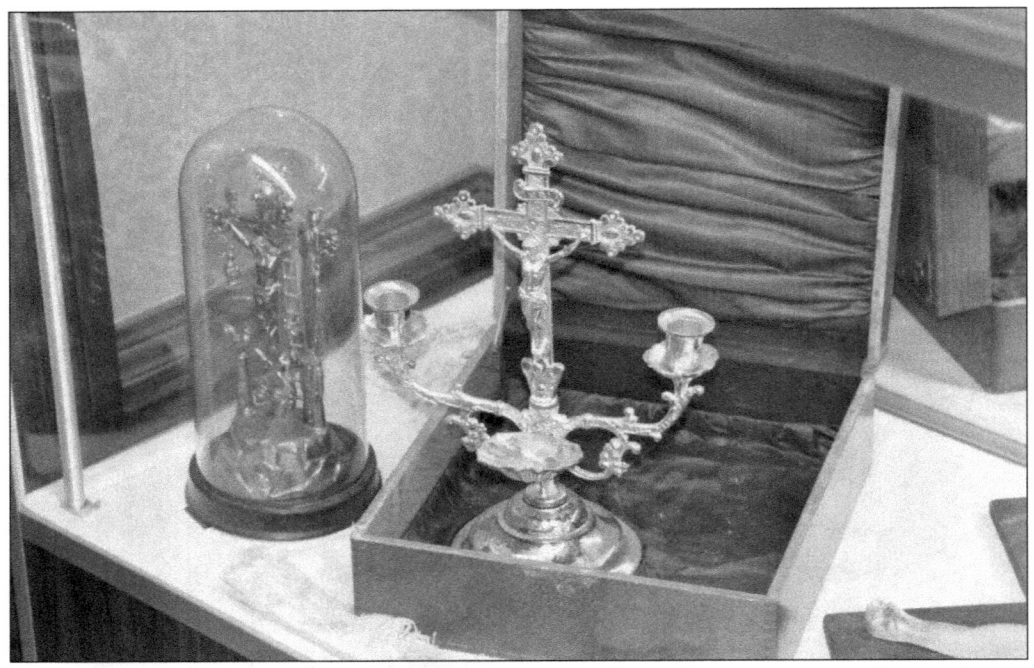

Shown here are two crucifixes and a kit used to administer last rites. The kit would also include two silver dishes for the Eucharist and a holy water bottle. The box was used to take holy water or oil to those who could not attend Mass. It also would have been taken to the hospital in order to provide Communion or last rights to inmates.

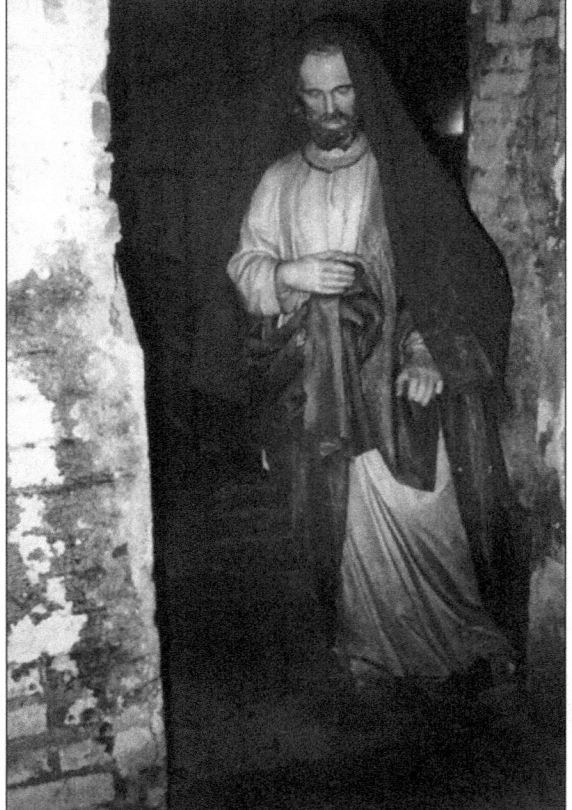

When the Catholic chapel was moved, this seven-foot-tall Jesus was placed in a basement alcove for storage. It was reported that newly employed guards would be assigned to the night shift so they could learn the procedures and building layout while the inmates slept. On occasion, a veteran would send a new guard to the basement to "retrieve" paperwork. With only a flashlight, the new guard would go to the basement and see this figure "hiding." The veteran guards would stand at the top of the stairs, waiting to hear a yell.

When inmates wanted to speak with administrators, request medical attention, or speak to a chaplain, they had to make an appointment. They did this through a "kite," a paper that was filled out and dropped in a box designated for that purpose. The kites would be collected and taken to the appropriate office. An appointment would then be made to meet with the inmate. Kites also referred to messages sent between inmates. For this purpose, a note would be tied to a piece of string. The inmate would swing the string underneath his cell door to the cell of another inmate. Shown here are an original kite form (above) and the box used to send it (below). Supt. Bennett Cooper personally read each kite sent to him and either responded or passed it on to the appropriate department. (Both courtesy of Scott Sukel.)

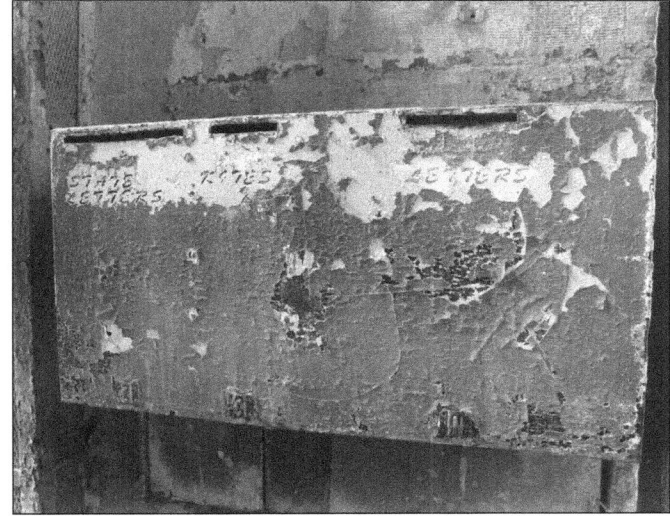

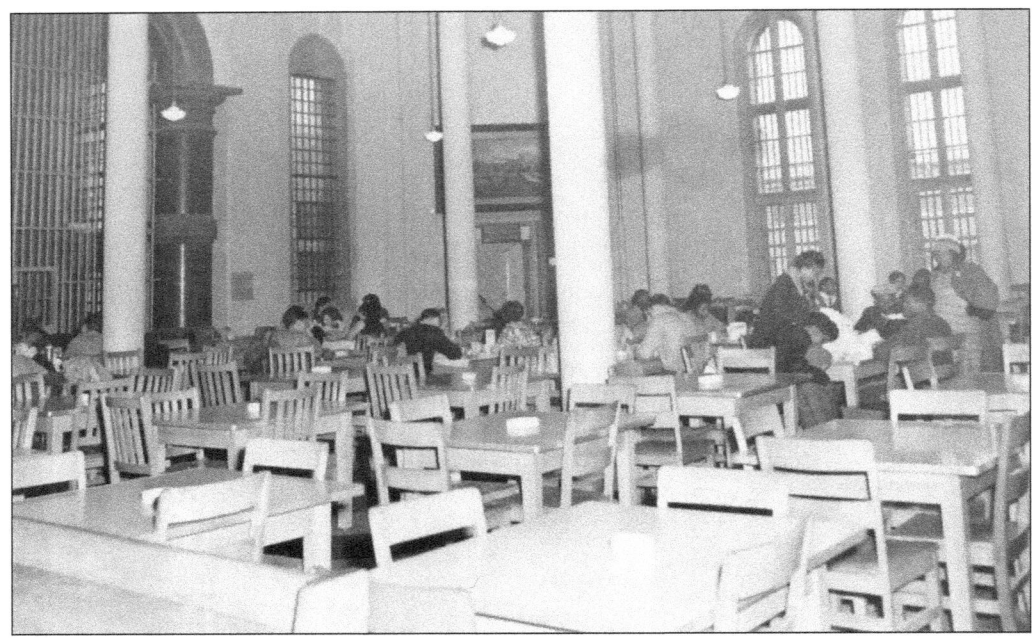

Visits from home were a welcome distraction from the strict routine of reformatory life. Some families were very devoted to the visits, which were allowed each month. The length of the visit depended on the number of families waiting. Visits were allowed if a family had to travel a distance to get to the prison. Families were permitted to bring in a picnic basket to share during the visit, but they were searched before being taken into the central guard room, where visitation took place. Family members themselves were not searched, but inmates were. No food was allowed to be taken back to the block after a visit, and inmates were searched to confirm that they were not smuggling food or other items.

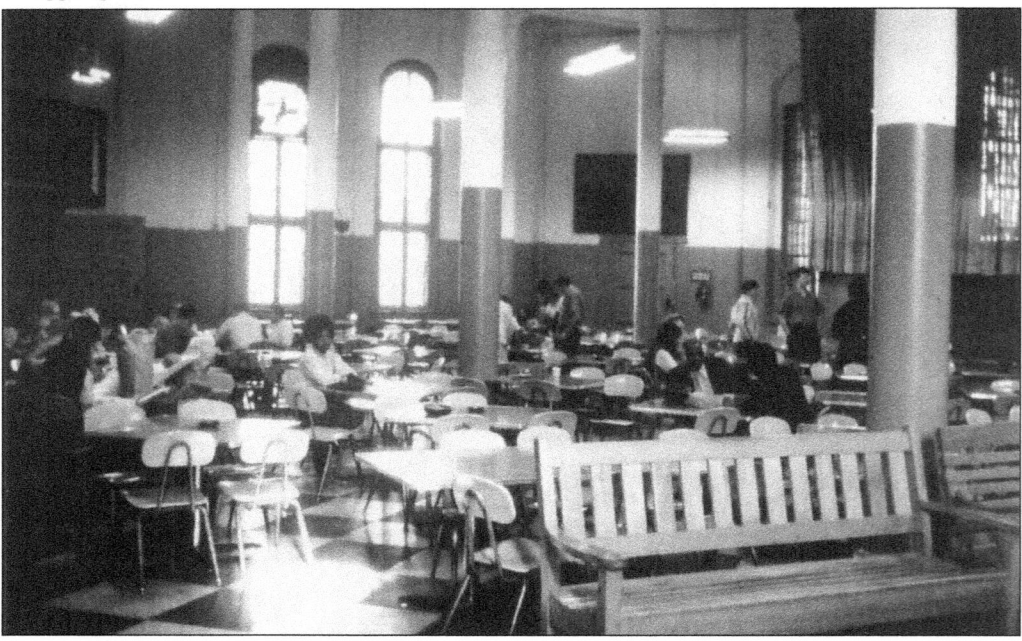

The commissary was vital to the inmate population. It provided many of the creature comforts that inmates were permitted to keep in their cells. One of the most prestigious positions for a prisoner was as a commissary worker, selected by the officer/manager. Inmates were taken to the commissary by guards once a week. They were marched there by block and tier and were then returned to their cells. Later, the commissary was open 12 hours a day so inmates who worked second shift, particularly at the power plant, the dining hall, and the hospital, were able to make purchases. Although a trip to the commissary was welcomed, it was not without risk. Inmates were vulnerable to being attacked and robbed when they carried their supplies back to their cells. (At right, courtesy of Jeff Sprang/*Mansfield News Journal*; below, Scott Sukel.)

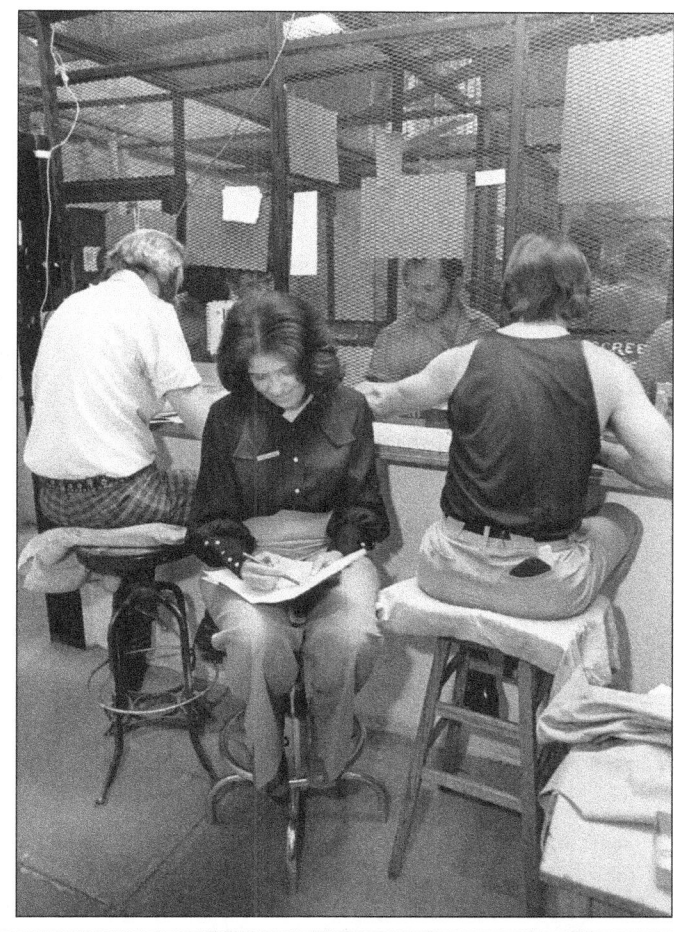

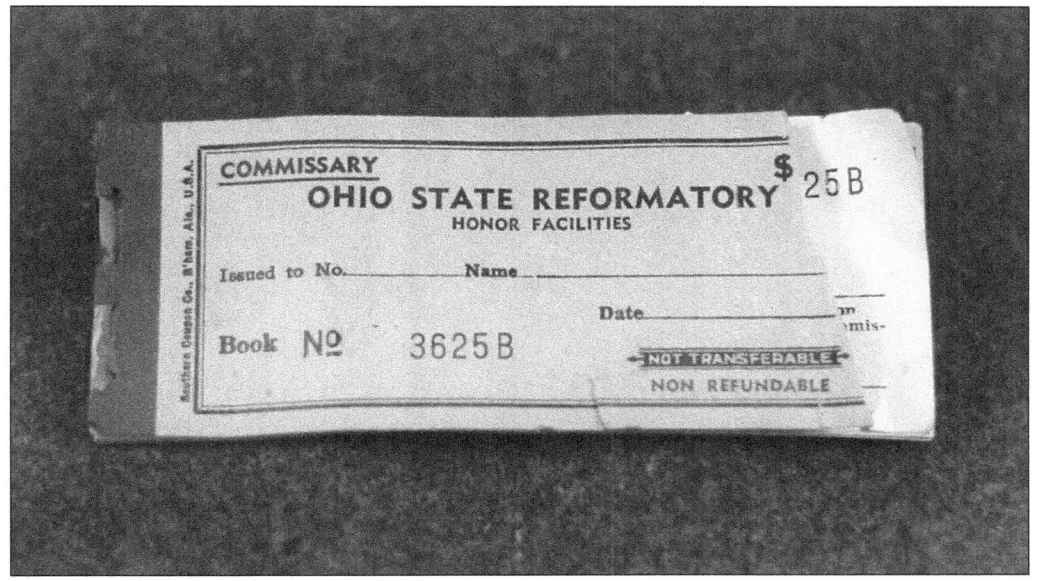

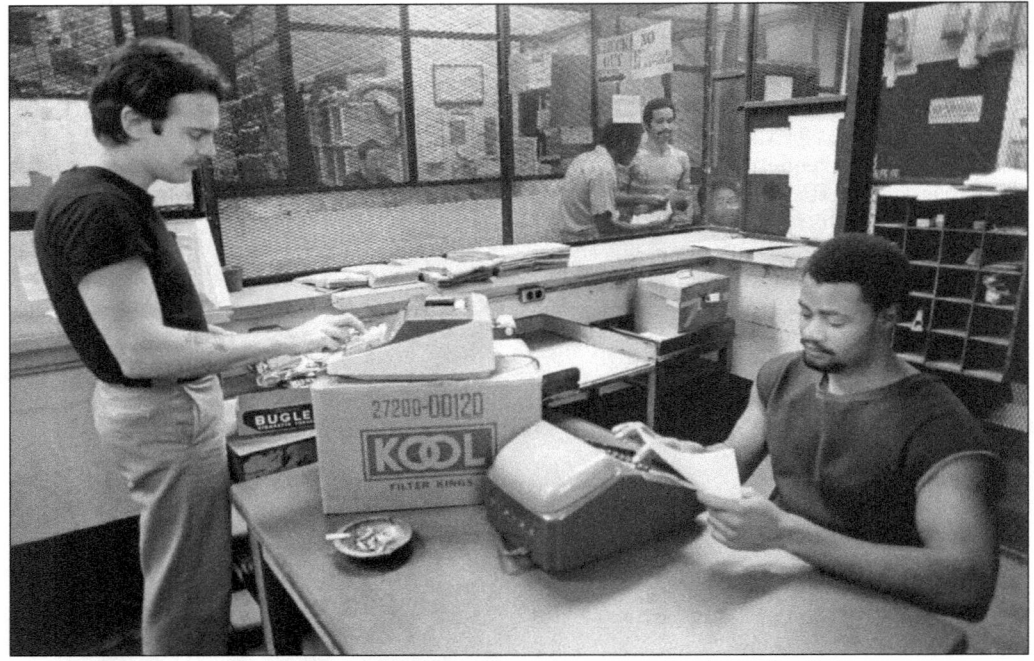

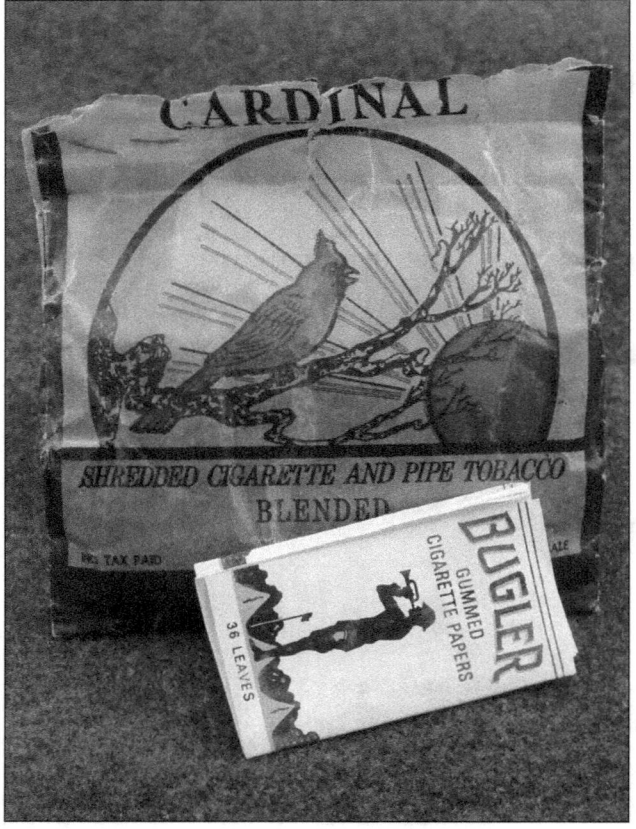

In the early 1970s, inmates typically made around 10¢ an hour and worked 40 hours a week. Typically, between $10 and $12 would be deposited into their accounts at the beginning of each month. This became the busy time for the commissary and its staff. A variety of items were available to inmates, including tobacco and rolling paper. One brand of tobacco was furnished for free, but it was of such low quality that other brands were also made available. A pack of cigarettes sold for 25¢, or a "quarter," which became a bartering term used by inmates. Flavored drink mixes, magazines, and nonperishable food items were also available for purchase. The prison provided toothpaste and soap, distributed by the commissary. (Above, courtesy of Jeff Sprang/*Mansfield News Journal*; at left, Scott Sukel.)

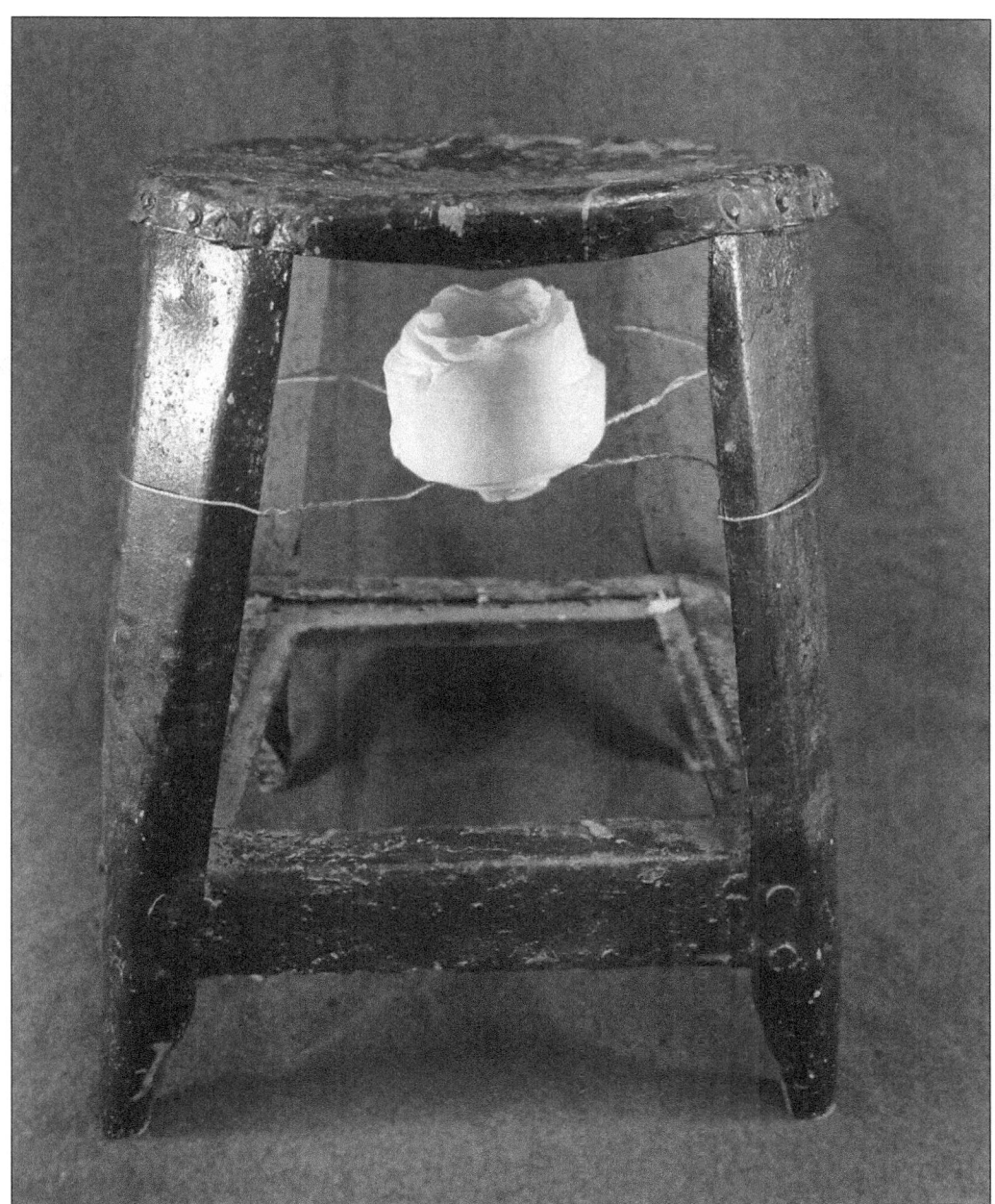

The life of the inmates was regimented and controlled 24 hours a day. Each man was assigned a cot and metal trunk. Each cell contained a shared sink, toilet, writing desk, and stool. The inmates did have ways of making their time more comfortable though. They could acquire all that was needed to make a toasted cheese sandwich. Using items easily accessible from within the prison, they were able to create a hotplate. They would wrap wire (undoubtedly from one of the shops) around the legs of the stool. Then, they would loosely wrap toilet paper and place it on the wire under the stool. When the toilet paper was lit, it generated enough heat to warm food. By this means, both sides of a sandwich could be toasted before the flame went out. (Courtesy of Scott Sukel.)

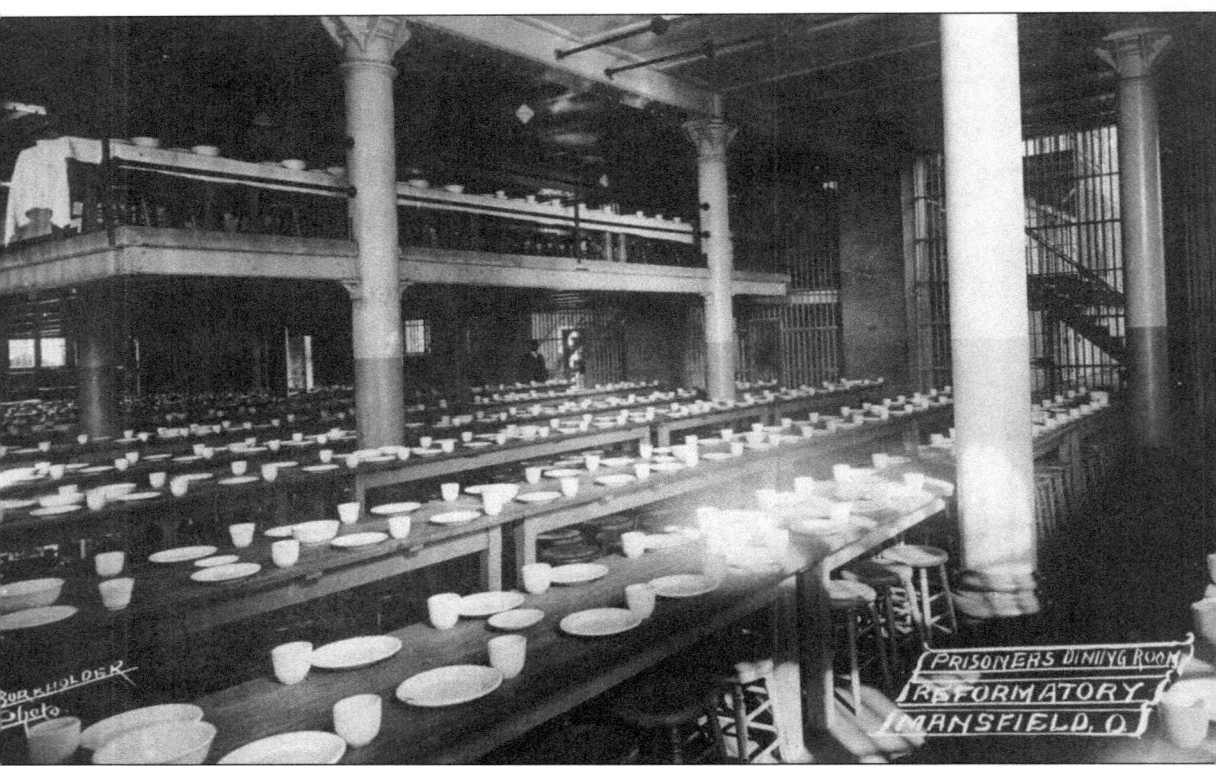

The original dining hall was on the main floor between the two cell blocks. The hall was divided into three sections. The first, for the most incorrigible inmates, provided minimal nutrition. They had to sit only on one side of the table and were not permitted to talk. The second section was for more well-behaved inmates. It offered the same diet, but the men were permitted to talk. The third section, for trustees, offered higher-quality food, and inmates were permitted to talk and take longer at mealtime. Through good behavior, inmates could move to a less-restrictive position within the prison and be allowed to dine on better fare. When a new hall was constructed, this space became what was called the bullpen: a pass-through from the cell blocks to all the outbuildings.

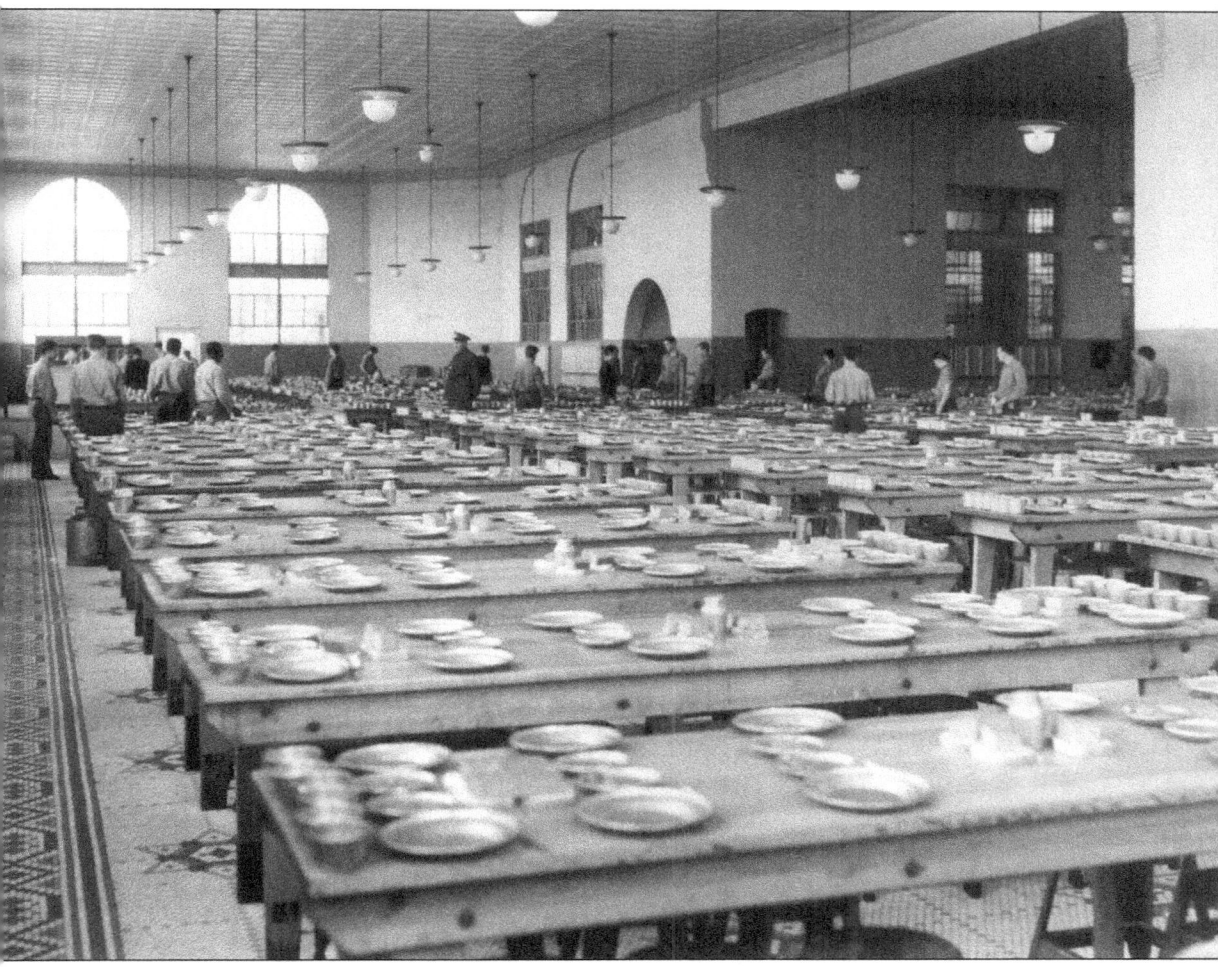

Another dining hall was constructed in 1938, but the meals served there were not considered a social time for the inmates. By this era, the men were going through a line and having food placed on their trays before sitting down. About five minutes later, a guard would pass by and rap on the end of the table, which meant it was time for the inmates to take their trays back to the kitchen and return to their cells. The prisoners learned to quickly eat any food that required utensils. Bread, a staple of each meal, could be taken and eaten on their way back to the cells. Later, inmates could purchase limited snack foods in the commissary. Mealtime was so regulated that 2,100 inmates could be seated, served, and led out in 50 minutes.

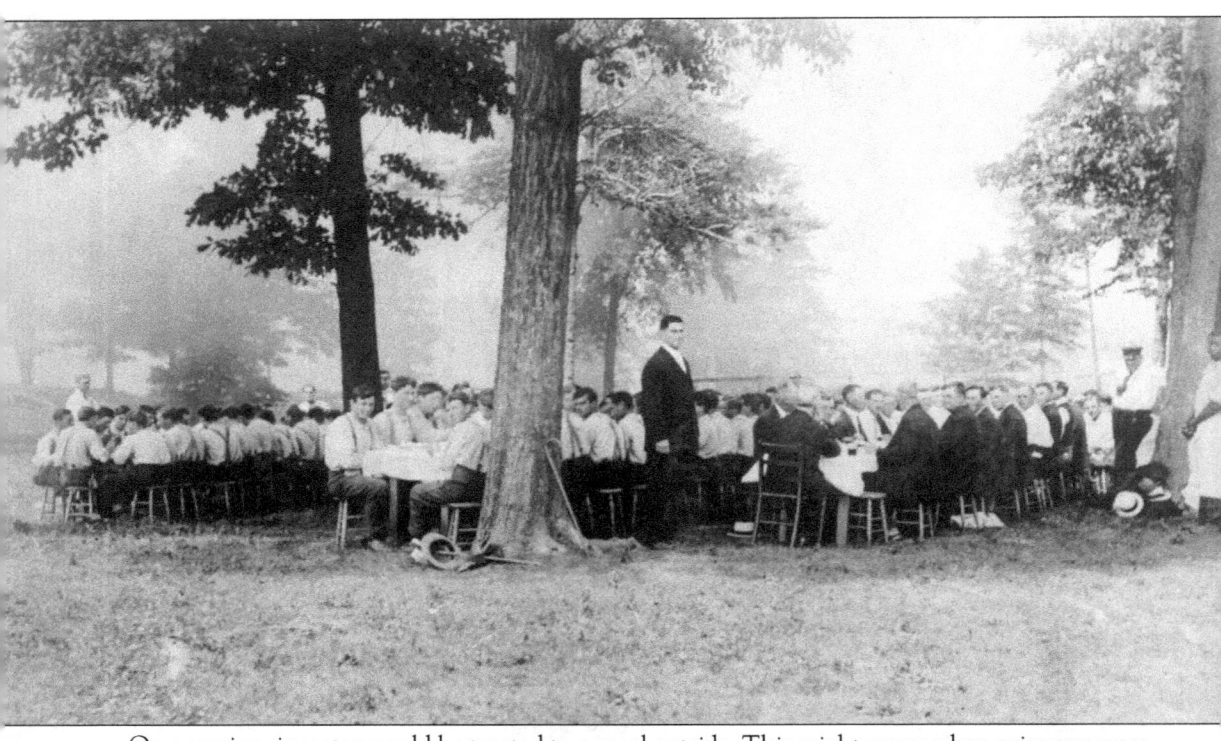

On occasion, inmates would be treated to a meal outside. This might occur when prisoners were on the road, traveling from one honors farm to another. On July 6, 1897, inmates were treated to a picnic to reward their good behavior. It was reported that only one instance of misconduct had taken place in the previous eight days, which was outstanding. Supt. W.E. Sefton organized a picnic for the inmates outside the walls of the prison as a celebration of Independence Day. After a speech by Chaplain W.H. Locke and the reading of the Declaration of Independence, the inmates were allowed to spend the afternoon participating in games and visiting with friends who had been invited. The July 7 edition of the *Xenia Daily Gazette* reported on the event, announcing it to be a "remarkable spectacle."

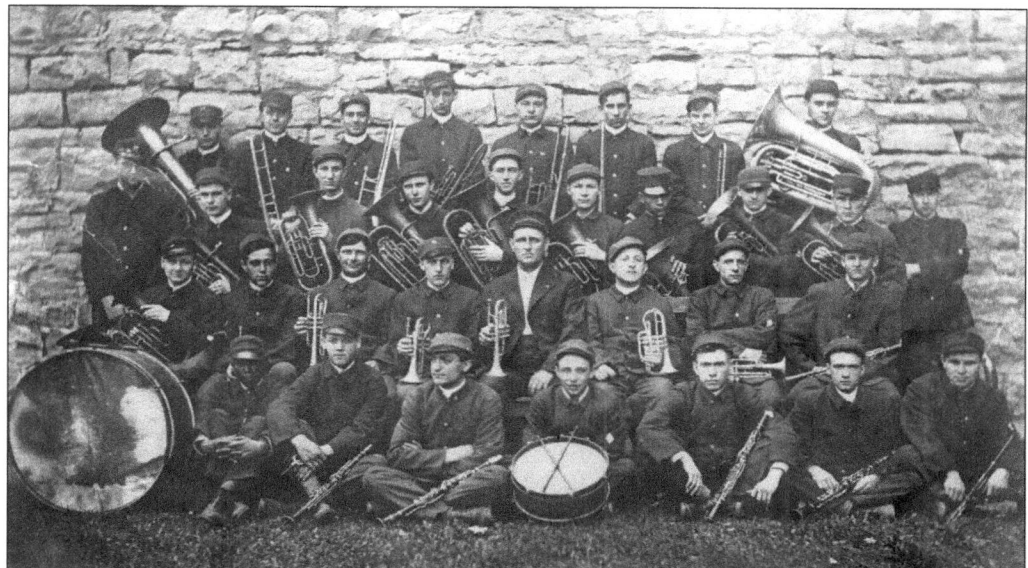

The Ohio State Reformatory band enjoyed a long history. Starting in the early 1900s, it played inside the walls at various ceremonies. Later, the reformatory band performed at local, regional, and state venues. An interesting event took place in Mansfield on October 24, 1921. The *Mansfield News* reported that a local church planned a concert called "Prison Sunday." The OSR band marched through town before arriving at the church for a well-received concert. On the same page of the newspaper was another item. Headlined "Musician Escapes," it reported that an inmate, Jean Mason, escaped following the concert. The escape was discovered when a head count of band members was made upon their return to the reformatory. Mason's horn was found sitting outside the guard's quarters. Other band members reported that they had seen nothing.

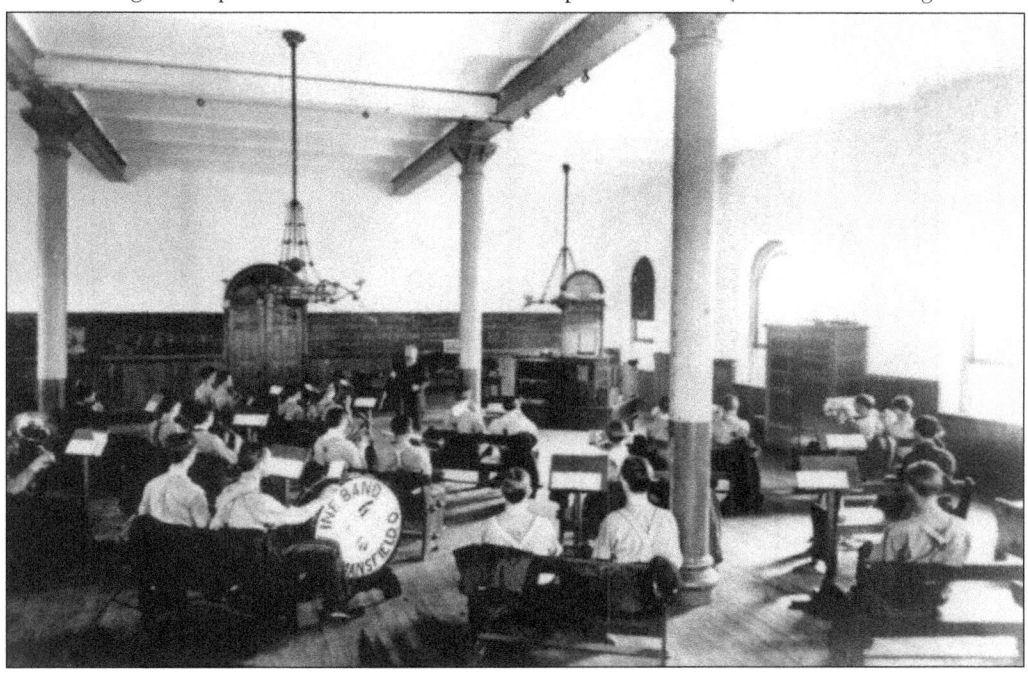

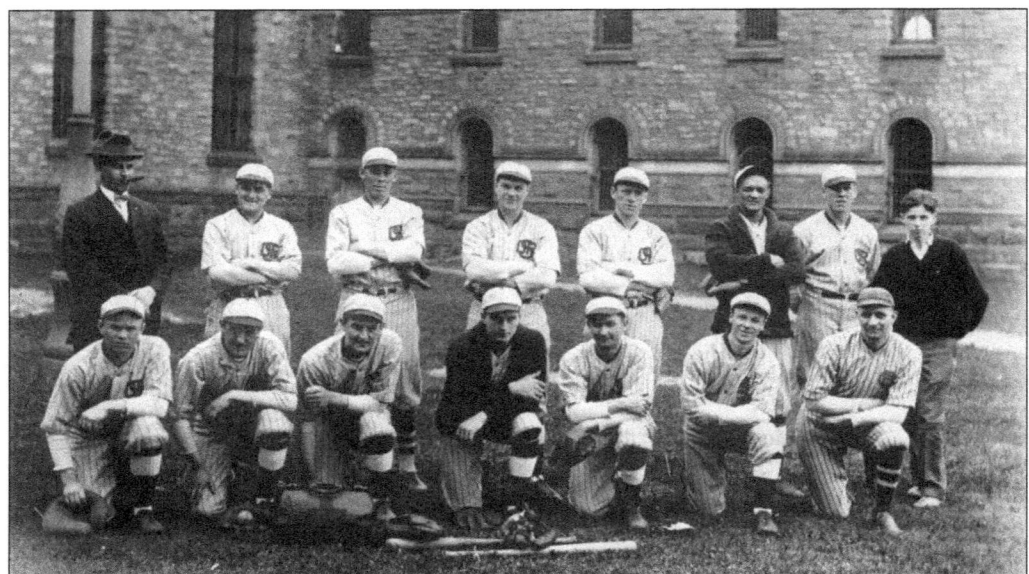

The Ohio State Reformatory fielded a number of sports teams over the years. Inmates became creative during their rec time, using balls of fabric and sticks from the wood shop to play baseball. The administration saw this as a positive way for inmates to spend their spare time. The first baseball team was outfitted through the efforts of the wife of warden Thomas Jenkins. Parents were allowed to send balls and mitts that had been used by the inmates prior to coming to the OSR, but new items were not permitted. Shoes were donated, and cleats were added to them in the shoe shop. Later, the baseball and basketball squads competed against local community teams. As early as 1933, the reformatory fielded a boxing team and would host matches, with the public in attendance. Shown below is the 1956 team.

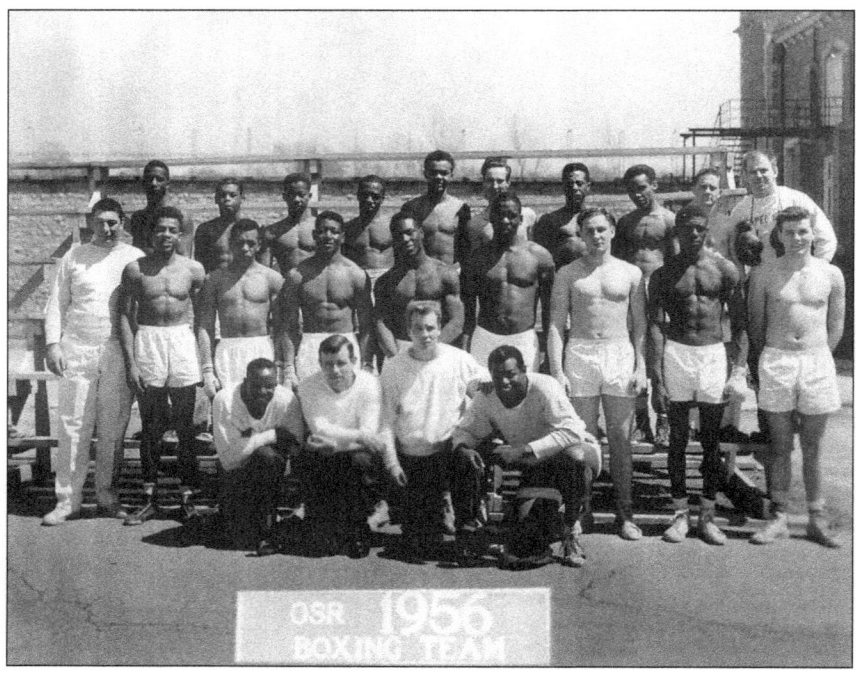

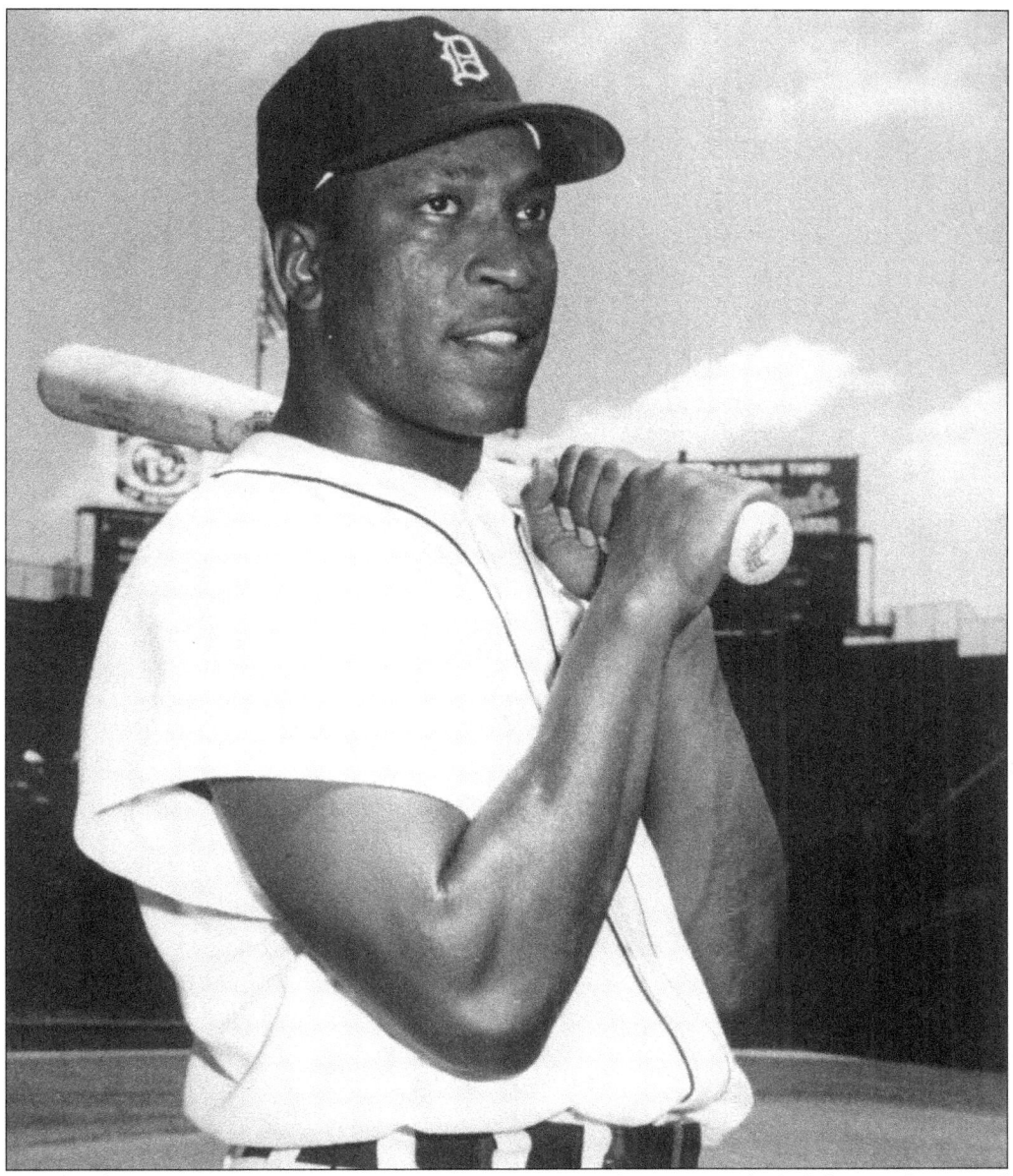

One of the many success stories of the reformatory theory of training and rehabilitation happened in the late 1950s. As a young man, Gates Brown was sentenced to the OSR for burglary. The guard/coach of the team saw real potential for this young man and contacted several professional teams. The Detroit Tigers, Chicago White Sox, and Cleveland Indians came to the OSR to scout Brown. The Tigers were so impressed that they petitioned the parole board for his release and signed him to a contract. Over a 13-year career (1963–1975) with the Tigers, Brown was part of Detroit's 1968 World Series championship team. He still holds the American League record for career pinch hits (107) and pinch-hit at-bats (414).

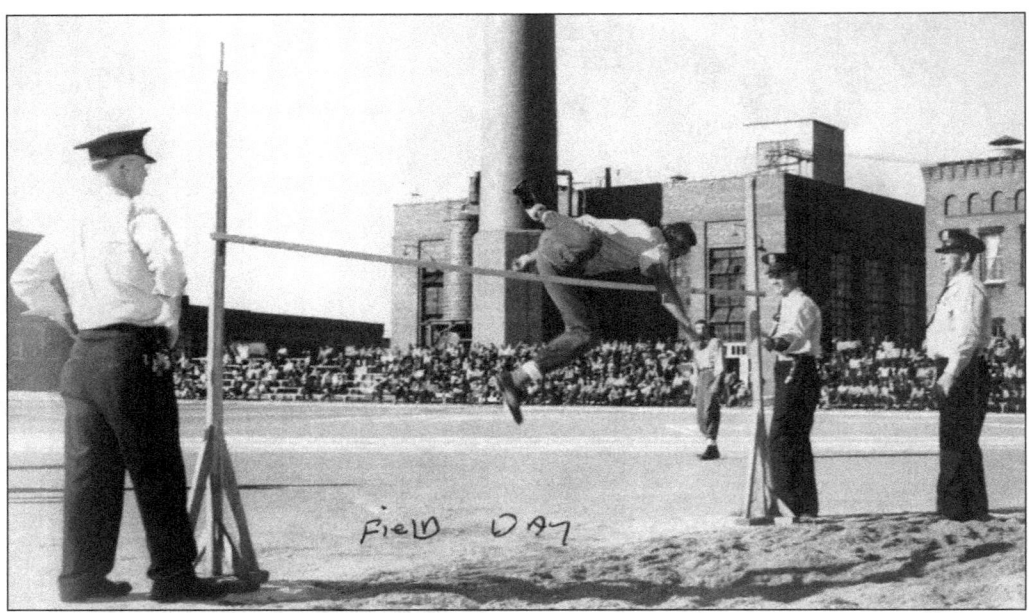

Keeping inmates occupied in positive activities was an important part of prison life. The chaplain, along with other administrators, worked to provide opportunities for inmates to participate. The men were treated to movies and talent shows. Movies had to be approved by the chaplain for content, and those taking part in talent shows were required to have their talent approved by the administration. Each summer, an annual field day was held, featuring track-and-field events, as well as fun competitions like the three-legged race. The day started with the raising of the flag and the national anthem being played by the OSR band. Competitions were judged by officers from a local National Guard unit. These activities impacted prisoner morale and helped guards keep the prison atmosphere less tense.

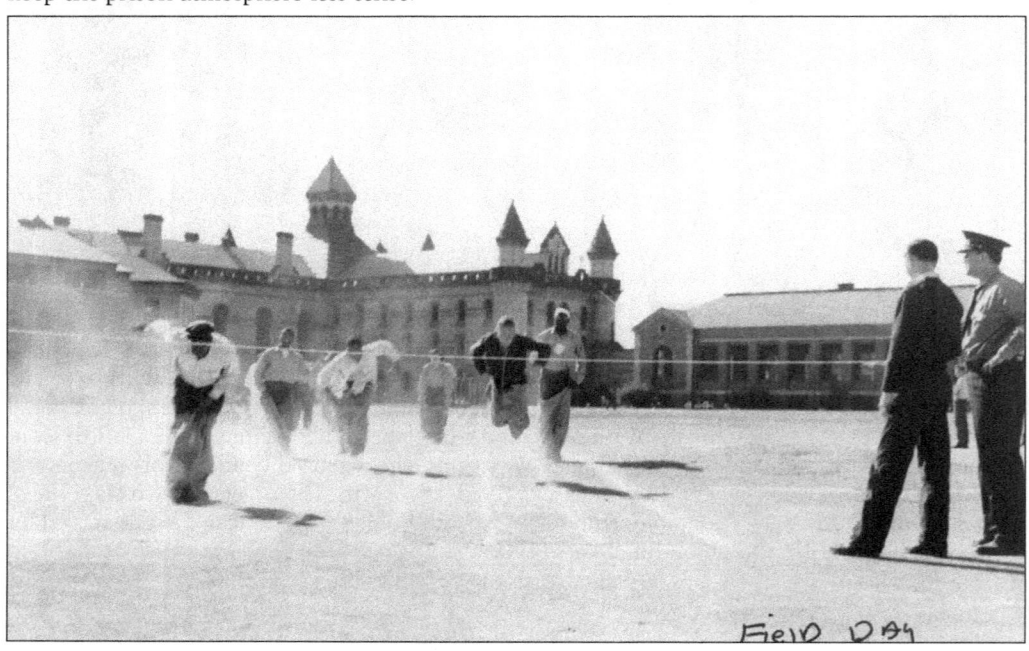

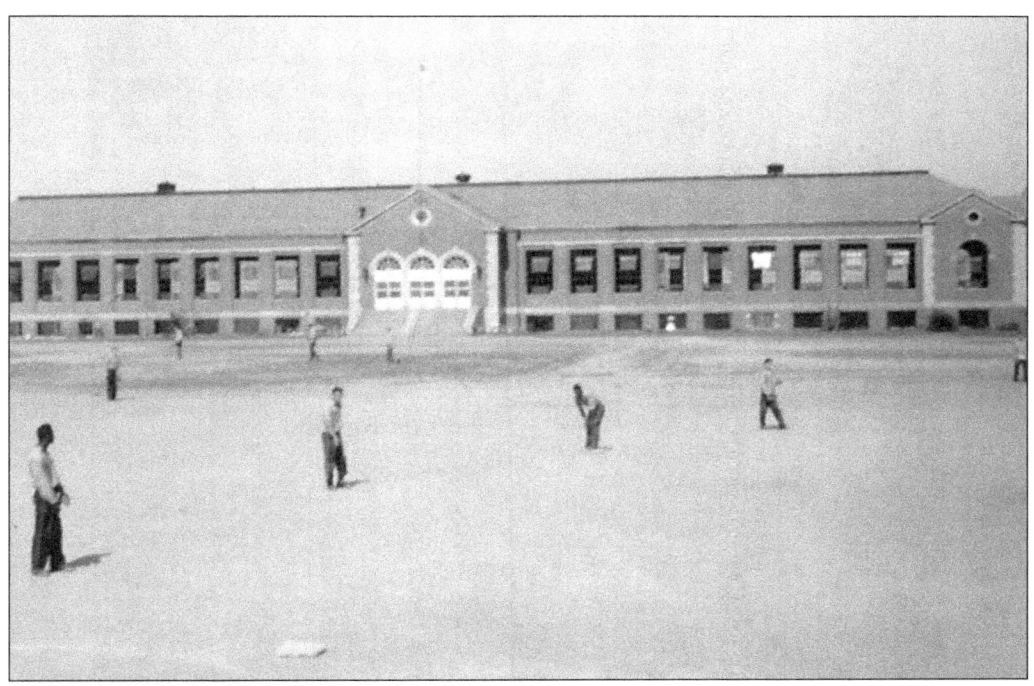

Recreation (rec) time was a way for inmates to socialize for a given period with little supervision. Inmates in the west cell block were allowed more time, as they were a lower security risk. Those housed in the east cell block were deemed more violent, not by the crime they committed but by their behavior within the walls. Prisoners could play baseball (above) and basketball (below) and could lift weights in the yard. By the 1980s, prisoners could go to the yard daily if they wanted. For those in disciplinary control or solitary confinement, cages were built above the west diagonal. These inmates were taken there in small groups for an hour each day; otherwise they were confined to their cells.

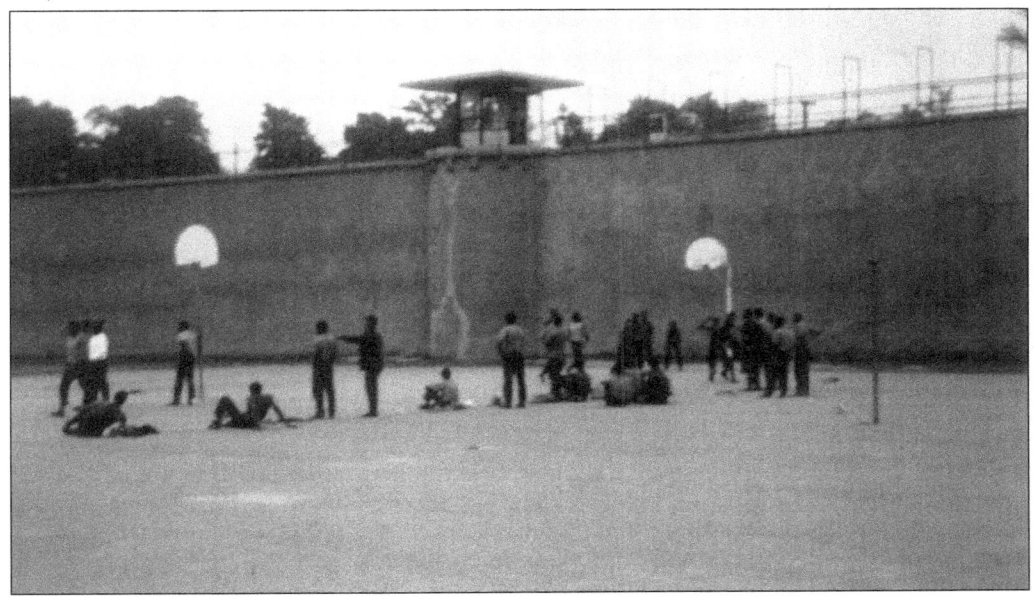

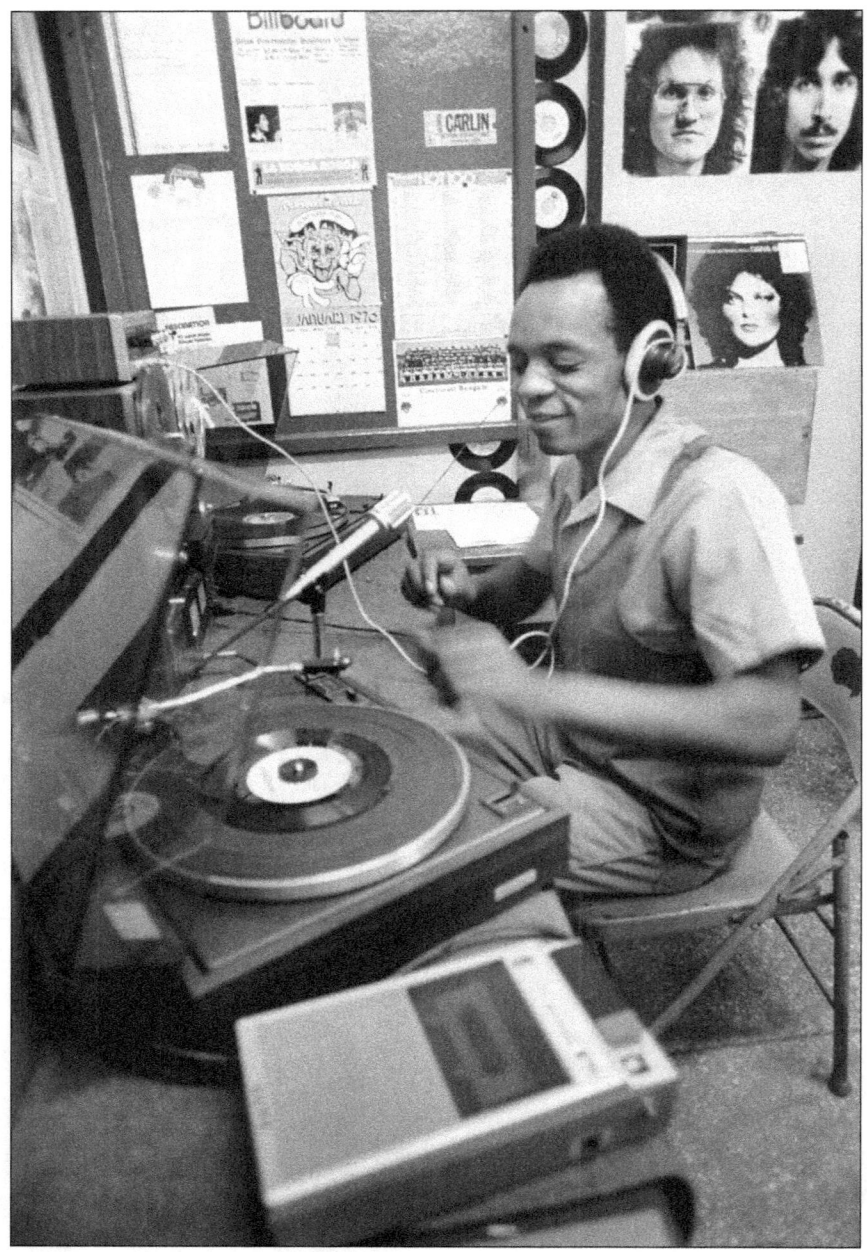

On November 1, 1940, Supt. Arthur Glattke flipped a switch that brought sound to the reformatory. It was the first system of its kind in the state. From a master control room, wires were laid to all parts of the building, including each of the cell blocks. Headsets were given to 2,200 inmates, allowing them to listen to the radio. Large speakers were placed in the recreation yard and in the chapel. Programs were prescreened by the chaplain to ensure that material was of moral or spiritual value. The prison station was later known as WOSR. Inmates replaced the prerecorded programs and played popular music and made announcements from the administration. Some inmates working as DJs aspired to careers in television and radio after their release. (Courtesy of Jeff Sprang/*Mansfield News Journal*.)

Along with sports, the reformatory allowed other forms of recreation for the inmates, including art. Inmates were not limited to oils and watercolors but created using a variety of media. The artwork shown below, created using tin and wire from workshops, hangs in the reformatory. With administration permission, inmates could have their families send canvases and paint. According to a former prisoner, inmates would "pay" artists for portraits by having money placed in the artists' commissary accounts. Many of the original paintings are at the reformatory today. Currently, the OSR hosts an inmate art exhibit each year for the adjacent prisons. Proceeds of sales from this event are placed in the prison art fund. The inmates are pleased when their artwork is purchased. (At right, courtesy of Jeff Sprang.)

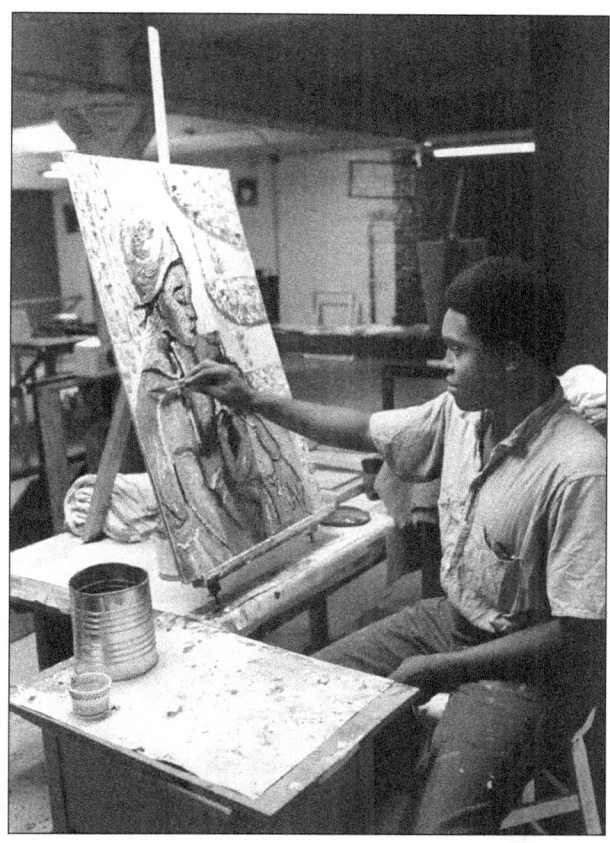

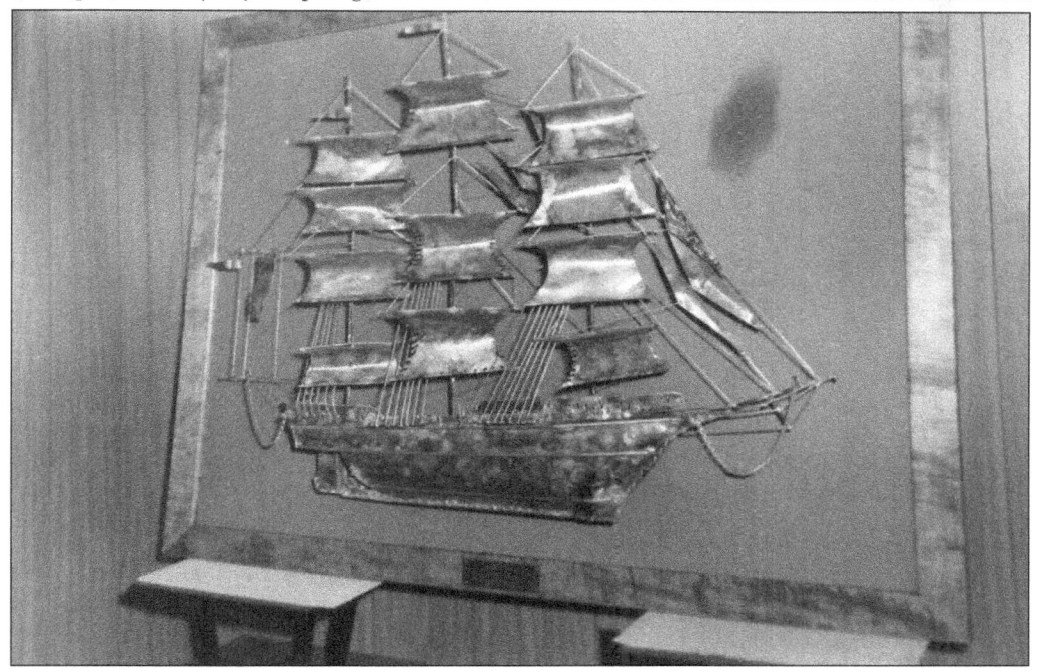

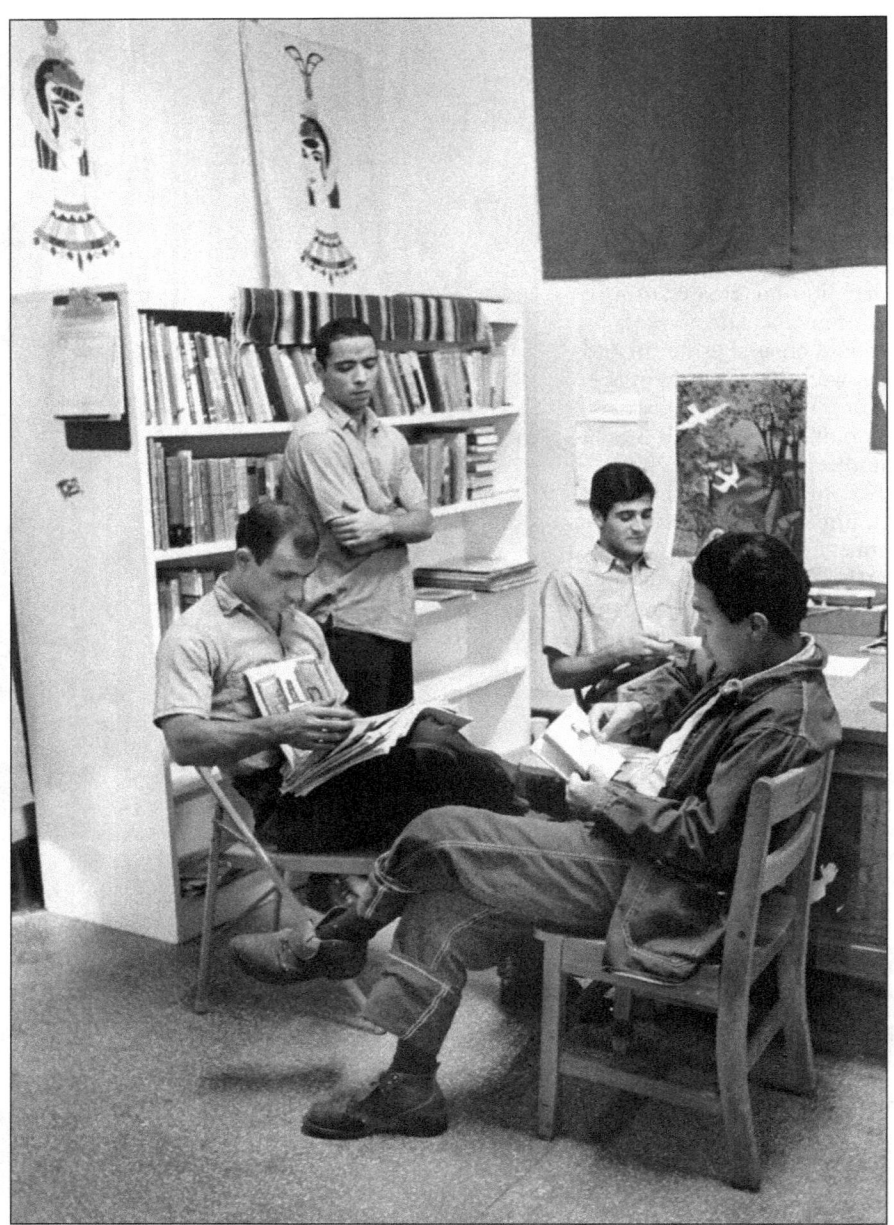

The Ohio State Reformatory continued to encourage inmates to improve their skills, even during the times they were in their cells. Contents of the prison library were available to inmates through delivery of reading material to their cells. Bob Besch reported in the March 22, 1959, edition of the *Mansfield News Journal* that over the years the library contained 14,000 books. Inmates could request up to two books and magazines for a one-week loan. Requests were processed by the librarian through his 16 inmate workers. Once a week, a tray would be loaded with the requested books and delivered to the cells. At the same time, books would be collected for return to the library. The librarian, a former guard, would accompany the inmate worker, called a runner, to ensure that no contraband changed hands as books were distributed or returned. (Courtesy of Jeff Sprang.)

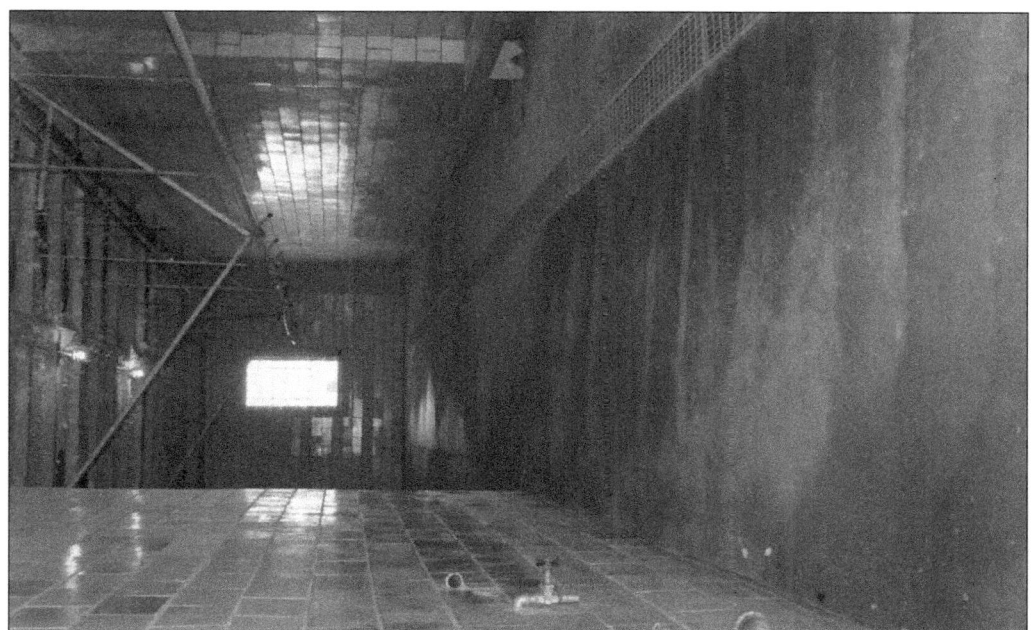

In 1903, during James Leonard's tenure as warden, showers were installed at the OSR. Up to 50 inmates at a time would walk into individual stalls, and the doors would be closed by a guard pulling a lever. Another lever would release the water for a short period of time. Later, the individual stalls were taken out, and men would shower in an open area with a line of shower heads (below). This became known as the "car wash." The frequency and length of showers were at the discretion of the guards. If inmates talked to one another, the shower could be shut down and all of the men would have to return to their cells. Inmates were always cautious of their shoes and clothing while they showered, as these items were subject to theft.

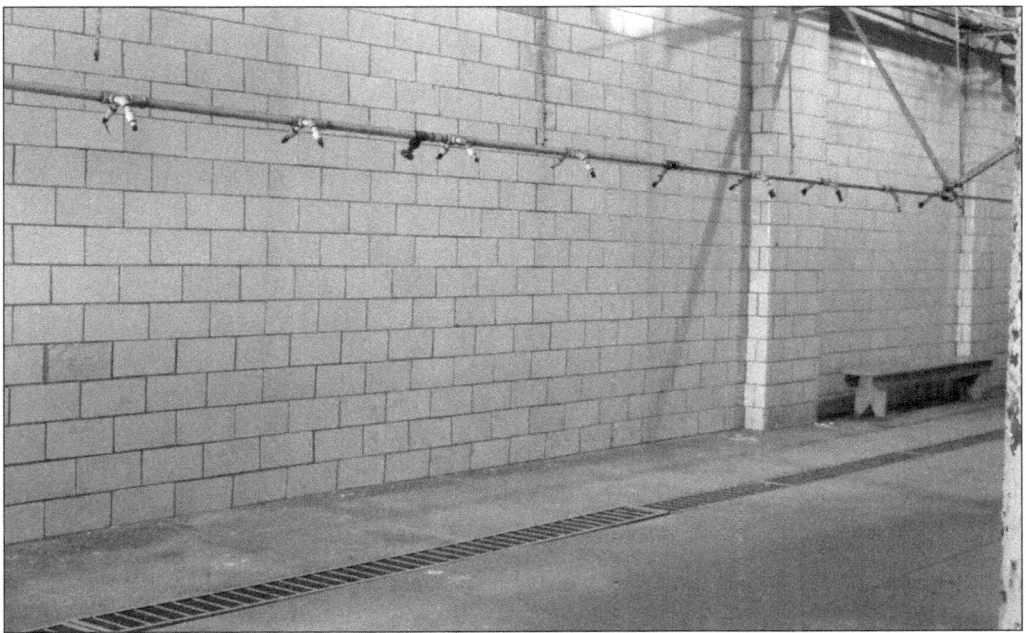

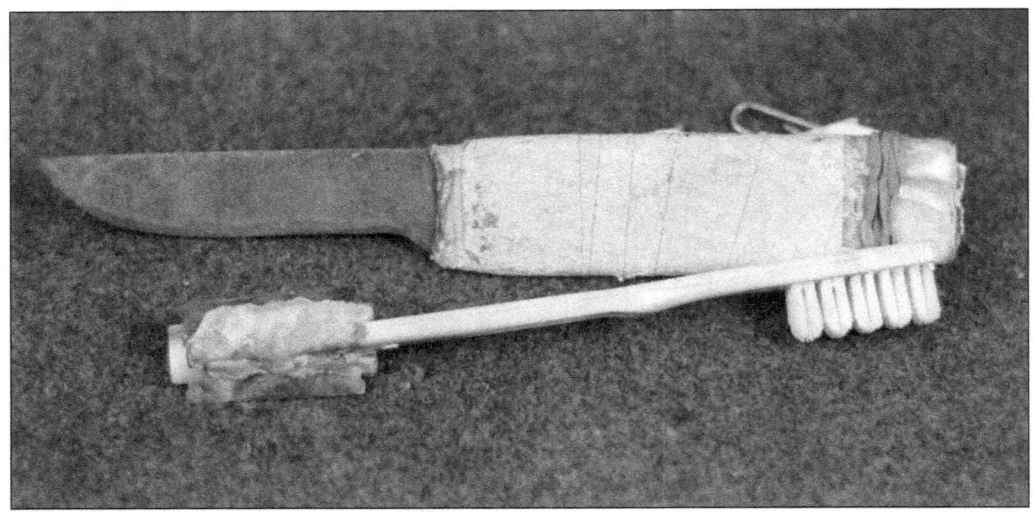

Shivs were a serious problem for guards and inmates alike. A shiv is a homemade weapon fashioned from items available to inmates on a daily basis. A prisoner, for example, could steal a small piece of metal from the workshop and take it back to his cell. Any item that could be sharpened to a point has the potential to cause great harm. Guards would routinely carry out shakedowns, or thorough cell searches, in order to find shivs and other prohibited items. Inmates found in possession of forbidden items would be subject to disciplinary action. In 2013, twenty-three years after it closed, a sixth-grade student taking a tour of the building walked into a cell and found a long-lost shiv. (Above, courtesy of Scott Sukel.)

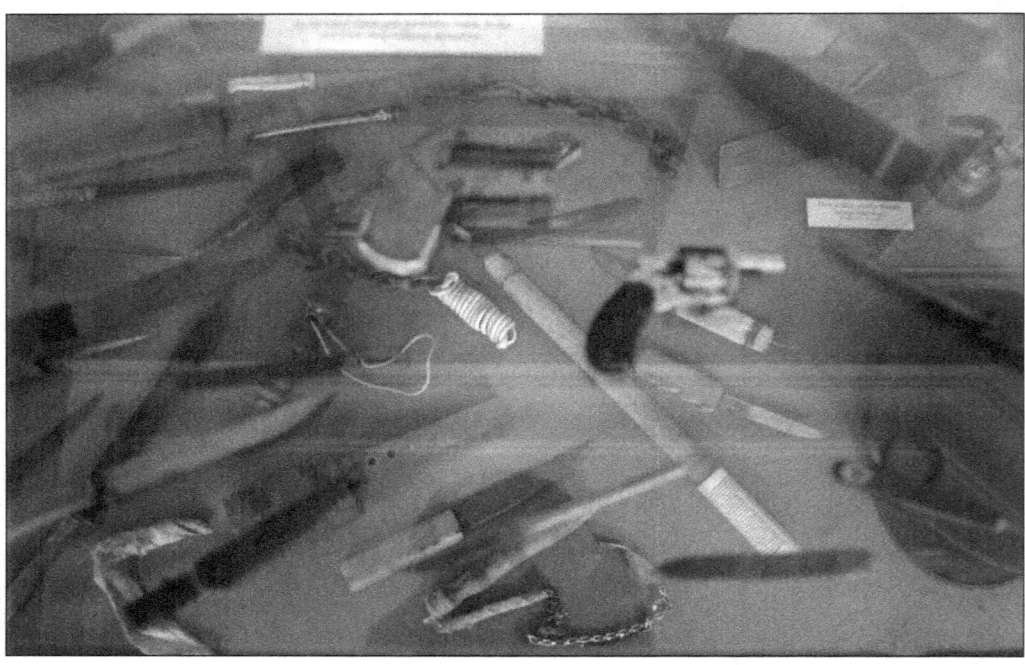

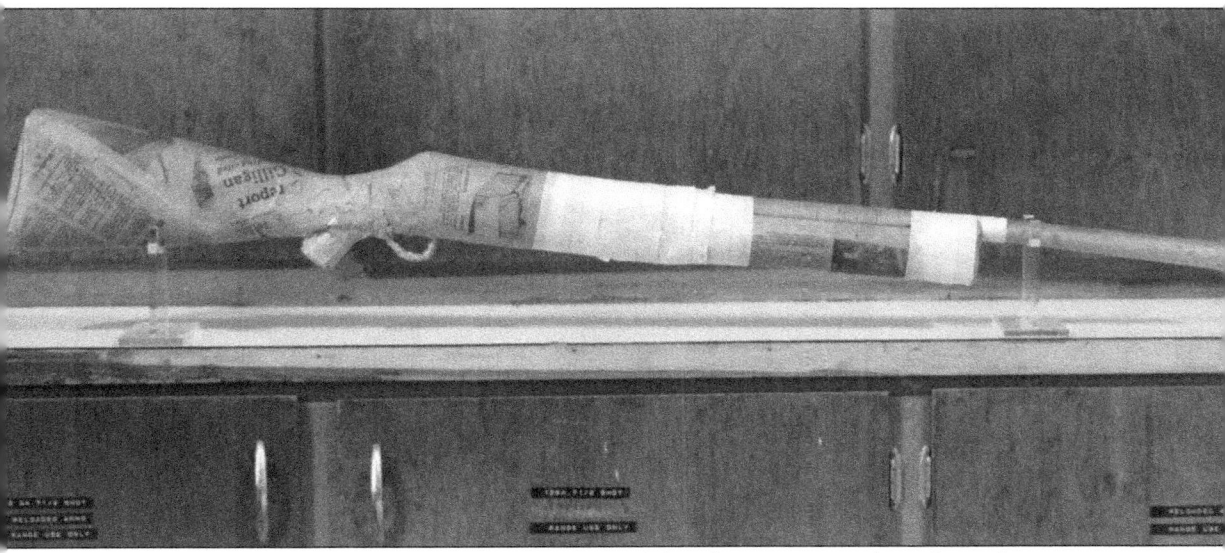

Weapons were always a potential threat. Inmates exhibited ingenuity as they planned escapes. On numerous occasions, inmates fashioned "guns" in order to attempt an escape. At the Ohio Penitentiary, two members of John Dillinger's gang unsuccessfully tried to escape using bars of soap carved to look like guns. Ohio State Reformatory was not immune to such attempts. A "gun" was fashioned from newspapers (pictured); in the dark, it looked all too real. Before it could be used, however, it was confiscated by guards and kept as a curiosity. Saved from being destroyed during the initial clean-out of the prison in 1990, the faux rifle was recently turned over to the OSR archive department. (Courtesy of Scott Sukel.)

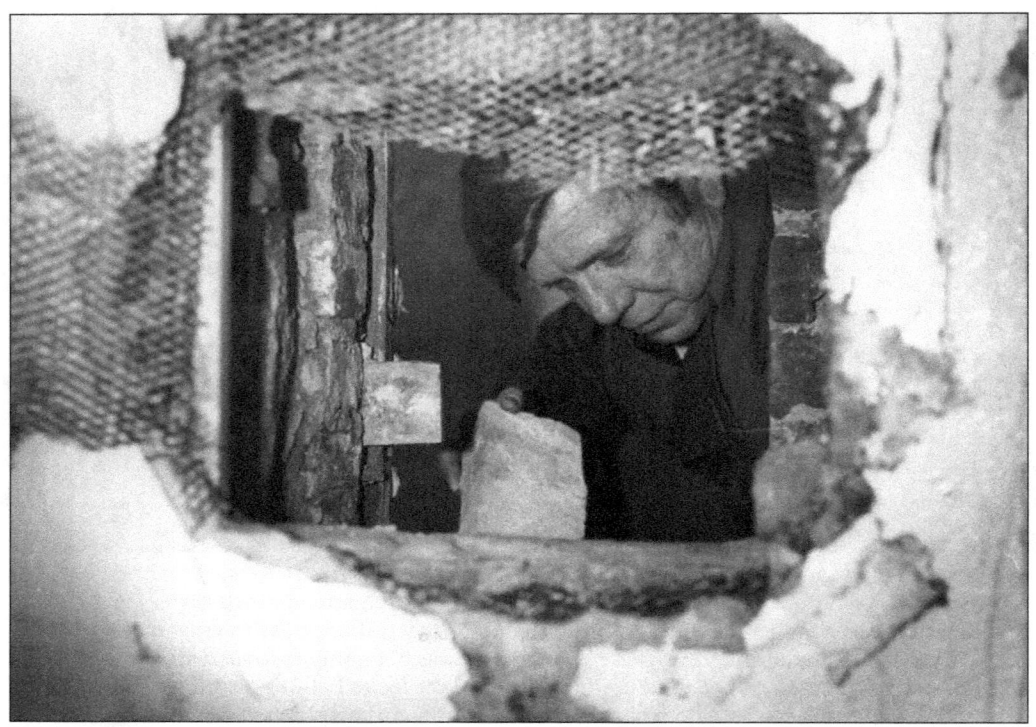

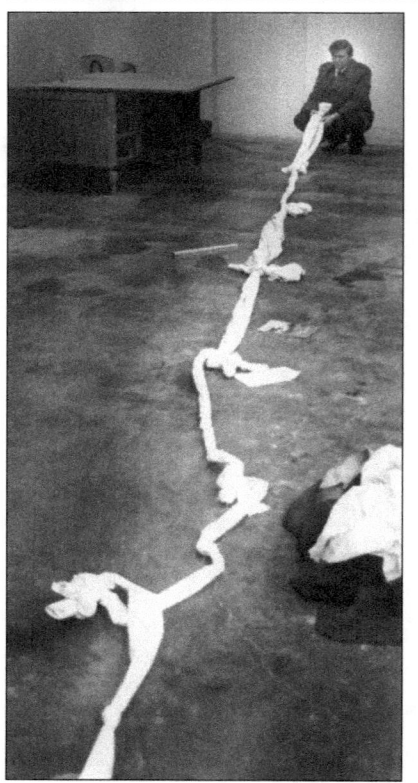

As with all prisons, escape is always a possibility—and sometimes becomes a reality. Most escapees from the OSR were captured within hours, days, or weeks. One escapee was able to remain free for 56 years before being apprehended in 2015. An inmate had himself nailed into a shoe crate that was scheduled to be shipped out to other state institutions. Things went perfectly for him until he kicked his way out of the crate and found that it ended up at the Ohio Penitentiary in Columbus. When he found himself surrounded by guards, he immediately offered to be returned to the reformatory. His offer was denied, and he spent the rest of his sentence (plus time added for the escape) at the Ohio Pen. Shown on this page are the remnants of an escape attempt in April 1990, just months before inmates were scheduled to be moved to a more secure prison. The photograph above shows the interior hole cleared by prisoners. Seen at left is a "rope" of tied bedsheets, intended to be used by inmates once they cleared the exterior wall.

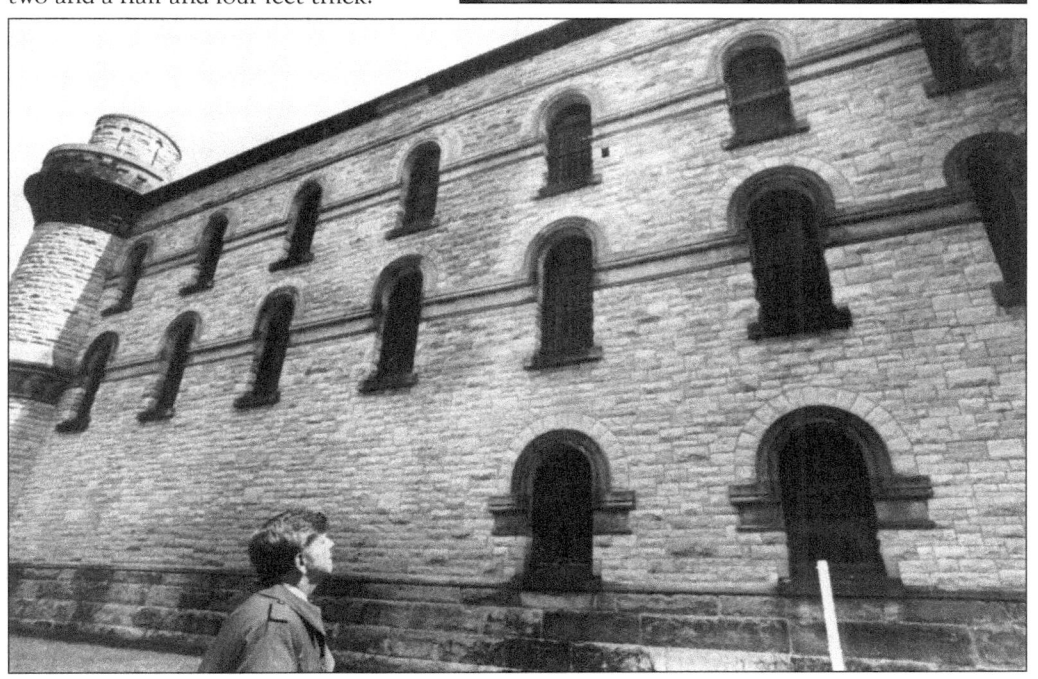

The photograph at right shows the hole inmates created for the April 1990 escape attempt. This would have been their view as they broke through the outer wall. The photograph below depicts the hole as it appeared from the outside. The final passageway was undoubtedly far too small for the inmates to squeeze through. The prisoners had managed to clear a wall that was between two and a half and four feet thick.

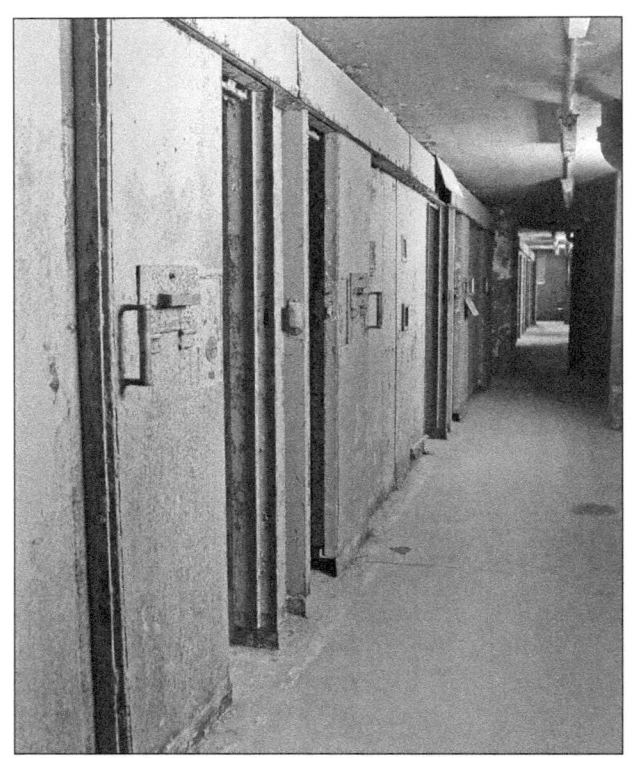

Inmates who broke the rules were subject to varying degrees of punishment. One of the most severe was "The Hole." This area of solitary confinement (below) is equipped with nothing but a toilet and a bunk. In some cases, prisoners had to sleep on the bare concrete floors. A small slot on the solid metal door (at left) was kept closed unless guards were serving meals or talking to or checking on the inmate. Lights to the cells were controlled by guards and could be kept on or off, depending on the sentence that sent the inmate to solitary. Because of their location within the building, the cells could be extremely hot or cold, depending on the time of year. (Both courtesy of Scott Sukel.)

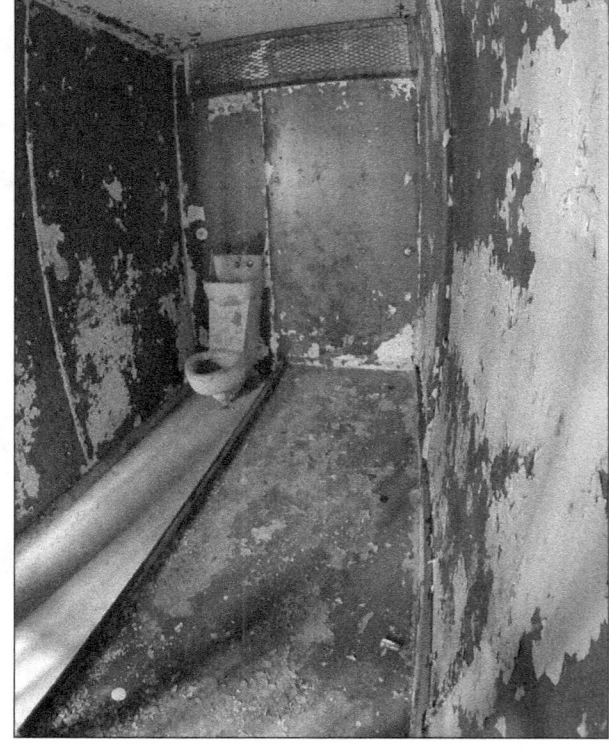

From 1896 until 1952, cells were individually locked and unlocked by guards in the morning and at night. This was time-consuming, and several guards were required. In 1952, remote locking devices were installed to control 594 cells in the east block. Unlike remote devices today, a lever called a slam bar (pictured) was placed at the end of each tier. A guard could then close the 50 cell doors from one location. Inmates were known to play a fairly dangerous game of chicken with this new system. They would remain outside the cell until the last possible minute, then jump into their cell. If they were seconds late, they ran the risk of getting arms or legs caught between the door and the jamb. The older cells of the west block were not adaptable to the new lock system. (Courtesy of Scott Sukel.)

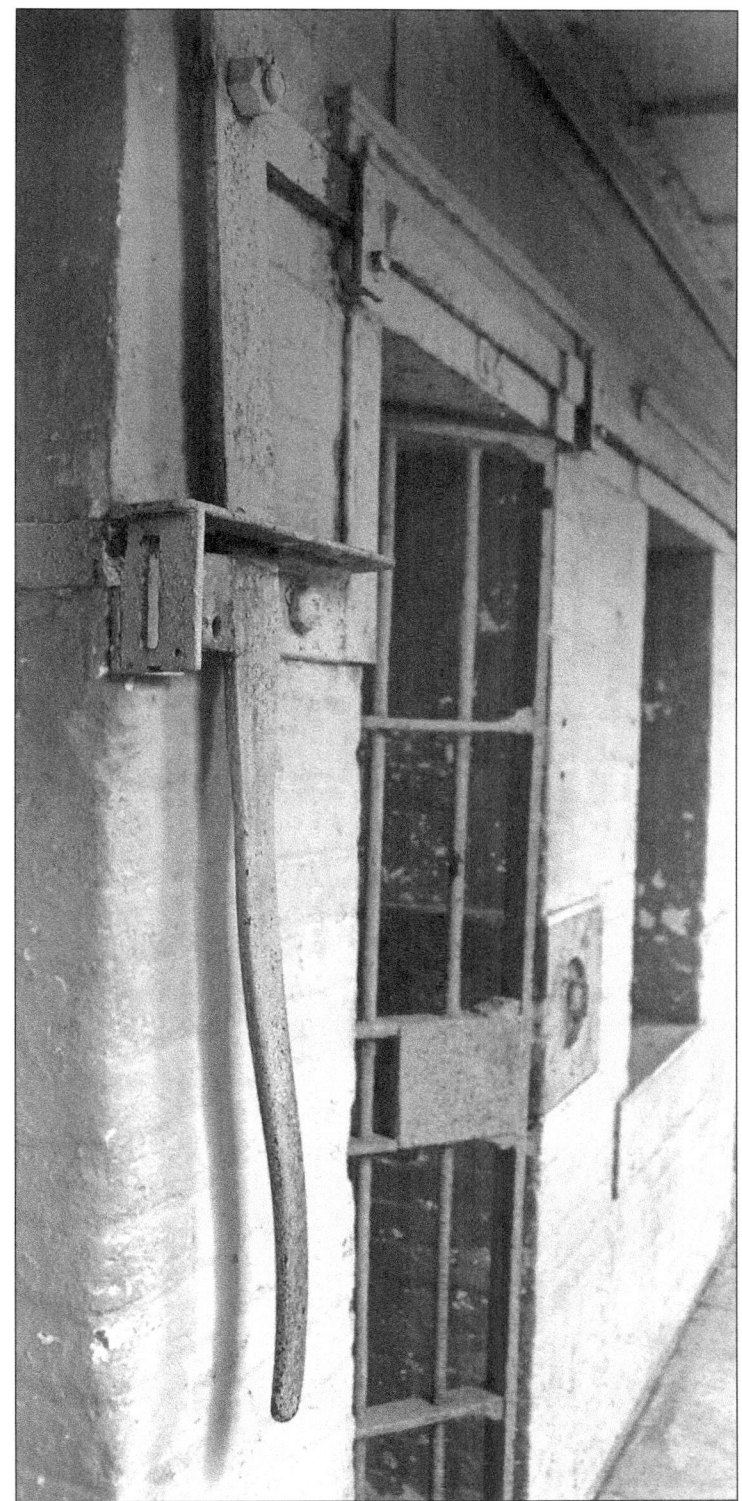

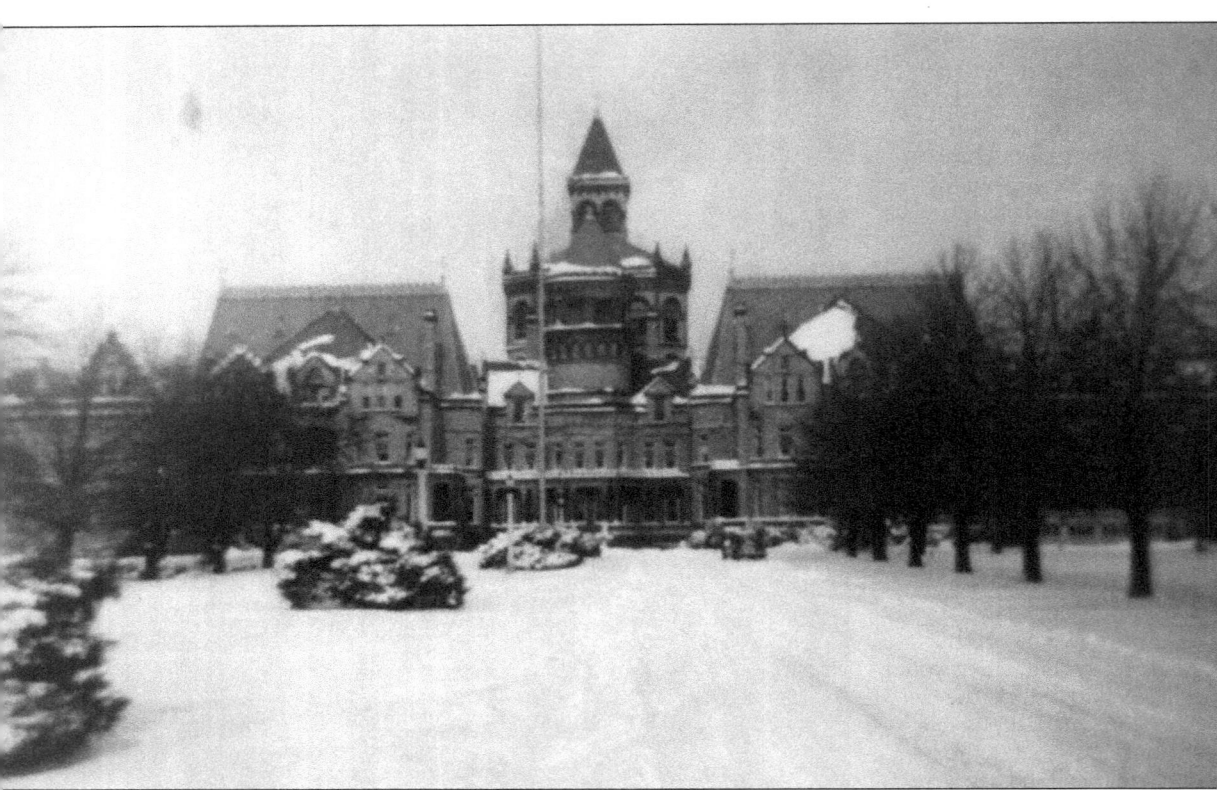

Christmas meals varied widely through the years. A more celebratory menu was offered on Christmas day. According to the December 25, 1963, edition of the *Mansfield News Journal*, for the first time prisoners could receive gifts from home. Families could send 20-pound packages of food, candy, and limited clothing and other gifts. Inmates whose families could not or would not send packages were given a superintendent's box with items from the commissary. Another tradition at Christmas saw inmates confined to correctional cells being released. Prisoners who violated rules were sentenced to 1 to 10 days in a special unit. At Christmas, these prisoners were released to return to their own cells. Those held in solitary confinement and could not be released were served a traditional Christmas meal.

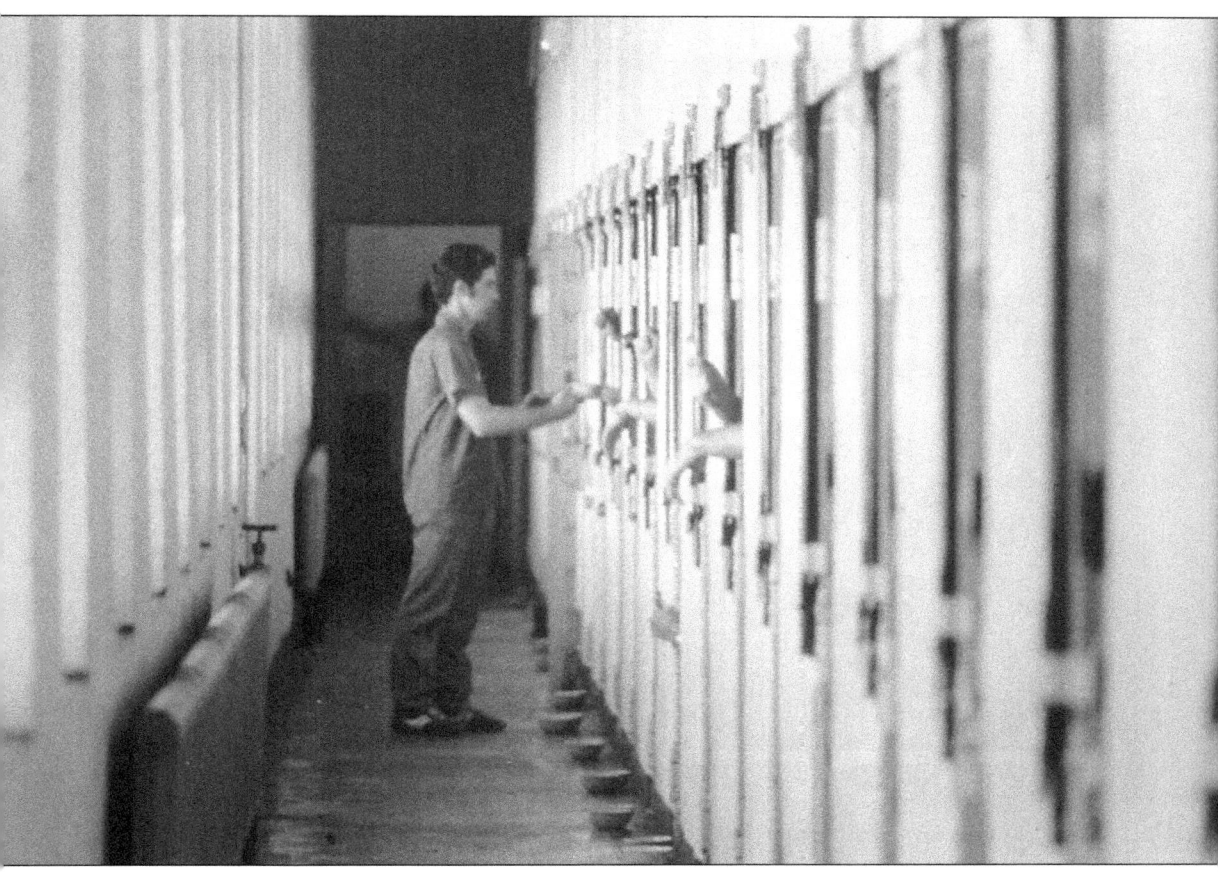

According to a 2015 interview with a former inmate, one worker had freer movement than other inmates. A "range man" had a number of duties and could be on the range at any time, except at lights out. He was responsible for keeping the range clean. Each morning, he pulled a large cloth bag down the range, collecting trash that the inmates had accumulated after cells were locked at night. This inmate had a range supply room at the end of the block next to his own cell. Stocked items included toilet paper, drinking water, and state-supplied soap and tobacco. The range man would also sell inmates sandwiches that had been smuggled out of the dining hall.

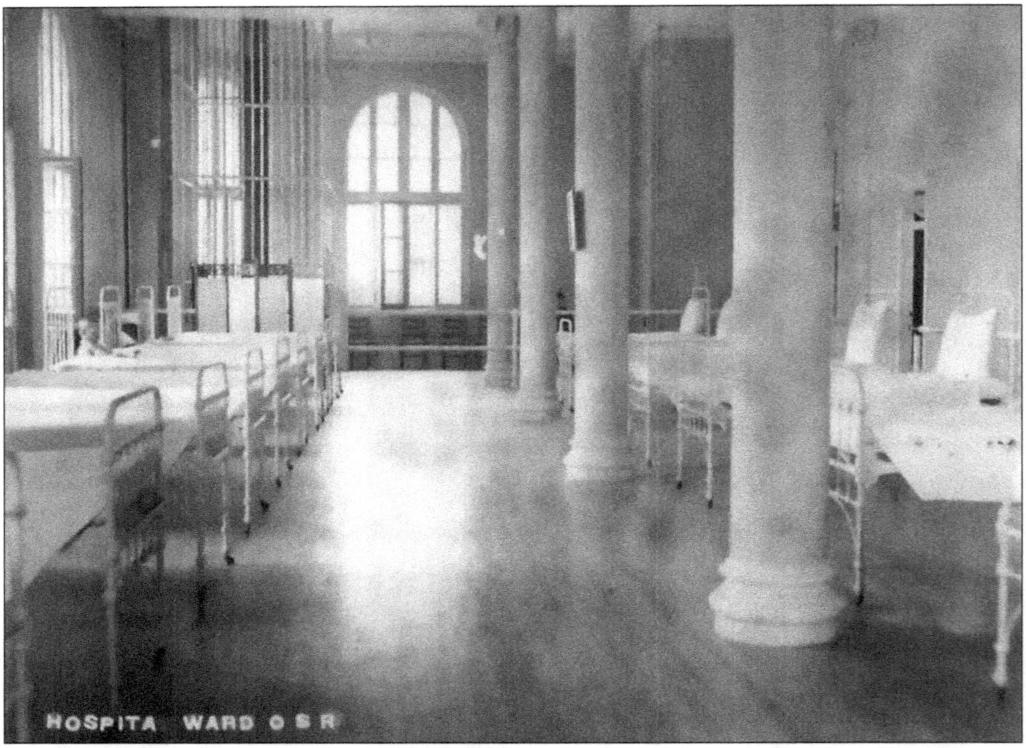

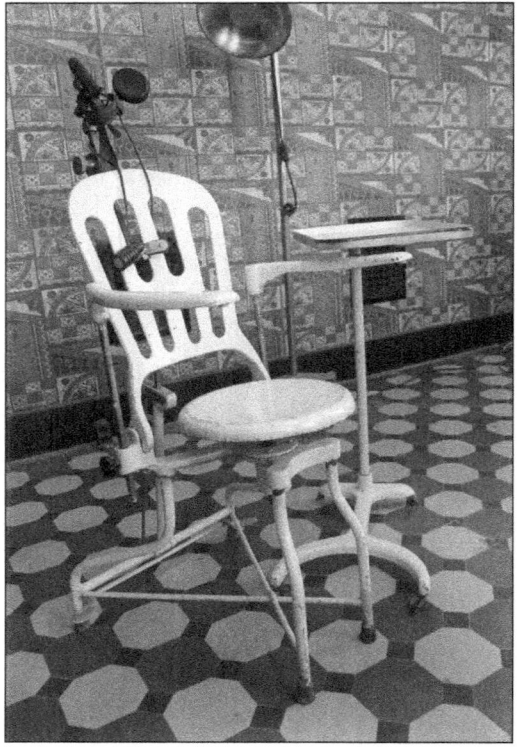

The prison hospital was a fully functional, 90-bed facility. It employed a surgeon, anesthetist, dentist, and eye-ear-nose-throat specialist, along with a guard-nurse and disciplinarian. In 1933, the hospital used 45 inmates as clerks, nurses, cooks, and kitchen help. Incoming inmates were inoculated as necessary for a number of diseases. Typhoid fever was a continuing concern, and inmates were given typhoid and paratyphoid vaccines. Other diseases required even greater vigilance. The tuberculosis ward was said to be always full, yet it was not large enough to accommodate all those diagnosed. In the 1934 report to the state, the reformatory cited the hospital's efficiency. While the death rate in the general Ohio population that year was 13 for every 1,000 patients, the rate at the Ohio State Reformatory was 5 for every 1,000 patients. At left is a chair used by the dental staff. (At left, courtesy of Scott Sukel.)

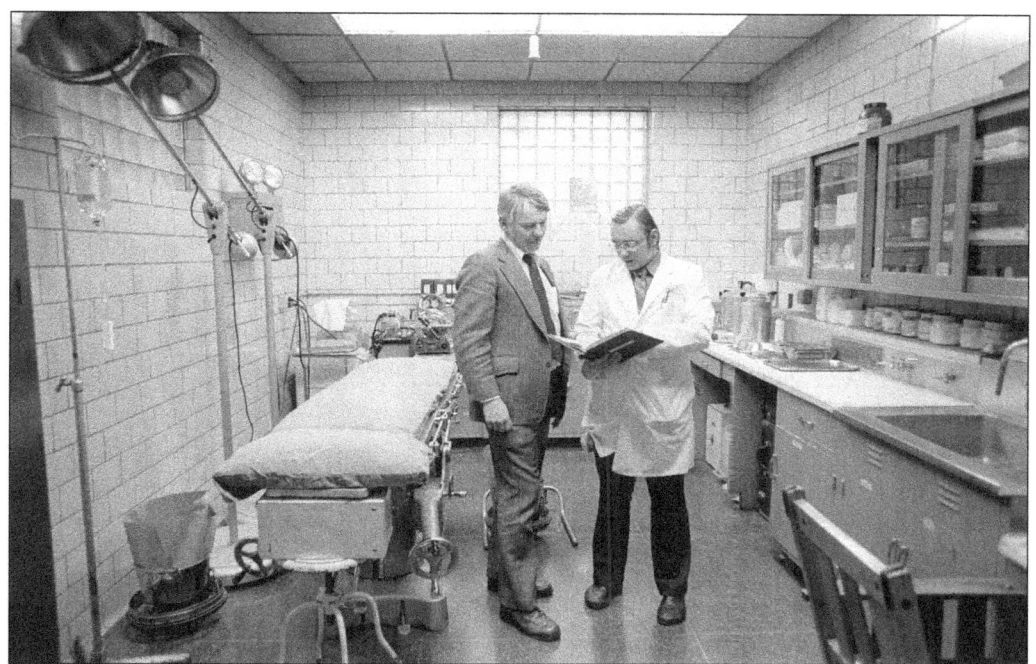

In 1948, a 90-bed facility was being planned. Completed in 1951, the separate outbuilding, three stories tall with a 175-bed capacity, cost $545,000. The new hospital was intended to include special wards dedicated to mental patients. According to Dr. John V. Horst, reformatory physician, this would meet the need to treat, yet isolate, inmates who had long been major problems for the institution. As with the original hospital, the new site would have an isolation ward for tuberculosis patients. Plans also called for two operating suites, one for major surgery and one for minor; a first-aid room; and a dental lab with six chairs. In the photograph above, Dr. John Catiller (right), director of the reformatory hospital, consults with an OSR administrator in 1978. Below, Catiller shows the handcuffs sometimes used to restrain prisoners in the mental ward. (Both courtesy of Jeff Sprang/*Mansfield News Journal*.)

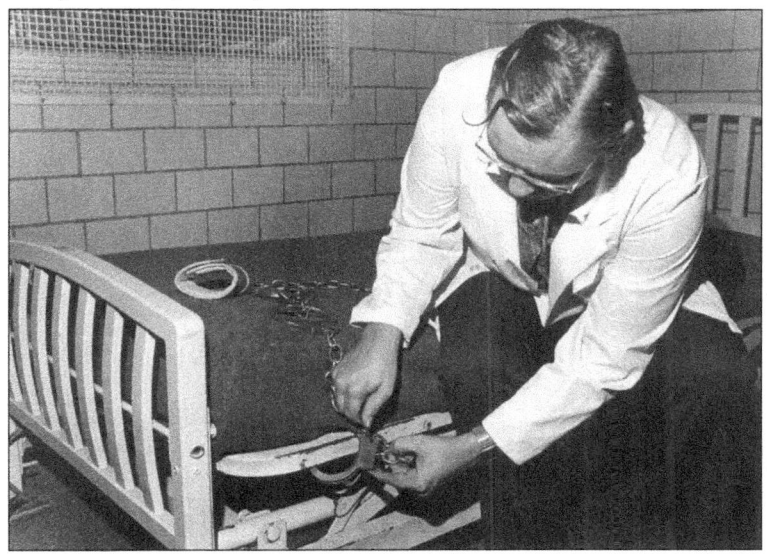

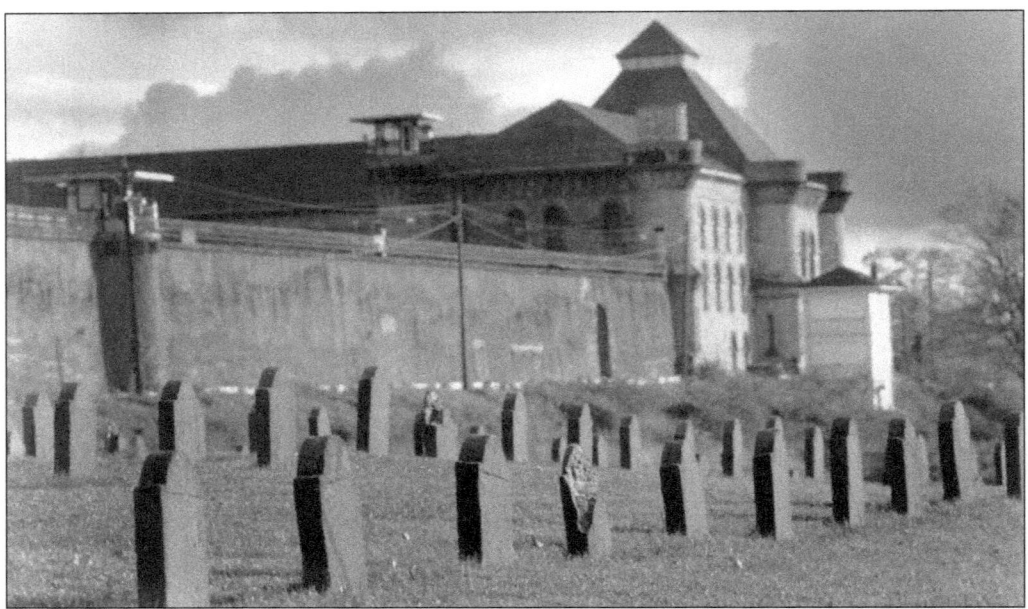

The cemetery has been in continuous use since the first prisoners arrived in 1896. The families of those who died while in custody had an opportunity to claim the body and have it buried in the cemetery of their choice. If, however, the family did not claim the body, it was buried in the OSR cemetery. Inmates were not identified on the stone by name, only by inmate number. When the reformatory closed in 1990, use of the cemetery was transferred to the Mansfield Correctional Institute (MANCI), northwest of the Ohio State Reformatory. The cemetery is maintained by the State of Ohio through MANCI.

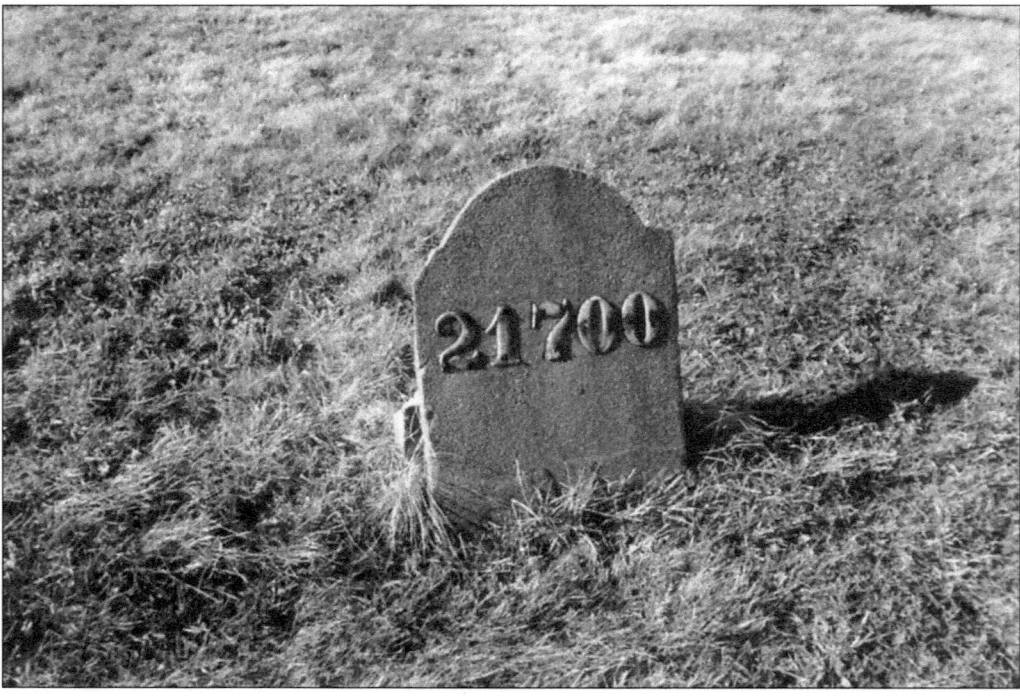

Five

HOLLYWOOD COMES TO TOWN

THE REFORMATORY ON SCREEN

The Ohio State Reformatory has become popular with the entertainment industry. Because of its Gothic appearance, it can be used as any number of settings. In 1976, the crew and stars of the film *Harry and Walter Go to New York* spent time in Mansfield. In 1989, Sylvester Stallone and Curt Russell starred in *Tango and Cash* and spent time within the reformatory's walls. The OSR's most famous appearance is in the Oscar-nominated *The Shawshank Redemption*. Much of the movie was filmed in and around the Mansfield area in 1993. The 1997 Harrison Ford/Glen Close film *Air Force One* used the OSR for part of its filming. Finally, *Fallen Angels* (2006) and *The Wind Is Watching* (2013) found the reformatory perfect as a setting. Creators of music videos and television programs have found the reformatory to be a fascinating backdrop.

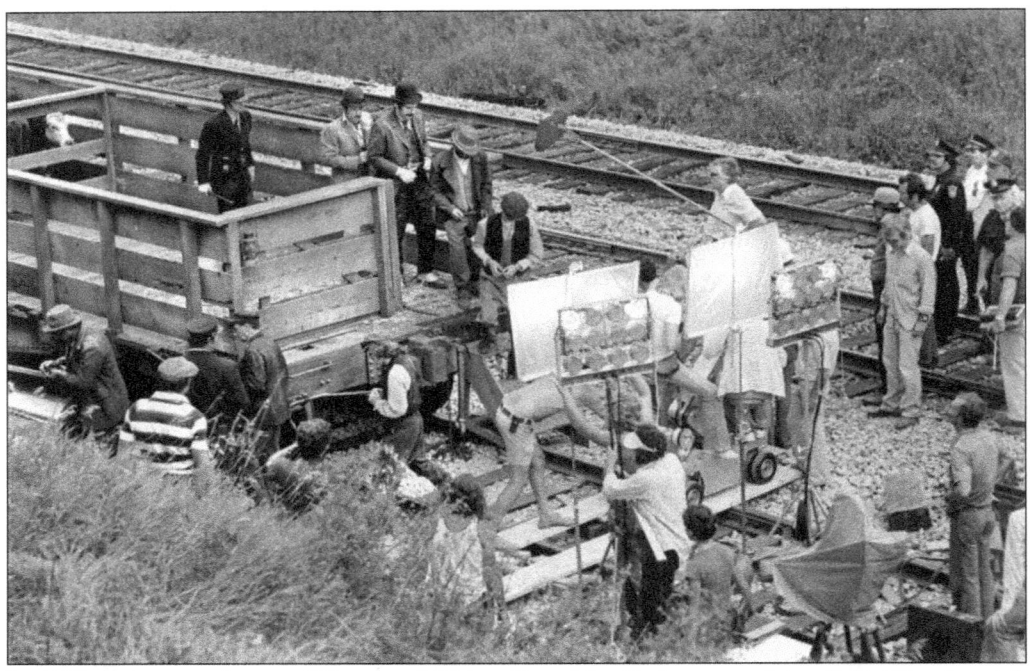

In 1975, the cast and crew of *Harry and Walter Go to New York* came to Mansfield. The slapstick comedy starred Elliott Gould, James Caan, Diane Keaton, and Michael Caine. Although some scenes were filmed inside the walls, other scenes were shot along the railroad tracks and at the front pond. In the film, Gould's and Caan's characters are taken to prison, and they step off a railcar just outside the northwest gate (above). In another scene, they plant explosives to knock down a prison gate (below). OSR inmates who were within 90 days of meeting with the parole board and were considered highly likely to be paroled and were first-time, nonviolent offenders, qualified to be in the movie. (Courtesy of Jeff Sprang/*Mansfield News Journal*.)

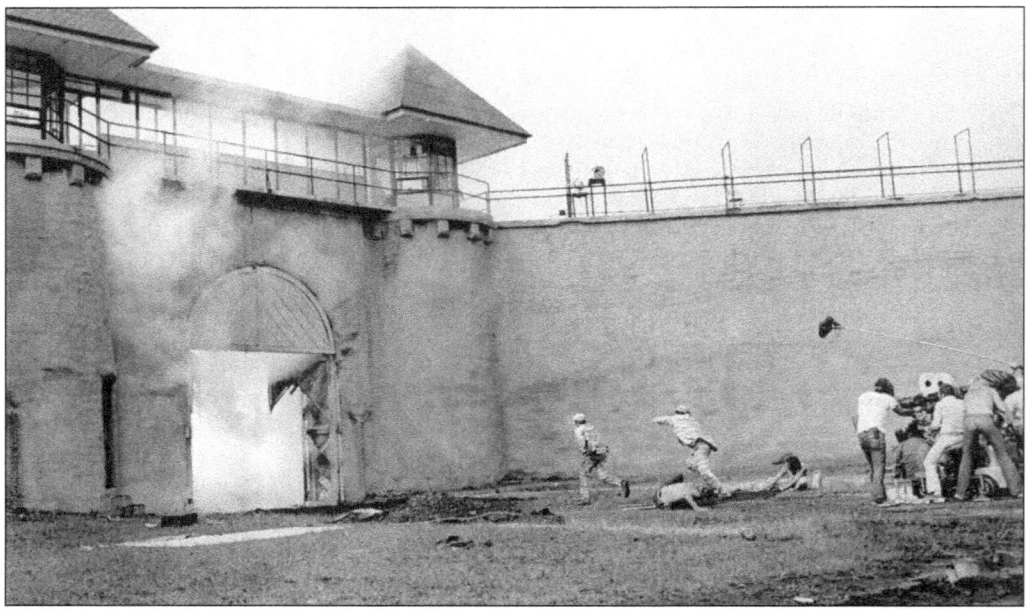

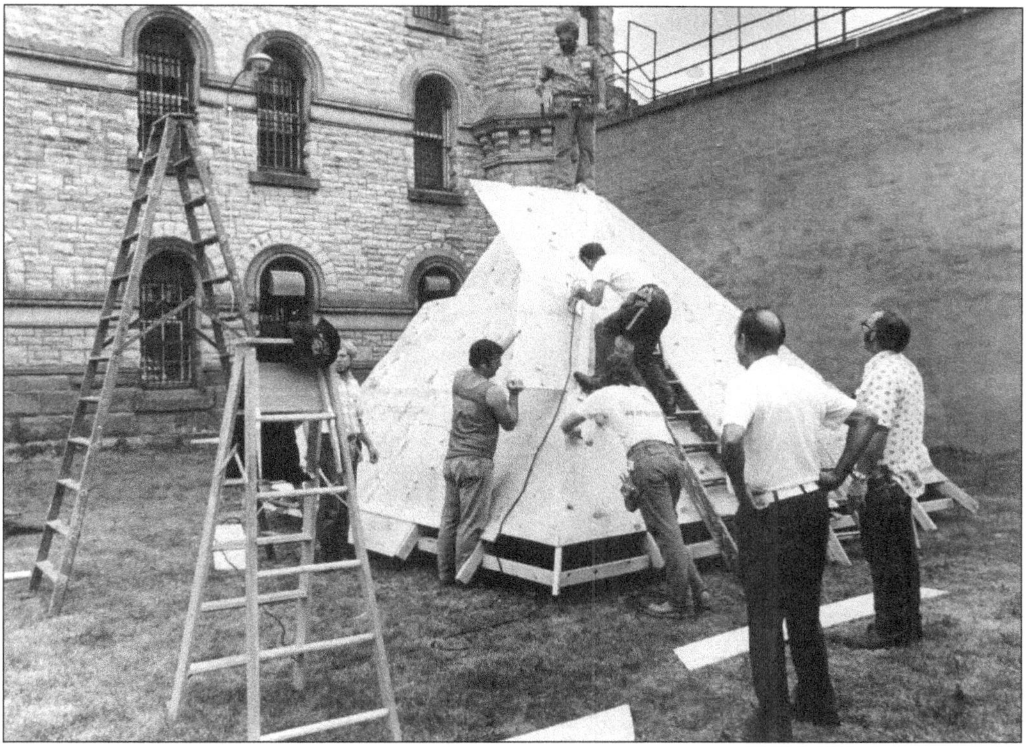

Some of the scenes for *Tango and Cash* (1988) called for a tree to be placed near the 25-foot-high stone wall. In the film, the tree was used by characters to escape from the prison. Immediately after the scene was filmed, the tree was removed because it could have facilitated escape attempts of actual prisoners. During filming, stars Sylvester Stallone and Kurt Russell spent time within the walls with OSR prisoners. The photographs on this page show the film's crew setting up scenes within the prison.

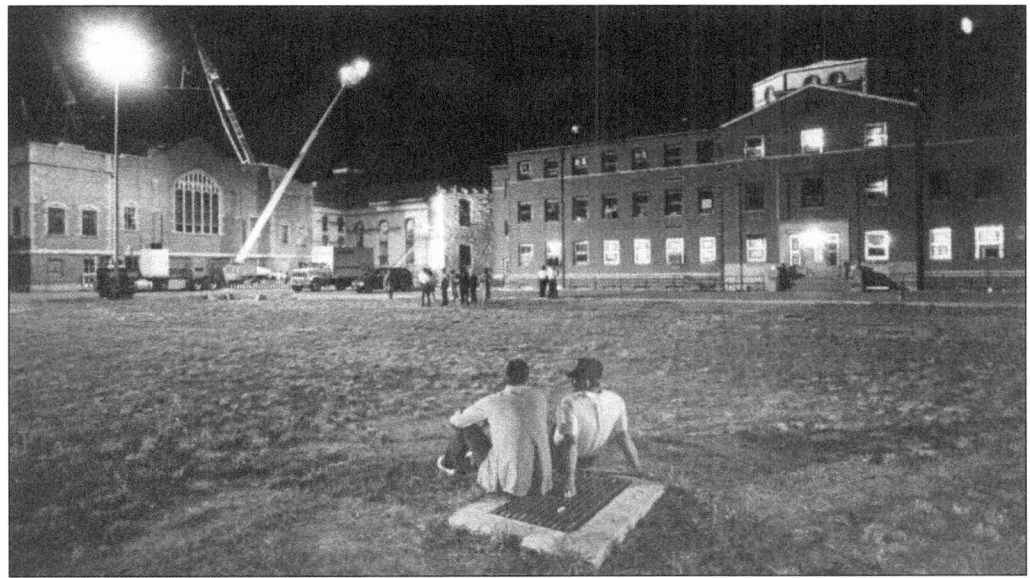

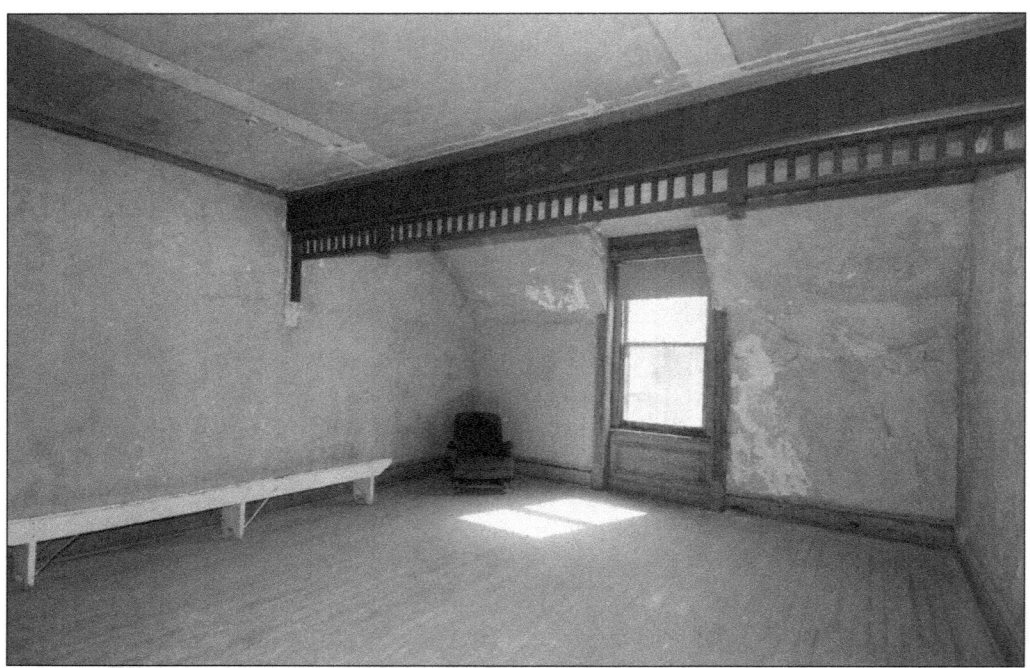

The Shawshank Redemption used the Ohio State Reformatory for much of its filming. A flyover shot took in the building proper and all of its outbuildings. The movie also used the showers, solitary confinement area, yard, and central guard room. The boardinghouse that Brooks Hatlen and Ellis "Red" Redding lived in after their release was filmed at the OSR. Also featured in the movie are the parole room, the offices of Andy Dufresne and the warden, the library, and the room that the new prisoners entered and lined up in when they were first brought to Shawshank Prison. The tunnels used in Andy's escape, as well as the wall safe in the warden's office used to hide the financial records, are still on display. Shortly after filming, the state began dismantling the surrounding wall and outbuildings.

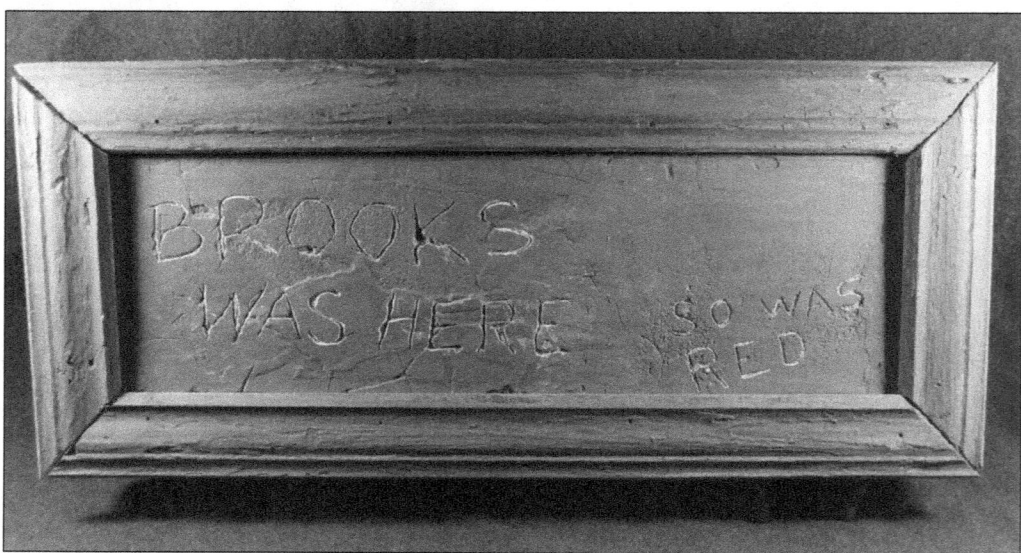

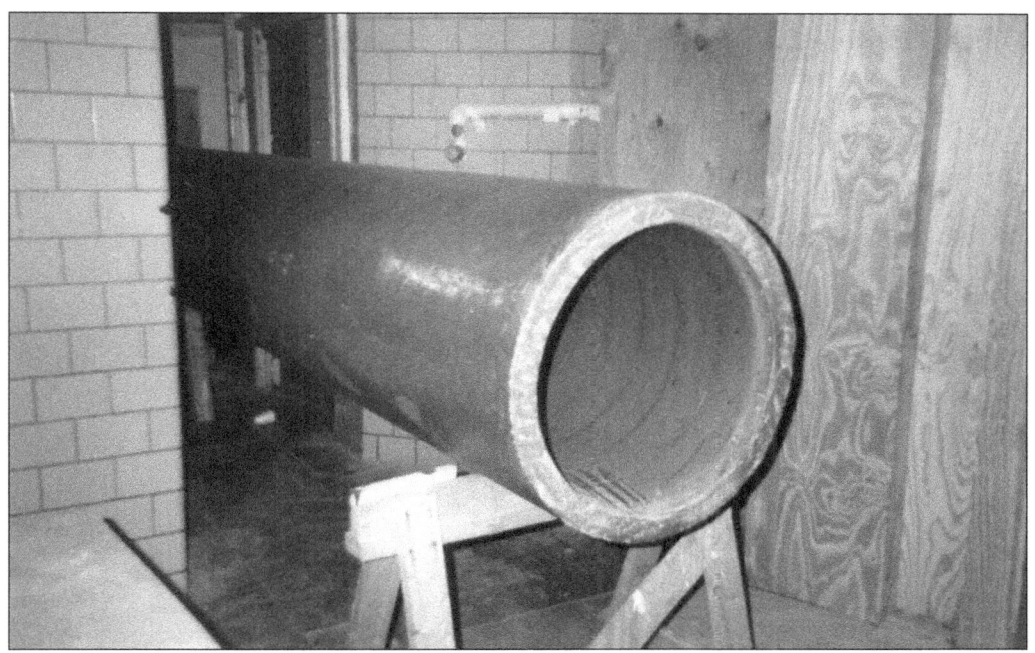

To make the sewer that Andy crawls through look longer than it really was, the cameraman used the cone-shaped object shown below. Portions of the sewer system used in the film (above) are on display at the reformatory.

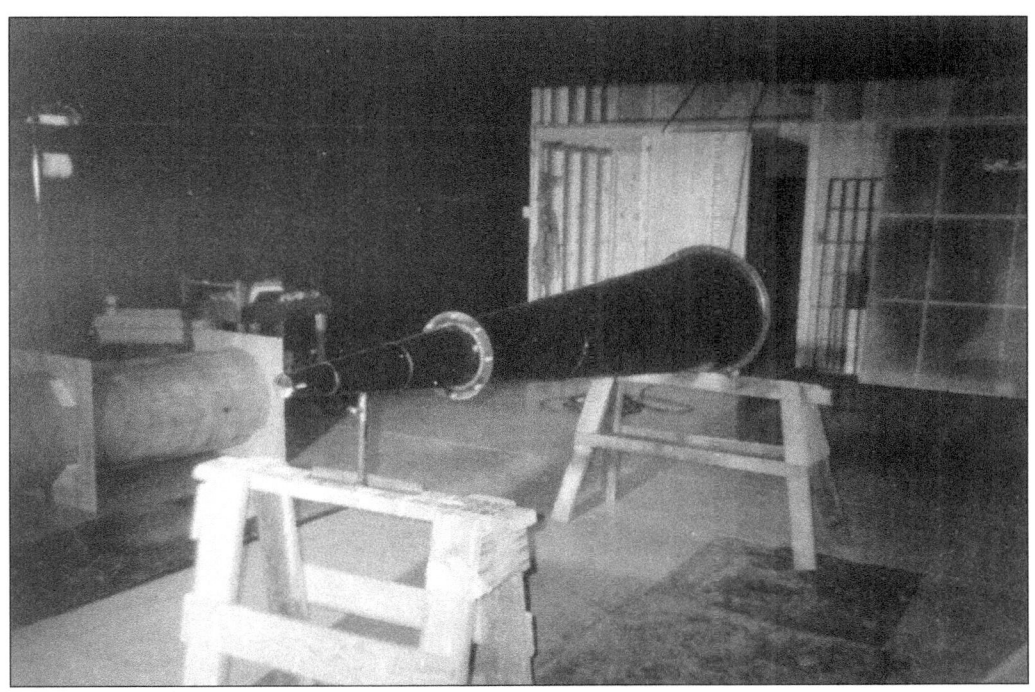

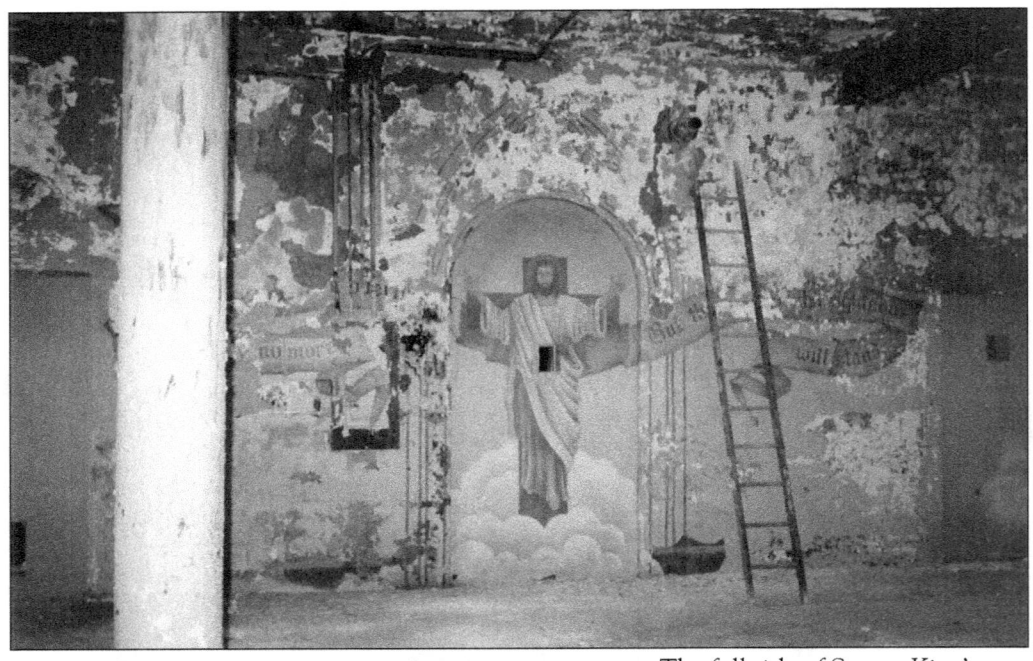

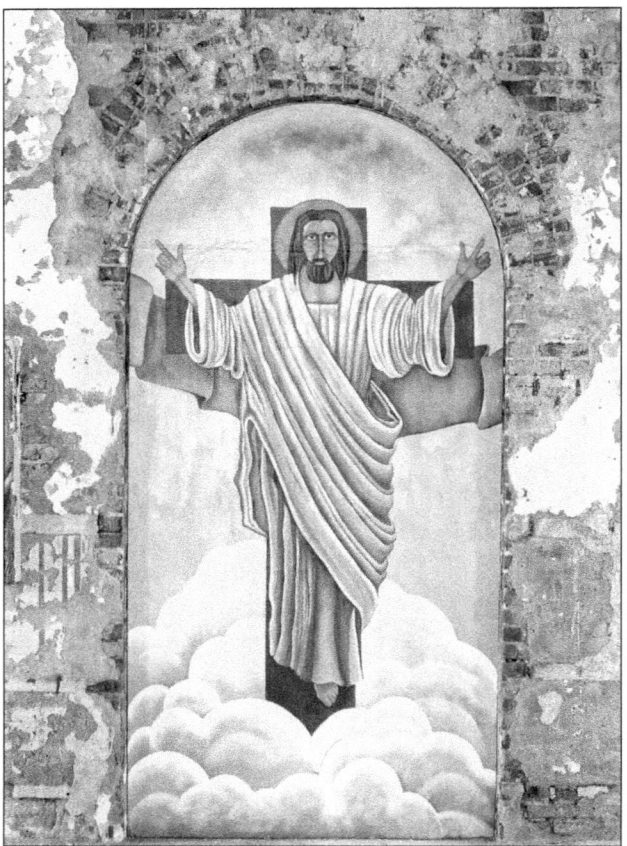

The full title of Steven King's short story is "Rita Hayworth and the Shawshank Redemption." The title refers to the movie *Gilda*, a favorite of the Shawshank prisoners. In the film, the prison's movie projector is behind a mural of Jesus. After filming, the mural was left behind. It has recently been restored and remains in the room used for filming the scene, referred to as the "Jesus Room."

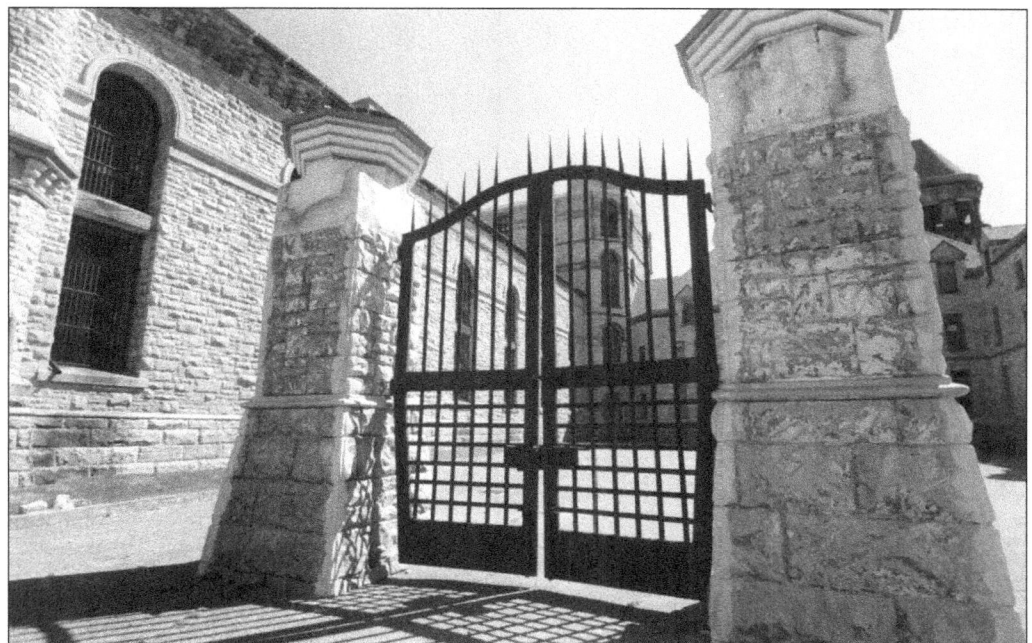

Although the portraits of Joseph Stalin and Karl Marx did not make the final cut of the 1997 movie, the portraits are lasting remnants of the filming of *Air Force One*. Visitors often ask why there are portraits of two communist leaders hanging prominently in the central guard room. In the film, the building served as a Russian prison that held the antagonist, Gen. Ivan Radek. The wall and gate were created by set designers. Molds were taken of the building and re-created using plywood and fiberglass. When erected on the site, they perfectly matched the building's facade. Even though the wall has deteriorated, the gate remains intact and is on display in the side yard.

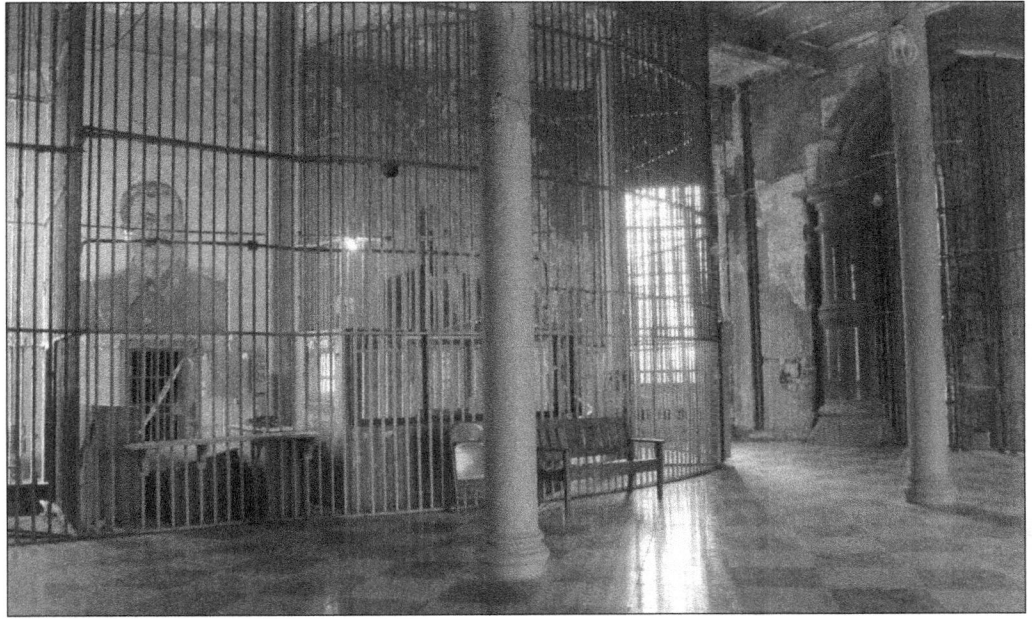

About the Organization

In 1990, the Ohio State Reformatory was planned for demolition. The outbuildings and wall were to be taken down, but the cell blocks and administrative building would remain standing because of the high cost of their destruction. A lack of funding serves as interesting bookends to the OSR's history: insufficient money slowed construction, and the same problem prevented the facility's complete demolition. The Mansfield community saw an opportunity in the suspended demolition. The Mansfield Reformatory Preservation Society (MRPS) was formed in 1995 as a grassroots effort to save and preserve the Ohio State Reformatory. By the time of its formation, the wall and outbuildings had been demolished. Because of the deteriorating condition of the building, the daunting task was at first met with skepticism. Over the next eight years, the state vacillated about plans for the building. Finally, in 2000, the State of Ohio gave the building to the City of Mansfield, which in turn sold it to MRPS for $1. This is when MRPS's work began in earnest. The goal of the society is to restore and preserve the building and its relics. In 2014, the reformatory was designated as the official museum for the Ohio Corrections Department and is currently preparing rooms to display items from throughout Ohio's corrections facility, including the original electric chair.

BIBLIOGRAPHY

Brown, Joan. "Female Guards at OSR." *Mansfield News Journal*. May 7, 1976.

Clay, Dwyer. "Staff Eagerly Awaits New OSR Hospital." *Mansfield News Journal*. July 5, 1948.

"Completing the Exterior of the Ohio State Reformatory." *Mansfield News*. September 24, 1900.

Domer, John. "OSR Graduation First in Ohio's Penal System." *Mansfield News Journal*. October 2, 1965.

"For the Intermediate: The Managers and Others before the Legislative Finance Committee." *Mansfield Evening News*. January 30, 1891.

"Law-Makers Return." *Mansfield Weekly*. February 12, 1891.

"Many Improvements Being Made at the Ohio State Reformatory." *Mansfield News*. August 17, 1903.

Miller, Marguerite. "Structure to Cost $450,000." *Mansfield News Journal*. May 12, 1950.

"New Chapel at Reformatory Formally Dedicated Sunday." *Mansfield News*. April 23, 1928.

"To Mansfield Reformatory." *Newark Daily Advocate*. September 18, 1896.

"The Ohio Liquor Law." *Norwalk Daily Reflector*. April 20, 1883.

The Ohio State Reformatory: Mansfield, Ohio, 1896–1934. Mansfield, OH: Ohio State Reformatory, 1934.

Three Decades of Progress: A Retrospective of Growth. Columbus, OH: Ohio Department of Rehabilitation and Correction, 2002.

www.oregon.gov/doc/OPS/PRISON/pages/osp_history3.aspx

Visit us at
arcadiapublishing.com

CPSIA information can be obtained
at www.ICGtesting.com
Printed in the USA
BVHW010422220720
584273BV00007BB/23